The Company Rule in India

THE COMPANY RULE IN INDIA

Some Regional Aspects

SHEELA SAHA,
D. N. SAHA

KALPAZ PUBLICATIONS
Delhi-110052

The Company Rule in India
Some Regional Aspects

Rs. 780

ISBN: 81-7835-251-6

Published in 2004 in India by
Kalpaz Publications,
C-30, Satyawati Nagar, Delhi-110052
E-mail : Kalpaz@hotmail.com

Laser Typesetting at : Shree Vaishnavi Creations, Delhi
Printed at : Mehra Offset Press, Delhi

Dedicated to the Memory of

Late Prof. K.K. Dutta of Patna University
&
Late Prof. K.K. Bose of T.N.B. College, Bhagalpur

Contents

Foreword

In this age of Globalisation it appears ridiculous to talk of regional history as it may to-day smack of localism and parochialism. However, the journey of history writing that began with Herodotus has to-day reached the same point from where it had begun. Herodotus began with the writing of history of Greece. The historical horizon widened with the coming of Christianity and Islam covering the history of Europe and parts of Asia. The enlightenment further widened the scope of history in the writings of Voltaire. With the emergence of Pragmatic and Idealist historians, H.G. Wells came out with History of the World and Spengler and Toynbee covered the rise one growth of the entire world civilization, However, K.M. Pauper came forward with Poverty of Historians and once again microscopic study of history began with subaltern historians and more so with Urban historical writings. Thus history has completed its journey from where it began

The first systemic history of India was written by V.A. Smith who influenced Indian historical writing and philosophy. He developed the thesis that whenever the centre was weak the country was disintegrated and therefore, made us believe that the Centre must be very strong . Even Nehru put emphasis on Unity in the midst of diversity. When the Republic of India was being born Ambedkar pooh poohed the idea of village Panchayat, local boards, district boards and indirect election leading to the Provincial and Central Legislature as suggested by Rajendra Prasad. He denounced it as the root cause of localism and parochialism that ultimately led to the ruination of India . So the Republic of India was born with a very strong central authority. But only within a course of last twenty years this top heavy central structure is crumbling with its weight and the country is no longer under the domination of Delhi but Delhi is being controlled from South, North and East. We have come to realise that there is Unity no doubt, but Diversity is as prominent which can no longer be suppressed or ignored. The emphasis must be on Diversity in the midst of Unity. The regional identity of India has come to be well recognised and the authors have, therefore, very appropriately tried to emphasise the regional identity of Bihar in the present venture, Bihar did play a very important role in the ancient period. It is essential to know the strength and weakness of Bihar for its revival.

I, therefore, congratulate the authors for bringing out a very comprehensive account of the history of Bihar under the rule of the Company and do hope that they will continue their efforts to search out the regional identity of Bihar with continued writing on this aspect of the history of Bihar.

(Dr.) Panchanand Mishra,
University Prof & Head (Retd.)
Deptt. of History, Bhagalpur University, Bhagalpur.

Preface

The Company-Rule in India is a regional study with a wider dimension. It is a full-length, in-depth study of political and administrative history of the Diwani Provinces with special imphasist on Bihar in Indian perspective covering the entire period of a century of tremendous historical importance from A.D. 1757 to 1857-58. The battle of Plassey in 1757 made the English king-makers in Bengal and Bihar and secured the foundation of the future British Empire in India. The battle of Buxar in 1764 and the consequent 'Diwanee' won them the legal status with the revenue of the three provinces which provided them with the sinews of trade, war and administration. Undoubtedly, it was from these three province that the English power first struck inland into the heart of the country and discovered the right road to supremacy in India. The Grant of Diwani to the English East India Company by the Mughal Emperor Shah Alam II in August 1765, and subsequent concessions conceded by the Bengal Nawabs through various treaties, engagements and arrangements made the British the sole ruler of the land, yet it was in 1772 that Company assumed the direct management of the government-both Diwani and Nizamut-of the three provinces of Bihar, Bengal and Orissa. The British Parliament also acquiesced in the political role of a private trading company by enacting the Regulating Act in 1773.

The rule of the Company came to an end in 1858 after the great revolt and the power was transferred to the British Crown riveting the shackles of slavery even more strongly. The people of the land, however, opposed the alien supremacy right from the time of Plassey and Buxar when the impact of the English ascendancy was first felt. The armed resistance became stiffer and widespread after 1772 with ever growing and ever tightening administrative control which was based on the policy of mercantilism and racial superiority. In fact, opposition forms a running theme of the history of the period. The people of Bihar, whether Hindus or Muslims, tribals or non-tribals, from plains or plateau, fakirs or farmers, rulers or retainers opposed the English rule at one time or the other. The opposition and resistance came in series by the cross-section of the people of the province manifesting itself in many ways, such as defying attitude, rebellions, resistance movements, plundering-raids, insurrections, conspiracies and revolts climaxed by the unprecedented upsurge of 1857-58 when practically the whole of Bihar, along with other provinces and people rose against the Company Raj. The people, however, had to taste defeat in their last and the biggest bid to overthrow the foreign rule. The revolt was suppressed with great violence and vengeance. Though the Company Bahadur was replaced by the British Crown as a ruler, yet no change was effected either in the structure of the government or in the plight of the people. On the other hand, consequent upon the failure of all the rebellions and movements, the yoke of slavery became still heavier not to be shaken off easily. The fate of Bihar became the fate of all Hindustan.

How a subject people could think of their glory, progress and prosperity, all which had become the things of remote past? The multifaceted degeneration which had started with the decline of the mighty Mughals was complete with a century of the Company-Rule. Evils of bondage with its entire natural corollary and the unnatural union of Bihar with Bengal as an inferior partner made the province backward and the people stagnant lagging behind in every field of human activity.

The book is divided into six chapters. The Chapter I depicts the advent, activities and rivalries of the European Trading Companies and their political designs kept under control by Nawab Alivardi of Bengal, gradual emergence of the English East India Company as a political power under rash Sirajud-daula, selfish Mir Jafar and communal Mir Qasim. It also highlights the beginning of dislike and resistance by the local rulers and Zamindars to the foreign domination. The Chapter also take a rapid survey of events in all their ramifications after the battle of Buxar leading to the grant of "Diwanee" by the fugitive Mughal Empeor Shah Alam II and 'Nizamut' by the titular Bengal Nawabs to the Company. It also takes note of the anarchy of 'Dyarchy' established by Clive.

The Second Chapter deals with the direct assumption of Government of the Diwani provinces including Bihar by Warren Hastings on the decision of the East India Company to end the Diarchy of Clive and to standforth themselves as the Diwan in 1772. It also depicts the pitiable plight of the people and high native officials as a result of the change of Government and growing resistance to the English supremacy by the cross-section of the people, such as the Hillmen and their chiefs, by the Rajas and Zamindar during the revolt of Raja Chait Singh of Benaras and by the Sannyasis and Fakirs through their plundering raids.

Chapter-III analyses the violent reaction of the tribal people, Chiefs and semi-tribal rajas of Chotanagpur and the Santhal Parganas on the sudden imposition of the English supremacy. A series of rebellions, such as the Chuar rebellions, the Kol-risings, the Bhumij revolt and even more fierce Santhal Insurrection in 1855-56, are the burning examples of the tribal resistance to the alien rule.

The Fourth Chapter brings to the forefront the Muslim-resistance to the rule of the 'Infidels' in the form of well organized, long sustained and the most remorselessly anti-British Wahabi movement in Bihar.

Chapter V deals with all its implications and impacts on the people of the province, of ever growing and ever tightening English administrative control which began with the anarchy of diarchy established by Clive, resulting in the direct assumption of the government on behalf of the Company as Governor of Bengal by Warren Hastings who tried to transform the machinery of merchants into the machinery of government laying down under Cornwallis and his succesors, of firm foundation of the Anglo-British administration which was based on racial superiority and class exclusiveness and, its results are also the subject matter of this Chapter. The period of Lord Moira to Bentinck, inaugurated in the wake of the liberal era of the Utilitarians in England, though constrained by the policy of economy, was a period of sweeping reforms. The period from

1835 to 1858 witnessed further changes in administration without undoing the unnatural union of Bihar with Bengal resulting in the under-administration of the province. Thesse changes and their impacts have also been reviewed in this Chapter.

Chapter VI narrates the glorious role played by the people of Bihar under the leadership of immortal Kunwar Singh and Amar Singh in the movement of 1857-58.

The argument closes with an epilogue.

Vijaya Dashmi
October, 2002

Acknowledgments

The authors owe a special debt of gratitude to Prof. Panchanand Mishra, their revered teacher, for writing the foreword.

The authors would like to thank the authorities and staff of various Archives, Record Rooms, and Libraries they visited for their kind cooperation and help.

Grateful thanks are also due to Prof, K.N. Das and Prof, V.K. Das of the Deptt. of English, T.N.B. College for going through the manuscript.

The authors' architect son Devendu Shreeharsh, his wife, Abha, and his assistants, namely, Sanjul, Kulbir and Sarvesh at Vasantkunj, New Delhi, deserve special mention for their assistance and designing the cover-flap.

The authors cannot help the temptation to place on record the warm asociation and cooperation of Devendu's in-laws at Sarva Priy Vihar, New-Delhi, namely, Mrs. Anita Shrma and Shri Akhilesh Naraian Sharma of Deepak Fertilisers & Petrochemical Corporation Limited, along with Dr. Aditya and Dr. Kirti. At this moment, we also wish to express all the love and affection for naughty Daksh and smiling Astha.

Sincere thanks are also due to Dr. Parthosarathi Ghosh, Director ICSSR, New Delhi, Prof. C.P.N. Sinha, Prof. P.N. Bhagat, Dr. Harihar Das and - all the relatives, colleagues, friends and well-wishers who have encouraged and helped the authors in many ways.

Last, but not the least, we are also thankful to Publishers, who took keen interest in publishing the Book well.

Sheela Saha
&
D.N. Saha

CHAPTER 1

The Rivalry, Struggle and Supremacy: The Beginning of Resistance

The Eighteenth century was a period of decline for India. This decline was multi-faceted—political, social, moral and fiscal. Politically, it witnessed the decline of the mighty Moghul Empire. With the death of Aurangzeb in 1707 A.D. and the weakening of central authority provincial governors began to assert their independence. At the same time there emerged new factors in Indian body politic. Taking advantage of the unsettled conditions of the country many ambitious Indian and non-Indian adventurers began to try their luck. In fact, mid-eighteenth century India proved a fertile land for such adventurers and fortune-seekers as many of them rose to eminence, and some of them could succeed in carving out independent kingdoms by noble or ignoble means. Moral values declined so much so that treachery reigned supreme. The economy of land was shattered. It was in this background that Alivardi rose to power in Bihar and Bengal, and the European Trading Companies, especially the French and the English, intensified their extra commercial activities.

With the Death of Alivardi Sets in Rapid Decline

Alivardi and his house, however, could not enjoy peace and power for long. Exhausted and ailing Alivardi closed his eyes on 10th April, 1756 A.D.[1] With the death of Alivardi disruptive forces, including the European trading companies, which Alivardi had kept under control by his tact and ability, began to manifest with greater force and swept the provinces and his successor, Siraj-ud-daula. The period of Alivardi, though comparatively and apparently peaceful and prosperous, was a trend-setter. It set in motion the multi-dimensional degeneration and decline through which eighteenth century India suffered subsequently.

Advent and Activities of Europeans in India

The fabulous wealth and the lucrative trade of India had always attracted the Europeans and they had trade relations with India from the hoary past. But the merchants of the west had no direct touch with the markets of the East. From the 7th century overland trade or sea-borne trade with India was conducted by the merchants of Venice and Genoa through Arab merchants who dominated the Red-Sea and the Indian Ocean. Indian goods and the luxuries of 'the East' had to pass through several shipments and hands before they reached European markets. The goods had to pay exorbitant tolls and taxes at various checkposts as they passed through many independent kingdoms. Even then they fetched enormous profits in European markets.[2] But the discoveries of the late 15th century and the opening of the direct sea-route to India by Vasco da gama (in May 1498) revolutioned the whole thing and proved to be epoch-making event. E. Denison Ross is perfectly right in observing that "perhaps no event during the Middle Ages had such far-reaching repercussions on the civilized world as the opening of the sea-route to India."[3]

With the beginning of this direct maritime contact, merchant-adventurers of many European nationalities, such as the Portuguese, the Dutch, the French and the English, forming trading companies at different dates forced their way to India. Originally they had come as traders. But the unsettled conditions of the country, dissensions, absence of the feeling of nationality and unity among the Indian powers, and gradual decline of the Moghul authority inspired them to aspire, with success, for sovereignty. These mercantile races of Europe now came to stay in India with all the echoes of their changing diplomatic relations at home as a decisive factor in the political life of India. This changed the course of Indian History. The English, one of these European traders, ultimately, supplanted the Great Moghuls as the Sovereign of India. Beginning with Bengal and Bihar, they subjugated the whole of India. She lost her independence for two centuries to come.

The Portuguese

The Portuguese were the first to venture in to the eastern waters. Vasco da Gama reached the port of Calicut on 17th May, 1498, with three vessels of cargo. He was received well by the local ruler, the 'Zomorin'. Subsequently, after some disasters and fighting engagements, the Portuguese established themselves on important ports of the West Coast, such as Calicut, Kannanur, Cochin; and they secured the firm footing on Indian soil. Gradually they also settled in Goa, Salsette, Bassien-Bombay, Daman and Diu.

Vasco da Gama could not visit Bengal, but he could gather information for the merchants of Lisbon that "the Country (Bengal) could export quanties of wheat and very valuable cotton goods."[4] And when the Portuguese started commercial transactions with Bengal, they found the report true to their satisfaction."[5]

The Portuguese in Bengal and Bihar:

Soon after the Portuguese had established themselves on the West Coast of India, they found their way into the Bay of Bengal and were well settled in Bengal before the arrival of the Dutch or the English there. Being first established at Pippli (Orissa), Hughli (Bengal) and Balasore (Orissa) by the year 1530 A.D., they were the frequent visitors to the Hughli and the ancient port of Satgoan. Later on they founded in 1537-38"[6] their factory at Golaghat, the future port of Hughli. 'Golaghat soon became the chief emporium and took the name of the river, that is Hughli town or port."[7] They soon began to send their merchants up the Ganges to Bihar. They retained their settlement in Hughli and being confirmed in the grant of 777 bighas of rent free land[8] by Shah Jehan developed the city of Bandel (Bengal). Robert Hughes, the second of the English factory at Agra, who visited Patna in June 1620, on an exploratory mission, 'found the Portuguese already in possession of the market.[9] They used to come in 'diverse frigatts' from Satgong, Hughli and Pippli and purchase all 'they can lay hands on'. But the Portuguese could no longer remain so prosperous in Bengal and Bihar as on the West Coast. Due to the nature of their working[10] and the superior forces of the rival Dutch at sea, they had to withdraw gradually from Bengal, their settlement at Hughli being destroyed in 1632 by the Moghul government.[11] Thus the Portuguese could not secure permanent footing in the Bay of Bengal and the Gangetic valley. Kasim Khan, governor of Bengal, appointed by Shah Jehan in 1628, took Hughli from the Portuguese and made it a Moghul Port under an independent Foujdar.

Patna as an Important Trade-Centre

Bihar at this time and onward occupied a prominent place on account of its commerce and manufacture. Patna, the capital and principal city of the province was a great international trade-centre of India. According to Ralf Fitch who visited Patna in 1583, it was, 'a very low and great town and a great mart of cotton and cloth of cotton, much sugar, very much opium and other commodities'. Mannucci, the Venetial traveller, who passed through Patna in 1663, found Patna 'a large city with Bazzars, the greater part thatched'.[12] Tavernier, who visited Patna in Dec. 1665, has described Patna as "one of the largest towns in India on the margin of the Ganga on western side, no less than two Cos in length, where merchants came from distant Tipperah[13]. Due to its geographical position and good connections of highways and waterways Patna had regular commercial intercourse not only with chief towns and ports of Bengal and Orissa such as Kasim Bazar, Maladah, Murshidabad, Hooghly, Satgoan, Balasore and Masulipattam, but also with towns of western India and upper India, like Surat, Benaras, Jaunpur, Agra and Lahore. Articles and goods from Nepal, Tibet, Bhutan and Sikkim also found their way to the mart of Patna. In fact, Patna attracted merchants not from distant tipperahas of India alone but also from distant foreign lands such as Egypt-Africa, Persia, Central Asia, West Asia and Europe. Thomas Bowray found Patna 'a country of very great traffick and commerce, and really the Great Gate that openeth into Bengal and Orissa, and consequently into most parts of India, viz., from the Northern Kingdom or Empires, namely, Persia, Carmania (Kirman), Georgia and Tartaria,[14] etc. Armenian merchants doing business in musk from Tartary to China frequented Patna enroute Hooghly. Again, Armenian merchants from Danzung and going to Bhutan were seen by Tavernier at Patna.[15] In fact, 'Bihar constituted a link in India's economic and commercial contacts with the three continents of Asia, Africa and Europe.'[16]

An idea of the briskness of the trade of the province may be gathered form the fact that the number of coins issued from the Patna mint was larger than that of all the mints of Bengal put together and upto 1655 it was the largest mint of the region.[17]

Patna and other important trade centres of Bihar had a number of sarais for the merchants and travellers. Peter Mundy found Saif Khan's Sarai at Patna as the best Sarai in India where merchants of all nations stayed.[18]

Chief commodities of trade at Patna were textiles, sugar, opium, agricultural products and above all saltpetre. Fitch has described Patna 'a great mart of cotton, and cloth of cotton, much sugar, very much opium and other commodities'.[19]

Manucci found Patna full of many merchants trading not only in white cloth of fine quality but also in 'bottles and cups of clay, finer than glass, lighter than paper and scented.'[20] Patna got an added significance after the discovery of saltpetre in making gun-power. Silk and saltpetre were the two commodities that especially attracted the English to Bengal and Bihar,[21] and their pioneer settlers in this region were directed not to lose sight of 'Patna and Petre'. It was, therefore, but natural for the Europeans to establish commercial intercourse with the region and to find permanent trade stations by securing farmans, parwanas and agreements from the Mughal Emperor, provincial-governors and local chiefs, and by resorting to force if necessary.

The Dutch

The Portuguese were followed by the Dutch. After challenging successfully the Portuguese naval supremacy and trade monopoly in the Eastern Waters and in the Bay, the Dutch established themselves on important towns and ports such as Pipli, Balasore, Dacca, Maldah, Kalikapur (Kasim bazar), Jugdeah, Chinsurah Baranagar, Patna and Fatwah. They even acquired territorial property as 'perpetual fief' at Chinsurah and Baranagar 'obtained by gift or rather by possession,[22] On account of the increasing commercial importance of Bengal and Bihar the Dutch -government at Batavia, in 1655, organised a separate Directorate of Bengal for the administration of its affairs in this region. The Dutch Directorate of Bengal with headquarters at Chinsurah governed the factories of Kasim bazar, Maldah, Dacca, Balasore and Patna besides number of trade establishments, even in the interiors of Bengal, Bihar and Orisssa. In October 1662, the Dutch obtained and Imperial firman for trading facilities not only in Bengal, Bihar and Orissa but 'within the limits of this Empire'[23]

The Dutch Factory at Patna

The exact date of the opening of the Dutch factory at Patna or trade settlements at other places in Bihar cant't be said with certitude. But Tavernier and Bernier while passing through Patna in Dec.1665 found the Dutch already settled there. Tavernier observes: 'The Dutch Company has an establishment there on account of the trade in saltpetre which it refines at a large village called Chapra situated on the right bank of the Ganges 10 Coss above Patna.[24] Owing to its better quality, Patna-saltpetre was in great demand and it formed the chief commodities of export to Europe from Bihar.[25] On the perusal of the Dutch records it has been discovered that in the year 1668 out of the 127,238 maunds of refined Patna saltpetre 105,238 maunds were meant for export[26]. Bernier has also testified the fact:'Bengal is the principal emporium for saltpetre. A prodigious quantity is imported from Patna. It is carried down the Ganges with great facility and the Dutch and the English send large cargoes to many parts of the Indies and to Europe.[27]' Though the English were equally interested in saltpetre but the Dutch share was far greater before the English got political ascedency after Plassey. Beginning from 1669-70 till 1705 they exported on an average 2, 381, 918 lbs., whereas during the same period (from 1701 to 1707) the English export of saltpetre was 757,097 lbs. per annum on an average.[28] The Dutch Company also exported from Bihar the Textiles, Opium and Ginger either to the East Indies or to Europe.[29]

Besides factory at Patna the Dutch had saltpetre refinery at Chapra (Saran) and trading agencies at Fatuwah, Baikunthypur, Lakhwar and other places. As in Kasim bazar, the Dutch factory at Patna had, contrary to the English factory, a well built house and garden and large godowns.[30]

On their petition in 1711, the Moghal Emperor Jahandar Shah granted the Dutch a sanad through which they received concessions for their trade in Bengal and Bihar: "That the faujdars and all other governors in Agra, Patna, Rajmahal, Murshidabad etc. on the banks of the Ganges to Hughly be ordered for future not to take double custom from the Dutch, but only 2½% in Hughly'. It was further granted that their sicca be first coined in the Imperial mints of Hughly, Mursidabad, Rajmahal and Patna. Again all the Hakims and Chaukidars were ordered not to make 'extortion and delays' in 'their cloth and silk', and not to evict them from their hired houses[31]. Even then the property and goods of Patna factory were seized in June 1712 as the Dutch Chief, Jacob Van Hoorn had died without any heir. However, they were engaged in enormous trade in the provinces sending 12 to 13 ships of cargoes annually from Bengal and they claimed premier rank among the Europeans at the Murshidabad Darbar[32], which was seldom disputed by the Europeans before Plassey. Events and facts are also indicative of their 'premier rank.'

In the year 1739 saltpetre bought jointly by the Dutch and the English companies in Patna was 'seized by the Dutch with an armed force'. In another case the Chief of the Dutch factory at Patna, contrary to the agreement, endeavoured to procure all the saltpetre he could to the (English) company's interest in 1741[33]. Again the agreement regarding saltpetre trade in Bihar in March, 1744, by the Chiefs of the Dutch, the English and the French factories of Patna, clearly shows the pre-eminent position of the Dutch. The said agreement stipulates that Mr. Drabbe, the Dutch chief of Patna factory, 'alone shall buy up all the saltpetre"..... and shall deliver to the other companies their respective shares of Dobara (refined) saltpetre[34]. But the situation changed altogether after the revolution of 1757, which definitely established the English ascendancy over other European companies. However, commercially in the pre-Plassey days the Dutch were the chief rivals to the English trade in Bengal and Bihar. In fact, the Dutch trade in Bengal was always larger than that of the English trade during the 1st half of 18th century[35].

The French

The English merchants in India had already a formidable commercial rival, the Dutch but from the last quarter of the 17th century, there appeared a new rival, posing all threats to their interests in India. It was the French East India Company. The Compegnie des Indes Orientales, founded in August 1664, under the Ministry of Colbert with the blessings of Louis XIV, embarked on eastern venture with all enthusiasm and high hopes. With great difficulty and sufferings, Francois Caron, on behalf of the Company, could establish in 1668 Comptoir or Agency at Surat. Soon, they were on the Coromandal coast with a factory at Masulipatan (1669), St. Thome (1672). The most important event of the history of the French Company in India, was the acquisition by Francois Martin in January 1673 from Sher Khan Lodi, the local governor, of a tiny village, the future Pondicherry, the French capital in India. Now the French ventured into Bengal and received in 1674 from Shaista Khan, the Moghul Governor, a site near the village of Chandarnagar between Hughly and Chinsurah. Within a few years the French developed the site[36] into a beautiful city (1688-92), Chandarnagar , which was finally ceded to them by Aurangzeb in 1688 and which became the chief centre of the French activities in eastern India. They also established their trade centres at Kasim bazar and Dacca. For various reasons, viz. the wars in Europe, the general history of the company at home and abroad itself, the first two decades of the 18th century were the period of inactivity for the French company in Bengal for which Capt. Hamilton had wittily remarked “A pretty little church to hear mass in....is the chief business of the French in Bengal.”[37]

The French in Bihar

But the French company got a new life from 1720 when it was reconstituted. It was at this time that the French factory was founded at Dacca in 1722,[38] and at Patna between 1722 and 1725. Capt. Hamilton in 1720 found only the English and the Dutch Factories at Patna,[39] whereas Cevalier D'Albert writing in 1725 mentions "the French and the Dutch had also factories at Patna"[40]. However, it was during the chiefship (1730-41) of Dupleix who came to Bengal in 1730-31 that the French trade in Bihar and Bengal reached the zenith of its prosperity[41]. Dupleix had not occupied the interdantship (of Chandarnagar) for four years, when in place of the half dozen country boats which on his arrival were lying unemployed at the landing place, he had at sea 30 or 40 ships, a numbers which increased before his departure to 72 engaged in conveying merchandise of Bengal to Surat, to Jedda, to Mocha, to Bussora, and to China." Nor did he neglect the inland trade. He etablished commercial relations with some of the principal cities of the interior, even opened communication with Tibet[42]". The volume of this inland trade must have been carried through Bihar, particularly Patna because by 1735 the French had made so much progress in their trade of Bihar that it worried the English Company to instruct their men: "Now the French were settled at Patna, our Chief and Council must double their diligence and keep all the 'assamies' they can, true to our interest and advance money liberally but with caution"[43]. The commodities of commerce and export were the same as of other Europeans, cotton goods and saltpetre forming the chief element. But for various reasons the French trade began to decline after the departure of Dupleix from Bengal in 1741. Dupleix was recalled to Pondicherry as the Governor of the French settlements in India. In fact, Dupleix after his elevation to the highest post in India began to think more in terms of conquests and Empire than that of the commerce. It was but natural for a man like Dupleix, over-cautions and a keen observer of the situation prevailing in the mid-eighteenth century India. He dreamed of making the French power supreme in India. But the attempt resulted in complete annihilation of their power from Bengal and Bihar. The French Factory at Patna was captured after the battle of Plassey and it ceased to exist after 1758[44].

The English

Excited and inspired by the profitable eastern trade of the Portuguese and the Dutch, the enterprising and adventurous English merchants, too, could not resist their temptation in the same direction. Though failing in their earlier attempts in the last quarter of the 16th century, the Governor and Company of Merchants of London Trading into the East Indies, started afresh on their eastern venture after receiving a Charter, with monopoly of eastern trade, from queen Elizabeth I on 31st Dec., 1600[45]. However, their first attempt under Captain Hawkins in 1608-11, to establish a factory at Surat failed, owing to the hostile Portuguesse influence at the Moghul-Court. Nevertheless, after some engagements and show of might at the sea, the Company secured the permission in 1612-13, to establish a permanent factory at Surat[46]. But more successful was the embassy of Sir Thomas Roe (1615-18) with letter from King James I, in obtaining important trade privileges from the Moghul Emperor Jehangir[47]. Though, Thomas Roe could not get his draft treaty ratified, yet he rendered a valuable service to the Company in its infancy by his sound advice and 'shrewd judgement' as to the line of conduct to be pursued by the Company's servants. The 'firmaun' of Jahangir, and the 'sage advice of Roe' long remained the sole authority of the English trade and their conduct in India. Before the departure of Roe in 1619, the English had thus trade establishments founded at, besides Surat, Ahmedabad, Agra and Broanch. Then following the example of preceding Europeans, the English also embarked on establishing themselves on the Coromondal Coast and in Bengal. With varying fortunes, and despite troubles given by the Dutch and the native officers, the English effected their settlement at Masulipattam. But more important was the acquisition in 1639 by Francis Day, of a piece of land near Madras wherein they built fort St. George[48], then the only fortified factory of the English in India, and which later on superceded Musulipattam as their southern headquarters. However, invaluable silk and saltpetre of Bengal and Bihar were still away from them. Hence, they tried their way to make into Bengal and Bihar.

From Surat via Agra to Patna and Early Failures

First attempt was made to effect settlement in this region through north by overland from Surat via Agra. As decided by the Directors of the English Company, the Agra Agency sent in 1620 two of its factors, Robert Hughes and J. Parker, to

Hagrepore-Pattania (Hajipur-Patna)[49] to explore the possibility of opening trade on account of 'Amberties, fine quality of white cotton cloth and Bengal Silk[50]. The English Merchants were well recieved at Patna by Muquarrab Khan who was 'wonderous pleased' with their arrival and gave them every possible help and protection[51]. For their establishment, 'a house in the great bazar near unto the Kotawali's Chowltry (office) on a rent of Rs. 6/12/- per month was also arranged. Purchases of cotton cloth and silk were also made[52]. However, Patna factory was dissolved in June 1621. The second attempt made under confusion in 1632 by Peter Mundy of Agra factory also proved a failure as he, after two months stay in this province of Bihar, found the maintenance of a factory at Patna not very profitąble[53]. Thus, though attempts to effect settlements in Bihar from the North ended in failures, yet the English merchants could not part long with the silk and saltpetre of Bengal and Bihar.

Firman form Prince Shuja, the Vicercoy of Bengal

What the agencies of Surat and Agra could not achieve was in fact, achieved by the agencies of Masulipattam and Madras. By 1651, the English from Balasore under Bridgeman were able to establish themselves at Hughly, and in procuring a 'firman' from Prince Shuja, the Viceroy of Bengal. This Firman, which was confirmed later in 1656 by a 'Nishan', allowed the English company free trade on and annual duty of Rs. 3000/-, and further ordered that 'the factory of the English Company be no more troubled with demand for customs for goods imported or exported by land or by water, nor that their goods be forced from them at under Rates but that they should be free to buy and sell without impediments'.[54]

The English Factory at Patna at Last

It was at this period that the English, again, established their commercial intercourse with Bihar. Though well established by 1652, Patna Factory was officially recognised in 1658. Richard Chamber Layne as the chief, and Roger Seymour, William Vassels, and Francis Farrier, as other factors, were appointed for the factory of Patna.[55] In the beginning the English factory had no house of his own, and the chief did not usually reside there, later on it rented one by John Marshal who had been at Patna from 1669 to 1671 as the second in the English factory.[56] It was the same reason that famous European travellers of the period, viz., Manucci, Tavenier and Burnier, while passing through Patna did not happen to see the Englishmen there.[57] The English chief lived at Hajipur in a hired house, rental being Rs. 38/- per month. They had a house of their own at Naunagar, nearly 8 miles south-east of Patna, and a factory alongwith saltpetre refinery at Singhee, modern Singhiya near Lalganj, 12 miles north of Patna.[54] Broad cloth, lead and quick silver formed the chief commodities of import to Patna and saltpetre the chief article of export. Besides saltpetre, Musk and drugs from Bhutan, Jurhusilk, Tinkall (Borax), sticklac and varieties of fine cotton cloth, viz. ,'Tafftas, Amberties, Sashes, and Elachis (a variety of silk cloth from - Baikunthpur near Patna) were also procurable at Patna and the English dealt in all these commodities' after they had been in Bihar for some time.[59] But soon there were changes in Patna staff, Henry Aldworth, Job Charnock and Pickring taking place of the 'fallen off' members of the staff.[60]

Job Charnock at Patna

With the appointment of Job Charnock as the chief of Patna in 1664, (Acting chief from 1661) and (pucca) permanent chief in 1671,[61] the English Company's trade at Patna increased rapidly. Though every change in the local rulers, which was frequent as a matter of policy during the Moghul-rule, was made the occasion of exactions and extortions, yet the English trade and Patna factory made considerable progress under the able and energetic chiefship of Job Charnock. Lately, the importance of Patna factory had grown considerably owing to the increasing damand of saltpetre. Patna saltpetre was found to be finer and cheaper, so the Company had discontinued its purchases on the west coast and at Masulipatttam. In fact, the English Company was now wholly dependent on Patna for saltpetre supply.[62] By the year 1668-69 saltpetre export of the Company from Bengal averaged 1,977,300 lbs. per year, and went on increasing.[59]

Job Charnock in Bengal with his Experiences of Bihar

Job Charnock left Patna in early 1681 to join as the chief of Kasim bazar factory. His long stay in Bihar had profound effects not only on the life and fortunes of Charnock himself and his Master's but on the destiny of India itself. His experiences of the people and polity, being in constant touch with the Moghul-Court and in direct contact with the people and Nawabs of Bihar proved to be of immense value for the English, and had decided influence on their future policy in India. He was a keen observer to watch the essential weakness of the Moghul Empire with all its imposing appearance. 'The king's hookim'(order) had as small value as an ordinary Governor's. It was on fast decline. The ' hasbulhukim or phirmaund' of Aurangzeb had not that great force and binding which it had in the days of Shah Jehan.[64] Khafi khan had also corroborated the view of Job Charnock: 'throughout the imperial dominions no fear and dread of punishment remained in the hearts of provincial grandees".[65] In the circumstances it was essential for the English company to give up Roe's policy of 'quiet trading'. Chaotic conditions and the weakening of the central authority in India gradually convinced them that they would have to resort to force if they were to stay in India. They could not depend upon the native authorities for the protection of their property and implementations of those 'farmans', 'hushbul hoookums' and 'Parwanas' so dearly procured .This view of the Company's Governors and Agents in India was approved by the Directors who were now free from financial and political troubles at home. A new charter granted by Charles II in 1661 empowered the Company to make peace and war with any prince or people, not being Christians, and administer justice within their own settlements; besides granting monopoly of the Eastern trade.[62] This Charter, as Sir Josiah Child had put it, transformed the London Company from 'merely trading merchants' into the condition of a sovereign state in India.[67]

The English Decides to use Force of Arms to Enforce their Privileges

Strengthened by these developments, the English Company now decided to 'use force of arms to enforce their privileges.[68] This marked change in their attitude and policy was soon to manifest itself in India under the leadership of Job Charnock and Sir John Child.

The English had differences with the Nawab of Bengal and Bihar over the payment of duties. They claimed duty-free trade save Rs.3000/- per annum as granted by Shuja, which the latter governors of Bengal and Bihar were not ready to recongnise. So they thought it wise to procure an imperial firman which they got from Aurangzeb in 1680. But here again the dispute arose over the interpretation of the Imperial firman. Shaista Khan, the Nawab of Bengal contended that by the Firman of 1680, a custom duty of 3¼ per cent was imposed on the English trade throughout the Mughul Empire and ordered to levy the same. The controversy led to crisis. The trouble started from Bihar where George Peacock, the chief of Patna factory, was imprisoned and saltpetre trade totally stopped. In Bengal also the English factories were 'in state of rigorous blockade'.[69] In the meantime, the Directors had sent an armed expedition in 1684 to enforce their privileges and to vindicate their position.[70] This was the beginning of an open rupture with the Moghal Government. Strengthened by the arrival of this task force, Charnock, now the Chief of the Hughly Agency, planned to retaliate. On the 28th October, 1686, explosion took place.[71] On slight excuse, Job Charnock pillaged and burnt the city of Hughly, sailed down the river, boarded a ship with his men and material, and reached Sutanatti, the site of future Calcutta.

The English Misfortune

On hearing the misconduct of the English merchants, infuriated Shaista Khan ordered to seize all the property and people of the English Company. This was followed by similar orders from the Emperor.

Patna factory, which was ordered to be withdrawn but could not, owing to various reasons, had already been plundered in 1684, and its chief, Joseph Dods, died subsequently. Now came the order of general confiscation. Buzurg Umed Khan, the son of Shaista Khan and new Nawab of Bihar, promptly carried out the orders. However, all the Patna factors escaped to safety.

The English comes to Terms:Privileges Restored

The English had miserably failed in wielding swords with the Moghal Emperor and his provincial viceroys. They now realised that they were rash in underestimating the power of the great Moghuls and came to terms with most humble submissive petition[72] by 1690. The Emperor and his Viceroys on their part realising the value of foreign trade granted pardon to the English. The English were allowed to trade with previous privileges. On the invitation of Ibrahim khan, 'the bookish nawab', Job Charnock returned to Bengal but he neither reopened outlying agencies of Patna, Dacca, etc., nor went to Hughly. Instead, he settled at Sutanatti with all the English business. Thus, he laid the foundation of future Calcutta. However, some sort of trade relations were established with Patna to meet the pressing demand of saltpetre. Whereas on the one hand, the Company had troubles during the rebellion of Shobha Singh both from the rebel and from Zuburdust Khan, son of Ibrahim Khan the, Nawab of Bihar, on the other, the English company received permission to fortify Sutanatti. More fateful was the acquisition in 1698 of the Zamindari rights of the three villages of Sutanatti, Kalikata and Govindpur from Prince Azim-us-Shan, the new Governor of Bengal, Bihar and Orissa[73], on a nominal annual rental of Rs.1125/-. This was a great advance for the English company, as it raised them at once from the position of mere adventuring traders, dependent on the caprice of the reigning nawabs to an assured status as landholders paying yearly rental of eleven hundred and twenty-five rupees to the Emperor at Delhi, and receiving in return authority to collect rents and to administer justice under the Mohammadan laws within the boundaries of the three villages.[74] Patna factory, called 'Residency', was re-opened formally by the United Council in 1704 to meet the Court's urgent order for saltpetre. During the embargo on saltpetre trade, George Redshaw, the incharge of the Patna factory, had found discreat means to secure....the company's saltpetre in the merchants' hands.[75] On account of heavy exactions of Prince Azim-us-Shan Patna factors were directed to come over to Calcutta. Redshaw was to be followed by William Cawthrop and William Lloyd. But the Calcutta Council had been reluctant to withdraw factors from Patna.[76]

The War of Succession after Aurangzeb and the English-Precautions

Hearing the illness of Aurangzeb, Azim-us-Shan left for the Imperial capital in the beginning of 1707, appointing Sarbuland Khan, the Dewan, as his deputy in Bihar. Sarbuland Khan was suspicious of the English. In the death of Aurangzeb, the English apprehended the war of succession and consequent disturbances and hence they adopted precautionary measures. Agents in the inland factories were directed to come away to Calcutta. Patna factors were at the same time, ordered to "get all the petre in as fast as they could" and to bribe, if necessary, to get the petre through".[77] But Patna factors were unable to leave Patna with their valuable petre as there was little or no water in the river, and should they make the attempt they expected the Dewan's (Sarbuland Khan's) people would stop them.[78] In fact, Farrukh Siyar who was in Bihar at this time, was making forced contributions from the merchants. Company's Vakeel at Patna was arrested on their refusal to comply with the demand of the Prince. In the circumstances the Company thought it unprofitable to retain the factory at Patna. But the Calcutta council found it unwise 'to abondon it too suddenly',[79] and decided on 19th January, 1708, that 'it were best of the Company's interest to continue the factory and to make a small investment, so as to get all things together to come away the first of next seasons, if the affairs of Government do not appear better than at present'.[80] Exactions continued even after. In August 1708 Cawthrop's boat of saltpetre were seized at Rajhmahal by the order of the Prince and were released on the payment of Rs.14 thousand.[81]

After the victory of Muazzam in the war of succession and on his accession to the Moghul throne as Shah Alam or Bahadur Shah I, the situation was somewhat calm. In the absence of Murshid Quli Khan, Sarbuland governed the three provinces till Nov., 1709 and granted and Sanad of free trade in Bengal, Bihar and Orissa to the English.[82] New Naib of Bihar, Sayyed Hussain Ali and Murshid Quli, the Dewan, confirmed the sanad granted by Surbuland.[83] In the changed situation the Council at Calcutta was directed by the Company' to keep on the Patna factory if they possibly could[84] and as such factory at Patna was retained.

By December of 1710, Lloyd and Cawthrop left for Calcutta on their new assignments and their places were taken by Edward Pattle who managed the Patna factory till its closure in 1715, and Samuel Brown as the second. But there was no end to their troubles. They had to submit to extortions by the new Faujdar of Rajmahal and had to suffer at the hands of rebel Pathan Zamindar of Chuprah who plundered and burnt 500 mds. petre of the Chuprah godown. At the same time their boats with 8,086 mds saltpetre were swept by a violent strom at Patna in October,1711.[85]

English Factory at Patna withdrawn

Still troubles were in store for the English. Bahadur Shah died in Feb.,1712 and they rightly apprehended disturbances during war of succession. Azim-us-Shan declared himself Emperor but soon he was defeated and killed. Jahandar Shah ascended the Imperial throne but his authority was challenged by Farrukh Siyar, Azim-us-Shan's son, who proclaimed himself Emperor at Patna with the help of its Governor, Syed Hussain Ali, one of the Syed brothers, 'the king makers'. Farrukh Siyar laid contributions on all the rich men of the city and expected 4 to 5 lacs from the English and the Dutch.[86] Pattle, the English chief at Patna, was also afraid of the coming of new Emperor's son and of "plundering on both sides.[87] However, they had to pay only 22 thousand to the Emperor and Rs.6500 to the Nawab whose good offices were utilized for the deal. Still apprehending further troubles at Patna, they left the city and withdrew to Singhee wherein also they did not feel safe. Fortunately, the trouble blew over. Farrukh Siyar alongwith Syed Hussain Ali marched to Delhi with sufficient men and money. Jahandar Shah was dethroned and Farrukh Siyar was proclaimed Emperor. Ghairat Khan, the new Governor of Bihar, till 1751, restored normalcy. But Patna factory had become too expensive owing to exactations, presents and bribes which the English had to pay to carry on their trade including private trade of the servants of the Company.[88] By the middle of 1713 order was sent for the withdrawal of the Patna factory but it took nearly two years to carry on the order.[89] In order to avoid the capricious demand of the native authorities, the Company thought it wise to obtain an Imperial farman and it was successful, under the Embassy of Surman, in procuring the same from Emperor Farrukh Siyar in 1717.[90] By this Imperial farman the English company obtained, besides confirmation of previous privileges, new ones, most important being use of 'dustuck'. A Dustuck or passport signed by the President of Calcutta Council exempted the goods it specified from being stopped or examined by the officers of the Bengal Government on any pretence.[91]

Dustucks were intended, as was justifiably contended by Murshid Quli Khan, for the use of Company as a corporate body for their goods to be exported or imported. But they were being abused by the servants of the Company for their private trade.[92] This abuse of Dustuck later formed the Chief ground of conflict between the Company and governments of Siraj and Mir Qasim.

Patna Factory-Reopens, Privileges Allowed by the Bengal Nawabs

Thus, being armed with Imperial Farman, Patna Factory was re-opened in July, 1718, 'under favourable conditions'.[93] Sarbuland Khan, during his second governorship, had restored order in the province. Murshid Quli Khan, the Diwan of the three provinces and the Nazim of the two, understood the value of the foreign trade[94] and his attitude towards the English was generally favourable.[95] But he resented the possession by the English Company of the privilege of being exempted from the payment of duties which others were obliged to contribute. He made it plain that the Company must either forgo this privilege or compensate for it by making him considerable and frequent presents.[92] Fakhr-ud-daula, Governor of Bihar, (1727-32),[93] left the English unmolested. The business of the English company being pretty easy with the country-government, notwithstanding the unsettled conditions of the country,[98] flourished. The branch factories at Fatuwah, Chandee and Begusarai were re-established and five new sub-agencies were started. The only trouble the English had to encounter with at this time was from the Chakwar Rajas of Shambhoo who "laid everything that passed on the river by Monghyr under contribution and put the European Settlements to an annual expense of a large armament to escort their trade to and from Patna.[99]

Murshid Quli Khan was succeeded by Shujauddin Khan in July 1727,[100] in the government of Bengal and Orissa. In 1732. Fakhr-ud-daula was dismissed from the Government of Bihar and it was added to the Bengal Subah by Emperor Muhammad Shah in 1732-33 A.D. and thereby was automatically placed under Nawab Shujauddin.[101] Shujauddin appointed Alivardi Khan his Deputy in Bihar who assumed his post at Patna in 1733.[102]

Nawab Shujauddin Khan allowed the English and other Europeans to enjoy the privileges that had been granted to them by the Emperor Farrukh Siyar, or by the former governors.[103]

Alivardi Khan as the Nawab of Bihar adopted the same policy of his Master's towards the Europeans and made the roads and rivers safe for traders by suppressing the unruly elements, viz., Chakwars, Banzaras etc.

Though the Company's business progressed considerably but the abuse of Dustuk and inland trade remained always an issue. And, the English in Bihar at this time had to face a new rival, the French, in Bihar.

In 1739, a devastating fire 'entirely consumed Patna factory, with broad cloth-godowns and the chief Mr.Cole's apartments.[104] After this fire a spacious building of more substantial nature was built for the factory.[105]

Alivardi, when he became the Nawab of the three provinces in April, 1740, continued the same old policy of let the Europeans alone as far as possible but kept them under strict control. His occasional heavy exactions, not meant to injure them or their trade made under pressing financial difficulties, were justified.[106]

The Maratha invaders and the Afghan rebels, though plundered the Dutch factory and the people in Bihar, left the English largely unmolested.[107] However, the political disturbances in and out of the provinces, the Maratha invasions, the Afghan insurrections and rebellions of refractory zamindars, certainly told upon the trade and commerce of the Company.[108] Under these political conditions and malpractices of the Company's servants, Patna factory was again closed in 1750, to be reorganised again in the middle of July, 1757, by

Peaks as an important trade centre, but with a significant change. The Battle of Plassey changed the status of the English in Bengal, and as such it also changed their status in Bihar. It transformed the trade settlement into a political residency. The chief of the English factory at Patna was no longer a mere traders, he was the Resident at the Durbar of Patna "whose advice the Government of the country sought and acted upon.[109]

These European Companies had a keen commercial rivalry among themselves but while dealing with native authorities and merchants they occasionally tried to present a united front to prevent any encroachment upon their 'Right and Privileges', to safeguard and to promote their commercial interests. However, they had more of jealousy than of brotherhood. In the beginning , their rivalry was confined to commerce but from the forties of the eighteenth century it was extended to politics as all of them began to tend political ambitions with the weakening of Imperial as well as provincial authority. Their diplomatic relations, rivalry, their wars and peace in Europe and elsewhere in the world had their echoes in their mutual relationship in India which had a decisive effect on the history of India.

Alivardi and the Europeans

By the time of Alivardi the European Trading Companies, viz., the Dutch, the French and the English were settled in the three provinces of Bengal, Bihar and Orissa. Alivardi understood the value of external commerce as had understood the Moghul Emperors who reflected their general desire to encourage foreign trade by granting to these Europeans privileges and lower range of export and import duties on their goods.[110] In conformity with the policy of his immediate predecessor, Shuja Khan, Alivardi pursued the policy of let the Europeans alone but kept them under strict control. He was, wrote Jean law, 'zealous of his authority". He especially effected great independence whenever there was question of any affair between him and the Europeans. To speak to him of firmans or privileges obtained from the Emperor was only to anger him. He knew well how to say at the proper moment that he was both king and wazier".[111] His attitude towards them was strict but not harsh.[112] He allowed them privileges but not at the cost of his prerogatives.

He was ready to accept them as mere traders and 'favoured the poor merchants,[113] but not to tolerate their political ambitions.[114] He valued their trade but was conscious of their power and had ability and means to keep them under control. He used to compare the Europeans to a hive of bees whose honey you might reap but that if you disturbed their hive they would sting you to death.[115] Under pressing financial difficulties, Alivardi laid under contribution all the Europeans including the English; his object being 'not to injure the hive of bees, but only to 'reap a benefit' as a 'bee -keeper'.[116]

Alivardi knew the strength of the English and compared them with 'the fire of the sea, which could consume' the prosperity of land and water in all Hindustan if disturbed and yet he did not allow the English and the French to enact the drama of the Deccan in his provinces. 'He saw with equal indignation and surprise the progress of the French and the English nation on the Coromondal coast as well as in the Deccan. He feared that sooner or later the Europeans would attempt similar enterprises in his government.[117] But he was on alert. He did not allow them to strengthen their fortifications telling them, "you are merchants what need you have of a fortress? Being under my protection you have no enemies to fear'.[118]

The alleged charge of Holwell pertaining to Alivardi's advice in his death bed speech to Siraj to root out the Europeans, has been proved to be concocted even by the contemporary English writers themselves.[119] On the other hand, he is said to have advised Siraj not to quarrel with the English.[120] Nevertheless, Alivardi did not permit Europeans to extend their political ambitions to his provinces. But situation changed after his death.

The death of Alivardi Prompted the Europeans for Political Adventures

The death of Aurangzeb not only hastened the decline of the Moghal Empire but also signalled the decline and degeneration of all aspects of Indian life as a whole. This provided the Europeans with an opportunity to realise their wild dreams and to aspire for political power. Nevertheless,

Bengal and Bihar in the first half of Eighteenth century was fortunate to have capable and strong governors in succession. Murshid Quli Khan, Shujauddin Khan and Alivardi Khan were powerful enough to prevent the Europeans from making their dominions a political arena. But the situation changed altogether immediately after the death of Alivardi Khan, for behind the facade of power and prosperity there had set in the weakness in the whole system, which the Europeans were astute enough to grasp. It now proved an opportune moment for them to embark on long cherished political venture. They came out with political designs and novel schemes which found ready welcome from the debased aristocracy selfish to the core, devoid of any sense of unity and nationality (patriotism). 'This, indeed, whetted the political ambitions of the European trading nations in India and made their penetration into her politics quicker, bolder and deeper than before.[121]

The opportunity was provided by the young but profligate, and rash but cowardice, Nawab Siraj-ud-daula who ascended the Masnad of Bengal in April, 1756 after the death of his grandfather, Mahabat Jang Alivardi. With the passing of Alivardi passed away all the wisdom and bravery. The line of wise, strong and independent Nawabs of the three provinces came to an end.

Siraj-ud-daula as Nawab

It was the misfortune of the three provinces that when it needed a capable and strong nawab, it was placed under inexperienced and young Siraj-ud-daula who 'came to his long assigned throne in a house divided against itself with a hostile faction in the army and a disaffected subject population."[122] The Europeans have depicted Siraj-ud-daula to be devoid of all the virtues of a ruler but full of all the vices of a spoilt prince. Even if we do not concede to this, he was not strong, wise, cool and calculated. Though he "seemed to be ambitious of military fame,[123] he was neither a warrior and general , so essential quality those days for a ruler to keep him in power, nor wiser 'to distinguish the faithful from the unfaithful.'[124] Insolent and rash as he was, he had offended the commoner and the courtier, the military, landed and mercantile aristocracy alike. Hill has aptly remarked: 'In fact, the cruelty and the folly of the Nawab had turned his court into a nest of traitors'.[125] He had a few friend around him to give him wise counsel when needed but many more to misguide him to ruin. Such was, then, the Nawab and the court destined to doom. And the people in general had little interest in what government came and went.

Siraj Unable to Keep Disruptive Forces Under Control

Though Siraj-ud-daula's accession had been smooth, his difficulties were enormous and events after his accession moved with marathan speed leading to his complete and tragic ruin.

Siraj-ud-daula could not, unlike his grand-father, keep under proper control the disruptive forces which had already appeared during the previous regime and which Alivardi had wisely utilised to his benefit; though Siraj attempted but perished in the attempt. In fact, 'his career as a Nawab', remarked K.K. Datta, 'was a big tragedy."[121]

Siraj Against the English:Calcutta Captured

Siraj was beset with enemies, not only claimants of the Masnad, like Sahukantjag and Ghasiti Begum, and treacherous aristocracy but also the intriguing English. The English were there with all the hostile intentions, designs and defying attitude.[127] Though, 'people knew', as M. Law had observed, 'Long before the death of Alivardi Khan that Siraj-ud-daula was hostileto the English,"[2] yet Siraj-ud-daula after his accession, had every reason to be hostile against the English.[128] Instead of manifesting any sign of the recognition of his accession the English were rightly and "strongly suspected of being in league with his opponents.[129] To add to the wrath of Siraj, the English did not surrender his offenders and did not demolish additional fortifications, which they had erected taking advantage of the illness of Alivardi at Kasim bazar and Calcutta. Moreover, they were abusing their trading privileges causing loss of revenue to the Government and misery to the native merchants.

Suspending his march towards Purnea, Siraj-ud-daula resolved to deal with the English first. He first reduced the

English factory at Kasim bazar and then took possession of Calcutta by assault on 20th June, 1756. But the young Nawab in his pride and ignorance and exhibiting the lack of all military and political wisdom, did not further consolidate his victory over Calcutta and left the English unmolested at Fulta where they had taken shelter escaping from Calcutta. [130]

Raja Ram Narain—Faithful Deputy of Siraj-ud-daula in Bihar

There were opponents of Siraj's succession in Bengal, but for the Deputy Governor of Bihar, it was a fait accompli and in turn Raja Ram Narain was confirmed in his governorship of Bihar by the new Nawab of the three provinces. Raja Ram Narain not only himself remained faithful to the last, but he also exacted allegiance from the refractory Zamindars and Chiefs of his province for his new master. However, trouble arose from Purnea which had lately been made a separate Faujdaree independent of the Nawab of Patna. Immediately after the accession of Siraj, his cousin, Shaukatjang, the faujdar of Purnea, equally profligate, rash and ambitious, staked his claims for the Masnad of Bengal. He had also supporters at the Darbar of Murshidabad and in the palace. At the same time, he managed to procure from the Imperial Vazeer the permission to seize the Masnad of Bengal.[131]

After the capture of Calcutta, Siraj-ud-daula was free to deal with Shaukatjang. At the end of September, 1756, he marched on to Purnea with an advance party under Mohan Lal, asking his Deputy in Bihar, Raja Ram Narian, to come to his assistance. Leaving Patna in charge of his brother, Dhiraj Narain, who was always alert in the fort of Azimabad with his 3000 horses, and 6000 foot, and 50 field pieces,'[122] Raja Ram Narain set out with Raja Sunder Singh of Tikari, Pahalwan Singh of Nokha and his brother Suther at the head of a force of Azimabad which alone could not be less than the double of the forces of Shaukatjang.[133] The battle fought on the 16th October, 1756, near Manihari resulted in the defeat and death of Shaukatjang owing mainly to the half hearted cooperation of the 'principal commanders'.[134] Purnea troops was completely routed and huge wealth of Shaukatjang was seized. For their services, special favours and rewards were bestowed on Raja

Ram Narian and Mohan Lal who received the Faujdari of Purnea to be ruled through his son.[135]

Miscalculation of Siraj and his Waning Fortune

Thus, acting promptly, decisively and energetically Siraj-ud-daula, within six months of his accession, miraculously relieved himself of all his enemies. It seemed as if fortune smiled on him, but infact, it had began to wane. He was so sure of the good fortune which protected him that he could not foresee the fire coming out of the sea. Scrafton wonderd why the Saubah permitted them to continue so quietly at Fulta, till they were become formidable to him and himself answered 'I can only account for from his mean opinion of us, as he had been frequently heard to say, he (Siraj) did not imagine there were ten thousand men in all, Firinghistan and had no idea of our attempting to return by force."[136] The result was inevitably unfortunate. The English forces under Admiral Watson and Colonel Clive from Madras regained Calcutta in early January of 1757. As if the recovery of Calcutta were not enough to vindicate their claim and national honour, they sent a small force to Hughli to impress the Nawab. The city of Hughli was plundered and burnt and the fort stormed. It was a hard pill for the Nawab to swallow. He proceeded against the English at the head of a strong force. But he blundered to meet the English on their own ground at Calcutta where, on the 5th February, he was 'so terrified' that under the advice of his treacherous minister, he granted the English every thing they asked for, the full restoration of all their privileges and restitution of all they had lost in the sack of Calcutta.[137] This was the treaty of Alinagar, both 'Honourable and advantageous for the Company'.[138]

Cunning Clive: all out to Dispossess the French and to Dethrone Siraj

Under the apprehension of impending European War, Clive had come to Bengal with the intension to dispossess the French of Chandranagore. Further, apprehension of a French alliance with Nawab induced him to remove both the French and Siraj-ud-daula.. 'The dethronement of the Nawab', observed M. Jean Law, 'had become absolute necessity. To drive us out of Bengal was a preliminary piece of work.[139] Siraj was now a ruined man. Only chance of his safety lay in a loyal alliance with the French against the English. But he would do nothing as the terror of the English arms , remarked law, had 'put him in a condition in which he was unable to follow, and even to see his true interest."[140] In fact, from now on Siraj, far removed from his former self, displayed pathetically lamentable lack of resolution, decision, proper judgement and boldness. There were reasons for the bewilderment of the young and inexperienced Nawab. On the one hand, he found traitors all around him, on the other, diplomacy and entreaties of cunning Clive, and threats of haughty Watson to 'kindle such a flame in the country not be extinguished by all the water in the Ganges, and even more, 'to make him prisoner to carry him to England.[141] The impending invasion of Ahmad Shah Abdali further complicated the issue for the Nawab. It was in such a situation that Siraj could not prevent the English çapture of Chandranagore and subsequent expulsion of M. Jean Law and his party. The loss of Chandranagore not only dealt 'an inexpressible blow to the French company' by depriving it of certainly a large, rich, and thriving colony',[142] but also crushed finally the French power and influence in Bengal and made the unfortunate Nawab all the more enfeebled to withstand the English in ensuing contest.

Clive's Conspiracy with Disgruntled Elements

Though, by now the English had gained all the things they had desired, and the Nawab had fulfilled most of the treaty obligations; the French power was crushed in Bengal, yet they did not find their position secure as there were still possibilities of the French making a fresh bid of come-back with a Nawab, sympathetic to them and hostile to the English. To avert this danger, the English needed a revolution in the Government.[143] They actively engaged themselves in a conspiracy in close cooperation with the disaffected elements of the Durbar, chief among them being Jagat Seths, the great bankers without whom the revolution of 1757 would never have been accomplished, Mir Jaffar, Rai Durlabh Ram, and Omichand. As a matter of fact, observed Law correctly, 'except Siraj-ud-daula himself, one may say, the English had the whole Durbar in their favour."[144] It was decided by the conspirators to replace Siraj-ud-daula by Mir Jaffar as the Nawab. The principal movers in the conspiracy were guided solely by their narrow self-interest keeping aside the greater national cause, and quite unmindful of the ill-consequences. The conspiracy took a definite shape in the form of a secret treaty with Mir Jaffar in early June, 1757.[145] 'Though, in the know of the conspiracy, vacillating, wavering and timid Siraj-ud-daula did not take action against the conspirators. On the contrary, he made entreaties with Mir Jaffar, with the natural result that the conspirators were emboldened.

The Battle of Plassey and (Mir Jaffar as Nawab) its Results

The opposing armies of the Nawab and the English, thirteen times different in numerical strength, met at Plassey on the 23rd June, 1757. The battle of Plassey which was not a battle but a grand show of betrayal, and a sordid story of, as Clive himself observed, 'fighting, tricks, chicanery, intrigues, and politics,'[146] was won by the English. The revolution was accomplished. Clive conducted Mir Jaffar to the 'Masnad' of Murshidabad on 29th June, 1757,[147] and Siraj met his tragic fate. And the fate of Siraj-ud-daula and his provinces, subsequently, became the fate of all Hindustan.

With the death of Siraj-ud-daula the troubles of the English were at an end. The new nawab lost no time in sending to Calcutta the indemnity promised to the inhabitants for losses and sufferings. From the depths of poverty and humiliation', rightly wrote Kathleen Blechynden, 'they were raised at once to wealth and power."[148]

Plassey reversed the position of the English vis-a-vis the Nawab in Bengal. Before Plassey the English stayed in Bengal during the pleasure of the nawab, after Plassey the Nawab sat on the Masnad at Murshidabad during the pleasure of the English. They were now the king-makers, power behind the throne. From commercial body, they were now raised to a political and military body—the 'Company Bahadoor.' In fact, Plassey secured the foundation of the future British Empire in India.

The Centre of Interest Shifts to Bihar

1757 Revolution in Bengal, naturally, shifted the centre of

interest from Bengal to Bihar where was the deputy-governor, Raja Ram Narain who had been a faithful adherent to the house of Alivardi', and where was the brave M.Jean Law, the exiled French chief of Kasim Bazar, having real sympathy with an 'unfortunate man' and a sworn enemy of the English. At the time of parting with the Nawab Law is said to have been asked by the Nawab 'if anything new should happen he would send for him again,[149] and was secretly supplied with Rs. 1000/- along with an order on Raja Ram Narain to help him with money and supplies.[150] Law moved leisurely as wished by the Nawab, from Murshidabad towards Patna where he reached on 3rd June, and was well received by Raja Dhiraj Narain, brother of Raja Ram Narian,[151] and where he was within four or five day's march or sail from Sooty, the mouth of the Murshidabad river, and, therefore, in a position to join the Nawab whenever it might be necessary.[152] And, actually when Siraj-ud-daula saw events taking unfortunate turn, he sent for Law. But for the treachery of Nawab's Officers, letters did not reach him in time and Law, could send only M. Sinfrey, who had commanded the French party at Plassey and gave a good account of himself and his party.[152] Even after defeat at Plassey letter written by Siraj-ud-daula did not reach Law in time.[153] Of his own, Law had started at the first rumour of danger before getting the Nawab's letter, but when he reached Rajmahal on 1st July "he found that all was over".[154] Contemporary Bihar historian Ghulam Hussain, lamenting the system and 'etiquette', notes that Law would have been in time had the Nawab's last remittance been a bill of exchange and not an order on the treasury.[155] To preserve his liberty Law made a hasty retreat from Rajmahal. Colonel Clive and his puppet Nawab sent urgent letters to Governor of Bihar to arrest him, "but Ram Narain was no lover of Mir Jafar and he was not yet acquainted with Clive, so he allowed him to pass.[156] "Though, hotly pursued by Major Eyre Coote, Law and his party forcedmarch to get out of the dominions of the puppet Nawab till they reached Ghazipur in the provinces of Nawab Shuja-ud-daula of Oudh on 25th July. Major Coote reaching Patna on 26th July seized the French Factory there and followed Law upto Chuprah only to find gone in safety.[157] Law wandered long in the lands and courts of Shuja-ud-daula and the Moghal Prince expecting them to invade the English in Bengal.

Bihar Unamenable to the Results of Plassey

In fact, Bihar was not amenable to the result of the battle of Plassey. Raja Ram Narain, the Deputy-Governor of Bihar and many leading chiefs of Bihar were most unlikely to support the new regime as they were certainly averse to the extension of the English influence over Bihar. Law who was keen observer of the situation says: 'They had an understanding with Ramnarain, All these Rajas.....united to each other by the same religion, mutually support each other as much they can. They deteste the Mohammmadan Government and if it had not been for the Seths, the famous bankers, with whom they had close connection, it is probable that after the revolution in which Siraj-ud-daula was the victim, they would all have risen together to establish a Hindu Government from which the English would not have obtained the advantages they did from the Muhammadan."[158]

While at Chuprah in pursuit of Law, Major Coote had gathered intelligence that the several Rajas of the country after death of Siraj-uddaula..... were assembling troops, and taking every other measure to prevent any demand being made on them', and Dhaunsi Ram, the Raja of Petera 'was collecting forces, and every day people were joining him from the north, and that he already with him 3000 horse, 1500 foot, and four pieces of cannon'.[159] Not only Hindu Rajas but also Muslim Zamindars of Bihar, like Kamgar Khan, the turbulent Mai chief of Narhat and Samai, were not reconciled to the Revolution in Bengal.[160] He opposed and fought the English till his death in 1764. As a matter of fact, we find an open manifestation of resistance throughout Bihar, from north to south and from east to west. More serious was the revolt in Purnea where Hazari Ali Khan, with the help of Achal Singh, the Diwan of the late Nawab Sahaukatjang, proclaimed himself the nawab in all out defiance of the new regime.[161] The insurrection could subsequently be crushed sternly by Khadem Hussain Khan with a large force.[162]

Raja Ramnarian not Reconciled to the Bengal Revolution

Raja Ramnarain, the Deputy-Governor of Bihar, who was a faithful adherent to the house of Alivardi, though could not prevent the 'Plassey' as he was kept in the dark about the gravity of the situation and had been busy in the suppression of the disaffected Mai Chief, had not immediately reconciled to the Revolution of 1757.[163] Though repeatedly written by Mir. Jafar and Clive to help Major Coote, who had come to Bihar in pursuit of Law, met with obstruction instead of aid from Ram Narain'.[160] Raja Ramnarain was even suspected of being in league with the French and Nawab Suja-ud-daula of Oudh against the English and their puppet Nawab of Bengal.[165]

Clive, the villain of the drama of 1757, also was not well disposed towards Raja Ramnarain in the beginning. He wanted not only to 'chastise' Raja's 'treacherous' and 'turbulent' dispositions,[166] but also to wrest the government from Ramnarain.[167] However, both came to terms, later on, out of practical considerations. The Raja was convinced of the hostile intentions of Nawab Mir Jafar who was bent upon the Raja's destruction and appointment of his own brother, Mir Cazem Khan, as the Deputy-Governor of Bihar[168] and, therefore, 'concluded his own power and dominion could never subsist upon a solid foundation unless he made an alliance with the English.[169]

The Raja Acqiesces in

And thus, Raja Ramnarain acqiesced in the results of the battle of Plassey out of the "motives of self interest' and 'love of office', instead of acting with a feeling of righteous indignation, readiness, for revenge, and vigorous and determined efforts' to resist the wrong doer', as Prof. S.H.Askari puts it correctly.[170]

On the other hand, Clive feared that case of a French alliance with Nawab Shuja-ud-daula of Oudh, 'troubles might arise and affairs grow serious especially if the Bihar and Midnapur countries were not settled:[171] and 'it would be a constant check on the Subah to have the Nawab of Patna devoted to the English.[172]

Consequently, the Raja with great character', power and popularity,[173] was won over by Clive and disaffection of other principal chiefs of Bihar was also diplomatically neutralised by Clive to the interest of the Company.[174] A settlement was effected between the Nawabs of Bengal and Bihar. Raja Ramnarain was confirmed in the Government of Bihar under the nominal headship of Miran, the Chhota Nawab, the son of Mir Jafar.[175] Clive, as solmnly assured, protected the person and honour of Raj Ramnarain even at the hazard of his life.[176] But it was the irony of the situation that not only the Nawab of Bengal and his principal officers but also the governor of Bihar depended on the English support for offices and lives.[177] Nevertheless, 'no favourable opportunity was let slip, no single occasion lost that could be turned to the Company's advantage.[178]

The Invasion of Prince Ali Gauhar (Shah Alam II) and the Mood of Resistance to the English Power in Bihar

'The peace and tranquillity of this Kingdom' of Bihar effected by the genius of Clive proved ephemeral. Though its Governor remained faithful to his new patron, the whole of Bihar again rose with a mood of resistance during the invasions of the Shahzada Ali Gauhar, the future Shah Alam II, on Bihar and Bengal.

The Prince, exiled from his Imperial capital, planned to invade and to wrest the provinces of Bengal, Bihar and Orissa with the help of Nawab Shuja-ud-daula of Oudh, Muhammad Quli Khan of Allahabad and Raja Balwant Singh of Benaras. He even procured a sanad from his father Emperor Alimgir II. Principal chiefs of Bihar viz., Kamgar Khan of Narhat and Samai, Raja Pehalwan Singh of Bhojpur and Raja Sundar Singh of Tikari readily came to their aid. M.Jean Law also joined the Imperial Prince in April, 1759, with his French Party.[179]

The invasion came like a storm from the north posing a 'great danger' not only to Patna but 'as well as to the whole province of Bihar'.[180] Raja Ramnarain found himself unable to withstand the invading army,[181] and siege of the city of Patna was raised only after the arrival of Forces from Bengal under Clive and Miran.[182] The Imperial Prince retired beyond the Sone and Pahalwan Singh and other disaffected zamindars were subdued.[183] The English believed that the progress of the Shahzada was totally stopped and his designs frustrated by which means this province was 'now in perfect tranquillity and the Subah more attached to' them ever.[184] But contrary to this English belief, Shahzada, who had proclaimed himself Emperor as Shah Alam II after the assassination of his father, reappeared on the borders of Bihar by December, 1759.

Shah Alam II's Second Invasion: Combined Opposition to the British Sway

Early in 1760 Shah Alam II invaded Bihar for the second time. This time his position stood on a better footing, and at this time he was more powerful than ever, by the number of disaffected zamindars, who had joined him, and he was not only an Emperor, atleast in name, but he had also with him faithful allies and brave generals like Kamgar Khan, Asalat Khan and Diler Khan. Khadem Hussain Khan the Faujdar of Purnea, also rebelled against Mir Jafar to join the Emperor.[185] During active engagements the Emperor was also joined by Raja Pahalwan Singh, Murad Khan and Ahmed Khan Qureshi[186] betraying Raja Ram Narian whose position was very critical.

Though Raja Ramnarain fought gallantly but was defeated and wounded in the battle of Masumpur on 9th February.[187] Three English Officers including Capt. Cochrane were also killed.[188] The attack on Patna was repulsed by the forces of Major Callaud and Miran. But the Imperial forces soon proceeded to Bengal to fall upon Murshidabad. They were reinforced by the rebellious Rajas of Birbhum and Burdwan who had declared for the Shahzada and Maratha General Sheo Bhatt Sathe[189]. However, they were defeated in Bengal and the Imperial Party retreated to Bihar to attack its capital again.[190] Joined by the French Party under Law, a vigorous attack was made on Patna,[191] which according to Broome was very nearly captured. But the attack was finally repulsed by the end of April[192]. Major Knox along with Sitab Roy also defeated, in June, Khadem Hussain Khan, one of the chief associates of the Emperor[193], on the other side of the Ganges at Hajipur. Ghulam Hussain believed that if the arrival of Khadem Hussain Khan had "happened sometime before when Azimabad was besieged by the Emperor'......there is no doubt but that he would have possessed himself of that city (Patna)[194]. Khadem Hussain Khan was further pursued by the forces of Callaud and Miran up to Bettiah[195], where the young Nawab was ' taken off by the flash of lightning on 3rd July.[196] However, the Emperor remained long hovering over Bihar.[197]

The Results of Shah Alam's Invasions

The two invasions of Shah Alam demonstrated in more clear terms the fact that Mir Jafar, the Subahdar of Bengal and Raja Ramnarain, the deputy Sunbahdar of Bihar, depended on the English for the military support and could not maintain themselves without them. It also brought to prominence the widely prevalent dislike and spirit of Indian resistance against the growing English power and their puppet Nawab. Clive himself considered Mir Jafar 'a prince of little capacity', whose mismanagement threw the country into great confusion in the space of a few months and might have proved of fatal consequence to himself, but for our known attachment to himself....He was not at all blessed with the talent of gaining the love and confidence of his principal officers."[198] Even more, Vansittart 'found a general disaffection against his government and a detestation of his person and principles prevailed in the country, amongst all ranks and degrees of people."[199]

Mir Jafar Deposed: Mir Qasim Placed on Musnad

Thus the English were intelligent and wise enough to detect a general disaffection against Mir Jafar's Government, that it was their attachment that saved him, but, as was natural they could not or rather were insane and blind, to grasp that the general disaffection' was also directed against the English due to Mir Jafar's known attachment to them'. It has been well commented by the translator of Ghulam Hussain's Siyar-ul-Mqtaqherin, that the English came to be hated and opposed soon after the battle of Plassey.[200] In fact, it was also because of this hatred against the English that Mir Jafar was also widely disliked. Many treasonable projects were set on foot against him with the object of effecting his downfall and destruction.[201] But it was brought about by his English friends themselves. Even after becoming 'Colonel Clive's Jackal' and granting extravagant concessions unwarranted by pre-Plassey Treaty with him,[202] poor Mir Jafar could not satisfy the greed of the English. His greatest fault was that he tried to exert certain amount of independence and allegedly desired to 'reduce' the English power, instead of augamenting it'.[203] Consequently, the alien king-makers in Bengal deposed Mir Jafar and placed

Mir Qasim on the Masnad of Murshidabad under a treaty concluded with Mir Qasim on 27th September, 1760.[204]

Ideas and Attributes of Mir Qasim as Nawab

Thus, was accomplished another revolution in Bengal. But the revolution of 1760 was really no revolution, for it involved no new-principle, not even a new political approach. It was a change of rulers.[205] However, it was a change with two differences. Firstly, in 1757 a change was brought by use of force, in 1760 threat of force was enough. The difference in method reflected a change in the Company's position."[206] Secondly, the new ruler was quite opposite from the old, not only in age but also in character, nature, and in his ideas about the post he was advanced in. Mir Qasim, observes Ghulam Hussain, was ' the most extraordinary Prince of his age', without an equal in unravelling the intricasies of government, and especially the knotty mysteries of 'finance', and then, 'had admidrable qualities that balanced in his bad ones'.[207] This quality of Mir Qasim has been corroborated by Vansittart, the then English Governor of Fort William, who says 'Meer Cossim...was esteemed a capable man in business.[208] There might be dispute whether Mir Qasim planned from the very beginning on the means of driving the English out of Bengal,[204] yet it is certain that he wanted to be a strong Nawab independent of the English and their military support which had handicapped Mir Jafar. So he wished to be a real Nawab, though recognising genuine privileges of the English granted under the treaties and engagements. It was never his desire, as he himself wrote to Vansittart even on the eve of complete rupture, on 19th June, 1763, to interrupt either Company's trade or 'foreign commerce', and to have anything contrary to the old treaty."[206]

Extended Authority of the English Frequently Clashing with Nawabs

Kasim Ali (Mir Qasim) had a much better army than any of his predecessors. Though it was not trained in the European manner, several of the chief officers were Armenians, who effected great reforms in discipline. Three years later it made a really good fighting against the English.[211] In a sense, Mir Qasim wanted to be the Nawab of the pre-Plassey days. But much water had flowed in the Ganges since then to change the face of the country and to erode the power of the Nawab. Needless to say, the English had become de facto rulers, and their authority had extended itself so near the Nawab's that they were frequently clashing.[212] To add to this, the merchant-rulers had lately brought such innovations' in the name of privileges that they frequently encroached upon Nawab's authority and honour. To this position, Mir Qasim was not reconciled, he was not ready to forgo the just rights of the government. And for the servants of the Company, it was quite ruinous to retreat from the profitable and privileged position to which they had reached, and to desist from making wild claims. As a matter of fact, the conflict between the two was implied in the logic of facts, for the interests of the Nawab and the English were 'essentially opposite' and 'irreconcilable'.[213] After the overthrow of Mir Qasim, commenting on the unworkability of the system that had emerged after Plassey, Vansittart observed: 'I am plainly of the opinion that upon the present system, no friendship can be observed with any nawab. The two governments clash too frequently to stand upon friendly footing."[214]

Shah Alam's Invasion and 'Universal Revolt' in Bihar

Under the circumstances differences were bound to arise and one arose soon. Shah Alam II who was still hovering over the borders of the province after his last defeat, invaded Bihar for the third time at the end of the year 1760. He had 35 to 40 thousand cavalry under Kamgargar Khan, and the French party of muskets and artillery under Law.[215] They were joined by Buniyad Singh and other refractory chiefs. This was the time that Asad Zaman Khan, the Raja of Birbhum also revolted against the British power and their protege, the Nawab, and invited Shah Alam to drive the English. The English Governor describing the situation mentions that 'the two armies were in the field and waiting only the fair weather to advance, the Shahzada towards Patna, and the Beerbhum Rajah towards Murshidabad, the capital. The Rajahs of Bissenpur, Ramgur, and the other countries....had offered considerable supplies to the Beerbhum Rajah. The Rajah of Currukpore had committed open hostilities...In a word, the whole country seemed quite ripe for universal revolt.[216]

The invading army of the Emperor in Bihar had encamped at Bihar Sharif. Even 'the revenues of the province were collected in his name upto within a few miles of the city of Patna."[217] However, the Imperial forces were defeated by the joint forces of the Nawab and the English forces under Carnac in the middle of January 1761[21]. Thus, ended Law's attempt to maintain the French party in Bengal.'[218]

Shah Alam under English Protection, Proclaimed Emperor, Mir Qasim Suspicious

Amidst the pursuit and defeats the Emperor, Shah Alam sought the Enlgish protection from Major Carnac at Gaya on 6th February, 1761.[219] Hostilities were ceased and he was provided with a daily allowance of Rs. one thousand by Raja Ram Narain. In fact, the unhappy prince was reduced so low as to be much more an object of pity than fear', said Major Carnac.[220] The English also decided to come to terms with the Emperor and negotiations had already been started for the purpose. Even proposals to escort him to Delhi were discussed.[221] It naturally gave suspicion to Mir Qasim who feared that an understanding between the two would endanger his position, and he 'offered a persistent, though half concealed opposition to the design.' Dodwell remarks that Mir Qasim 'was clearly obessed with the fear that the English would obtain from Shah Alam a grant for the provinces on their on account,' and that there was not a shred of truth in the Nawabs suspicion.[222] But it is hard to accept this contention in the light of latter events and evindence.[223] It was under these circumstances that Mir Qasim was hesitant to 'proclaim Shah Alam as emperor till after his departure'(from the provinces), and was brought to do so by Coote's threat of doing it himself if Mir Qasim delayed any longer.[224] A Durbar was held in Patna on 12th March 1761 and Shah Alam was acknowledged Emperor in the presence of Mir Qasim, other principal native officers and chiefs, and all the civil and military officers of the Company.[225] Mir Qasim was confirmed in the Subahdaree of Bengal, Bihar and Orissa by the Emperor[226] and the revolution was legalised. In June, the Emperor was escorted beyond the borders of Bihar by Major Carnac.[223] An interesting and significant episode of this escort which manifests clearly the magnitude of the political designs of the English give evidence against Dodwell's contention of Mir Qasim's 'suspicion', is that during this march Major Carnac presented two arzees' before the Emperor for the confirmation of English 'possessions and privileges.[228] 'In answer, the Emperor even made voluntary' offer of Dewanee of the Subah of Bengal. The Council at Calcutta discussed the matter and came to the conclusion that the Dewanee "would be a source of continual jealousies between the Nawab and the Company, we do not think it advisable to sue for it at this time.[229]

The Cleavage on Increase

The cleavage between the Nawab and the Company remained on increase and was further intensified due to internal dissensions in the Council at Calcutta. Opposition and the party against the President and Governor turned out to be the opposition against the Nawab as he was supposed to be the Governor's nominee.[230] It became manifest in the case of Raja Ram Narain, the deputy-governor of Bihar.

After the confirmation of his post as the Subedar and departure of the Emperor from the province, Mir Qasim found himself at leisure to regulate the affairs of his government. He understood it well that he must improve his finances and reorganise his civil as well as military establishments, if he were to preserve his independence and authority as a strong Nawab free from the interference and encroachments of the English. With this twin object in mind he adopted a series of measures which brought him, beginning with differences on Raja Ram Narain's removal from the office as a natural corollary, on road to rupture with the English.

Differences on Raja Ram Narain's case

Mir Qasim was not well disposed towards Raja Ram Narain. Ram Narain's huge wealth made the Nawab believe that he must have embezzled government revenue.[231] The Deputy-Governor's sincere attachment to the English and at the same time defying attitude towards the Nawab[230] made Mir Qasim abhor the Raja. Apparently the Nawab had just demand on Maharaja Ramnarain of large sums on account of the last four years.[233] But he was evading the submission of accounts and payments on the protection of Major Carnac and Colonel Coote, in whose favour Ramnarain had ingratiated himself and who were supporting him against the wishes of their superiors.[234] As a matter of fact, for Mir Qasim, Raja Ramnarain was a base man', a 'wretch', an 'enemy', 'a traitor', 'a snake half killed', who was 'fomenting dissensions' against him, and making his 'life and fortune a prey'.[231] Mir Qasim, therefore, was bent upon Ramnarain's removal and destruction. Latter events proved, he intended to destroy' leading men of any rank or consequence' who had good connection with the English.[236]

The Raja Left at Nawab's Mercy

In the beginning, Vansittart's Government, pursuing the old policy of Clive had instructed Major Carnac[233] and Colonel Coote to secure Ramnarain's against all the attempts of oppression or injustice and to preserve the Government of Patna for him,[238] as Ramnarain had been 'remarkably steady in his alliance with the Company and had received from Colonel Clive particular assurance of his protection with respect to his person, fortune, and government'.[237] However, the tone of the Calcutta government gradually cooled,[240] as the Nawab expressed his total inability in complying with the pecuniary obligation of his government, and of the Company, and even threatened to relinquish his office, if he was not permitted to 'finish all the accounts' with his deputy and other people.[242] Raja Ramnarain was suspended in June[242] and ordered to be delivered over to the Nawab in September.[243] The measure was subsequently approved by the Court of Directors in their letter to the Council of 17th Dec., 1762. Thus, Ramnarain was absolutely left at the Nawab's mercy. What could be expected of the Merchant Rulers?

Raja Ramnarain put to Death after Long Ordeal

Raja Ramnarain with his family and bankers were imprisoned and their entire property confiscated.[244] After undergoing long ordeal at Patna, Murshidabad and Monghyr, he was put to death by throwing into the Ganges with a bag of sand fastened to his neck[245] in August, 1763.

Affairs of Raja Ramnarain also demonstrated very clearly the ill consequences of stationing in Bihar of the high military commanders who often clashed with the Chief at Patna who had assumed the role of political resident. As a remedy for this evil Major Carnac and 'Colonel Coote were recalled to Calcutta and a small contingent of troops under Captain Carstair was placed at the disposal of the Chief at Patna.[246] However, one evil produced another. It had the effect of making the Chief so powerful that now and then he even defied the authority of the Governor and the Council at Fort William.[247]

Governor of Bihar Relegated to the Position of Mere 'Naib'

After Ramnarain, deputy governors of Bihar were changed in quick succession. It was the misfortune of the province that the battle of Plassey and subsequent events had relegated the position of its Governor to a mere 'Naib' and placed them at the mercy of the Nawabs of Bengal and their English patrons. Patna, the capital of this province, from this time again became the centre of all sorts of jealousies, intrigues, treachery, assassination, rivalries, and even active fights and occasional plunder, enacting the Imperial capital.

Changes in Bihar Government in Quick Succession

Immediately after Raja Ramnarain was removed, Raja Rajballabh was advanced in the Deputy Governmentship of Bihar[248]. But he could not remain long in the good book and confidence of suspicious Mir Qasim who got him removed and imprisoned with his son in June 1762. He was succeeded by Raja Naubat Roy.[249] Raja Rajballabh's entire property and effects, even in Dacca, were confiscated.[250] Later on he was also put death at Monghyr in Aug. 1763, along with Raja Ramnarian and other prisoners of distinction.[251] Raja Naubat Roy, too, was removed within months and was succeeded by Mir Mehdi Khan.[252]

Mir Qasim Prepares to be the Real Nawab

It is true, 'the perpetual treasons and endless duplicities, which he had been seeing throughout so many preceding administrations, had soured his temper; and the perpetual infidelities of the troops as well as of the Commanders and Grandees of Bengal, had rendered him exceedingly suspicious, and every proof to confiscation of properties confinements of persons, and effusion of blood,[253] yet it goes to the credit of Mir

Qasim that within a short period he, observed Vansittart as a compliment, 'discharged the Company's debt, and the heavy arrears of his army; retrenched the expenses of his court, which had before consumed the income of his predecessors, and secured his won authority over the country by reducing the power of the Zamindars, who were before continual disturbers of the peace of the province'.[249] Thus, he overhauled the rickety system of administration, and even reorganised his army which was better appointed and better disciplined than any an English major had seen in India before,[250] with the help of Curgin Khan the Armenian, Sumroo, the Alsatian, and Muhammad Taqi Khan, who effected great reforms in discipline.[255] Arrangements were also made for the manufacture of arms and ammunition at Monghyr,[256] to be at a great distance from the English Settlements', further determined on removing the seat of his government to Raj Mahal.[257] As is well known, Mir Qasim, in fact, shifted his capital to Monghyr. All these he had done, truly, charged' Amyatt, the then Member of the Calcutta Council,' from no other motives but from distrust, and desire of being independent of us'.[258] However, this desire of being independent' and to assert his authority as a real Nawab proved his misfortune.

Abuse of Dustuck-Immediate Cause of Rupture

The immediate cause of the rupture was the question of inland trade and abuse of dustuck which had been 'scandalously prostituted'. It had long been the contention of Bengal Nawabs and even accepted by the Company and some of its officials[259] that the privilege to trade duty-free was meant for the Company as a corporate body, and for articles meant for export and import, and not for inland trade. But as a result of and encouraged by the 'Plassey plunder', the servants of the Company had brought many 'innovations' and were engaged in private trade on a scale, in a manner, and in articles, unknown before. 'English Gomostas and other servants of the Company in every district, in every gunj, parganah, village, carry on trade in oil, fish, straw, bamboos, rice, paddy, beetle-nut and other things: and everymen with a Company's dustuck regard himself no less than Company, complained Mir Qasim on March 26, 1762.[260] The complaint carried whole truth which was testified by the English officers themselves. Verelst wrote:

A trade was carried on without payment of duties in the prosecution of which indefinite oppressions were committed. English Agents and Gomastas not contented with injuring the people trampled on the authority of the gonvernment, binding and punishing the Nawab's officers wherever they presumed to interfere.[261] Country's government was not in Nawab's hands and the cause was, as was explained by Mir Qasim in his letter of 26th March to the English Governor at Calcutta, that from the factory of Calcutta to Cassim bazar, Patna, and Dacca, all the English Chief with their gomastas, officers and agents in every district act as collectors, seers, zamindars and talookdars, and setting up the Company's colours, allow no power to my officers'.[282] Hastings was convinced that no 'firm and lasting harmony between the Nawab and the Company was possible unless' certain boundary be fixed between the Nawab's authority and our privileges which clashed too frequently."[263] But the servants of the Company were not at all ready to forgo their assumed claims as it touched both their vanity and pockets. To take the matter to the climax there came at Patna Mr. Ellis, the haughty and headstorng member of the Calcutta Council and diehard opponent of its President and Nawab, as the Chief of the factory. Immediately after his arrival at Patna Mr. Ellis began to flout Nawab's authority and make him lose in respect and honour in the eyes of the people.

The Three basic Issues: Attempts at Reconciliation

Thus, three issues were involved from the standpoint of the Nawab:[264] (a) He lost a large revenue, (b) His administrative authority was exposed to serious encroachments. (c) The Nawab's subjects were forced into an unfair competition in inland trade with the holders of dustucks.

Hastings was sent from Calcutta to effect a reconciliation particularly between Ellis and the Nawab. But imprudent Ellis, who sought to commence open hostilities, left for Shinghia just before the arrival of Hastings at Patna. Hastings met the Nawab, who in a bitter mood complained of the acts of violence committed by Mr. Ellis before his face; insults on his people and the disturbances raised in the country', and his authority rendered contemptible to all Hindustan', and obstruction thrown in every business of the government of Bihar.[265] Thus Hastings' 'endeavours' to accommodate the differences between the Nawab and Mr. Ellis had proved ineffectual.[266]

However, well intentioned Vansittart, the Governor, was still hopeful of a settlement with the Nawab, and he alongwith Hastings met the Nawab on 30th Nov.,1762 in his new capital at Monghyr. Vansittart soon found that he (the Nawab) and Mr. Ellis could never be friends; yet wishfully hoped that 'their enemity be burried within their own breasts.[267] As regards the private inland trade it was agreed, besides other provisions, that duties of the rate of nine per cent on the prime cost, at the places where goods are provided, be paid.[268] But unfortunately the Calcutta Council which met as a full board from 15th February, 1763[269] wherein majority was hostile against its President, did not confirm the agreement as they attacked their material interests. The Councillors with the exception of Hastings allowed their material interest to colour and distort their policy.[270] They were of the opinion that the President in concluding this agreement with Mir Qasim had' assumed a right to which he was not aurhorised', that the regulations were dishonourable to Englishmen and that they tended to the ruin of all public and private trade.[271]

The Final Rupture

After his return from the expedition to Bettiah and Nepal, Mir Qasim learnt that his orders regarding the trade agreement with the Governor had been disregarded by the English factors and agents, that the Council had not approved the Monghyr agreement, and there had been serious affrays between his officers and Company's servants, and that even his Collector and high officers had been arrested. Outraged by these violent disturbances, Mir Qasim wrote bitterly to Vansittart on 15th March, 1763: 'such disturbances as the English have set on foot, were never known in any government till Meer Mohammad Jaffer Cawn:...... that they should send sepoys and seize the officers of the Government and carry them away, I can bear them no longer'.[272] In the circumstances, with the twin object of eliminating possibilities of disturbances due to clashes between his officers and the Gomastas, and to save the money spent on the maintenance of choukeys which hardly produced any revenue;[273] Mir Qasim entirely gave up the collection of duties and removed all choukeys; and duly informed Vansittart of this in his letter of 22nd March, 1763.[274] The Nawab was perfectly within his right to lay trade open. But for the hostile members of the Calcutta Council, 'this exemption was breach of Company's privilege'; and beyond Mir Qasim's authority as a Suhab, raised and supported by them without revocation of their grants by the King himself.[277] On the other hand Vansittart, justifying the measure of the Nawab said that the Nazim of every province had right to do anything for the relief of the merchants trading under his protection, without waiting an order from the (Imperial) court, particularly at a time when there was no court nor king'. If Siraj-ud-duala, Mir Jafar or Mir Qasim had a right to give upto us those duties which their predecessors received or permitted us to trade in articles we were before excluded from, of course, they have a right to made regulations in favour of trade in general.[278] Thus, the relation between the Nawab and the English was heading towards complete rupture; and the ' ill-fated' attack on Patna precipitated the war. Equally ill-fated deputation of Amytt and Hay to the Nawab leading to the murder of the former and confinement of the latter, accelerated the process instead of preventing it. Enraged by the capture and ruthless plunder of Patna,[279] Mir Qasim after the recovery of Patna, issued general orders to his officers to seize and make prisoners of the English wherever they were to be found.[280] Not only Patna was recovered but all the English prisoners were taken to Monghyr.

The Calcutta-Council Declares War Against Mir Qasim

The Calcutta Council declared war against Mir Qasim, and again proclaimed and acknowledged Mir Jafar as Subahdar of the three provinces on 7th July, 1763;[281] and a fresh treaty was concluded with Mir Jafar,[282] on 10th-11th July.

Defeats and Disasters for Mir Qasim

Mir Qasim's fate had taken tragic turn. Defeats and disasters came in a series for him, first being at Patna on 19th July, where Taqi Khan, though fought bravely, expired' with an unfinished course on the cowardice of his fellow commanders upon his lips'.[283] As a result, Murshidabad went out of Mir Qasim's hands. Another serious reverse that Mir Qasim's forces had to suffer on 2nd August was in the 'obstinately fought' battle of Gheria near Sooti.[284] But even more serious was the disaster in the battle of Udhuanalla on 5th September. Here Mir Qasim had prepared a 'mighty work' 'to block the only way to advance' into Bihar.[285] The victorious army proceeded to Monghyr. Hearing the approach of the enemy Mir Qasim, who had become cruel and suspicious of every one due to successive defeats and treachery of his generals and nobles, caused the murder of some of the prominent prisoners under his custody at Monghyr before retreating to Patna. These unfortunate victims included Ramnarain, Rajballabh, Jagat Seth brothers, Umed Roy, Zamindar of Tikari, Shah Abdulla, Gurghin Khan and others.[286] At Patna on 4th October,1763, Mir Qasim heard the unfortunate news of the surrender of Monghyr, as informs Ghulam Hussain, through the treachery of its Governor. This inflamed him to such a pitch of fury, that he resolved on the perpetration of an act of wholesale slaughter of the English prisoners, which according to Thornton, exceeded in 'enormity even the atrocities of the Black-Hole".[287] English prisoners about one hundred in number, including Ellis, Hay and notorious Lushington, were massacred on 5th and 6th of October.[288] Fullarton, the surgeon of the Patna Factory, was the only person who escaped the wretched fate of the rest.[289] However, Mir Qasim's fortune was now on fast decline. Though his forces fought gallantly, Patna was taken by storm on 6th November by Major Adams. Mir Qasim, compelled to 'fly the provinces', was pursued beyond the borders. He took shelter at the court of the Nawab Shuja-ud-daula of Oudh who alongwith the Emperor promised to help him recover his lost territory and title. The allied forces of the three marched into Bihar in April,1764.

The Battle of Buxar

After various indecisive and futile engagements, the final battle between the English and the allied troops was fought at Buxar on 22nd October, 1764. The battle, which has truly been ranked as one of the decisive battles of India by Colonel Malleson, ended in complete and crushing defeat of the allied troops. Major Hector Munro won a victory for the English which was, describes Mill, 'one of the most critical, and important victories in the history of British wars'. The Emperor joined the English camp, Nawab Vazir Shuja-ud-duala, finally threw himself on the generosity of the English, and Mir Qasim flying from the field,[290] died a miserable death in a village near Delhi on 6th June, 1777 after wandering from place to place.[291]

Circumstances had made Mir Qasim a hateful tyrant and inhuman murderer', yet it goes to his credit that his measures against the English were 'generally approved by his own subjects". Further observes Vansittart, "It is remarkable, that when the war broke out between us, altho' he wanted the courage to face his enemies in person, yet his soldiers fought for him with a bravery and fidelity rarely experienced in the undisciplined troops of Indostan; nor did any of his officers in the most distant part of his dominions revolted from his authority to join us till Patna was taken, and he was preparing to fly the provinces. This must be attributed to their for him unless we rather choose to place it to the account of their contempt for Mir Jafar or their resentment of our oppressions."[292]

'Thus, ended the famous battle of Buxar on which depended the fate of India, and which was as gallantly disputed as was important in its results', observed Broome.[293]

Far-reaching Effects of Buxar

Plassey had made the English king-makers in Bengal. Buxar and the Grant of Diwanee made them king itself. Plassey brought them power, Buxar won them legal status. More important than this was the fact that it was from these three provinces that the English power first struck inland into the heart of the country and discovered the right road to supremacy in India. The wealth of the provinces not only provided for the Company's investment, but furnished also the sinews of the various wars which brought the greater part of India under the British Rule".[288]

Engagement with Successive Nawabs and the English as De-facto Power

The English had won the contest, and had overcome a serious challenge to their position posed by a powerful and vigorous Nawab like Mir Qasim. Still there was a great deal to be done to secure their position beyond any challenge in future. The Calcutta Council had wisely contributed much in this direction when after Mir Jafar's death in February, 1765, his son, Nazm-ud-daula, was recongnised his successor only after he agreed by a definite treaty (20th Feb.,1765) to leave the management of all affairs in the hands of a Naib Soubah, namely Md. Reza Khan nominated by the Company and not to displace him without the acquiescence of the Company.[294] As a result of this arrangement the position of the Company was fortified, yet it lacked something. The Nawab could be reduced to a political phantom only when the Company had direct control over the collection of revenues.[295] Thus, the acquisition of Diwanee had become a political necessity which awaited the genius of Clive to be achieved.

Clive Again in Bengal

The Court of Directors sent Lord Clive with extraordinary powers for the second time in 1765 as the Governor of Fort William to solve the intricate political and administrative problems facing the Company in Bengal. Immediately after his arrival in Calcutta in early May, Clive seriously engaged himself in regulating the affairs of the Company and in negotiations with the Emperor and the Nawab Vazir of Oudh to whom he wisely restored his dominions except Allahabad and adjoining areas which were given in turn to the Emperor for the support of his dignity and expenses[296]. Political arrangements made by Clive regarding Bengal and Bihar were highly significant. Clive had come to the conclusion that, the perpetual struggles for superiority between the nawabs and the Company,' together with the recent proofs of notorious and avowed corruption among the servants of the Company, had rendered, 'that no method could be suggested of laying the axe to the root of all these evils than that of obtaining the Dewanny of Bengal, Bihar and Orissa for the Company. Moreover, division of power was impossible without generating discontent and hazarding the whole. All must belong either to the Company or the Nawab; .....no system, could less affect the Nabob's dignity, and at the sametime secure the Company against the fatal effects of future revolutions, than this of Dewanny'.[297]

Defacto Power of the Company Legalised by 'Diwanee':

The Diwanee of the three provinces 'offered' by the Emperor and declined by the Company in the past, 'was now solicited, bestowed and accepted'. The Emperor, Shah Alam ,due to the adversity of the times', was made to grant to the Company on the 12th Aug., 1765, (Supplemented on 19th) the Diwanee of Bengal, Bihar and Orissa for ever as a free gift on the condition of remitting twenty six lakhs of rupees as the Royal revenue, and providing the expenses of the Nizamut of the provinces. Here, one technical point is remarkable. 'Similar separate Phirmaunds were grantend for Bihar and Orissa',[298] indicating the separate identity of Bihar. Nevertheless, this highly significant deal, rightly observes Ghulam Hussain," which at any other time would have required the sending of wise ambassadors and able negotiators as well as a deal of parley and conference with the Company and the King of England, and much negotiation and contention with the Ministers, was done and finished in less time than would have been taken up for the sale of jack, or a beast of burden, or of a head of cattle.[299]

The grant of Diwanee legalised the de-facto power of the Company. According to Burke it was 'the great act of constitutional entrance of the Company into the body-politic of India. It gave to this settlement of Bengal, a fixed constitutional form, with a legal title.[300]

The Company gets 'Nizamut' from Bengal Nawabs but shrinks from Responsibility: the Double Government

By an agreement on 30th Sept., 1765, with Nawab Nazm-ud-daula a sum of Rs. fifty three lakhs eighty - six thousand, and odd was fixed as an adequate allowance for the support of the Nizamut'.[301] Nawab Nazm-ud-daula's brother and successor, Saif-ud-daula, agreed under the treaty of 29th May,1766, not only to accept the reduced annual stipend' of Rs. Forty - one lakhs, eighty - six thousand and odd (Rs.41,86,131,9), but also to leave the military control and protection of the three provinces entirely to the 'discretion and good management of the Company.[302] 'The Grant of Diwanee and the engagement with successive Nawabs of Bengal entitled the Company to the surplus revenues, estimated by Clive nearly at rupees 122 lakhs , and made them absolute master of the provinces of

Bengal, Bihar and Orisssa. In fact, this' left neither pretence nor subterfuge', significantly says Ghulam Hussain;[303] and the Company 'now lacked nothing of sovereignty but the name', observes Thornton.[304] Thus, the Company acquired Nizamat from their nominee, Nawabs of Bengal, and the Diwanee from the titular Moghul Emperor. Yet they did not recongnise 'the obvious moral', and shrank from responsibility. Clive understood the mind and interests of his masters. He had a definite plan and policy accordingly. He was sensible to grasp that "since the acquisition of Diwanee the power formerly belonging to the Subah of these provinces is totally, infact, vested in the East India Company. Nothing remains to him (the Nawab,) but the name and shadow of authority. This name, however, this shadow, it is indispensably necessary we should seem to venerate"...... It, therefore, always to be remembered, that there is a Subah (Subadhar); and that though the revenues belongs to the Company, the territorial jurisdiction must still rest in the chiefs of the country, acting under him (the Nawab) and this Presidency in conjuction. To appoint the Company's servants to the offices of Collectors, or indeed to do any act by exertion of the English power, which can easily be done by the Nawab at our instance, would be throwing off the mask, would be declaring the Company the Subah of the provinces. Foreign nations would immediately take umbrage; and complaints preferred to the British Court might be attended with very embarrassing consequences. Under the circumstances, immediately after the acquisition of Diwanee he came to the conclusion; 'The power of supervising the provinces though lodged in us, should not, however, in my opinion, be exerted'.[305] The Court of Directors, who were more interested in the revenues of the provinces than in the good government of the country, readily accepted the idea, and approved the acquisition of Diwanee and the scheme of strange system of dual government introduced by Clive, in their letter of 17th May, 1766. However, they were alarmed at the contemplation of added responsibilities.[306]

The Working of Double Government

Under this Double government, the Company only undertook the superintending the collection of revenues and receiving the money from the Nowab's treasury to that of the Company through their 'Resident at the Durbar under the control of the Governor and Select Committee'. The collection of revenue and the administration of justice, the appointment to offices, Zamindries, in short, whatever came under the denomination of Civil administration, were left in Indian hands, in the old machinery of the Nawab.

The Nawab remained the figure head and the business was conducted under the supervision of the Resident by the Naib Nazim, Md. Reza Khan who was also Naib Diwan, and was assisted by banker Jagat Seth and Diwan Durlabh Ram, all the three were the nominees of the Company,[307] and then Richard Becher served as the Resident. Later on a deputy Resident was also appointed.[308]

Changes in Bihar in the Wake of Diwanee

Changes in administrative set up of Bengal brought in the wake of ' Diwanee' were naturally followed by changes in Bihar. Mir Muhammad Kazim Khan, brother of Mir Jafar, who was ruling over Bihar since August 1764, was found by Clive as 'simple and plains and unfit for so weighty an office as the Government of Bihar, 'was pensioned off' in Sept., 1765, to lead a retired life at Rajmahal till his death there in 1981.[309] He was succeeded by his deputy, Dhiraj Narian, brother of Raja Ramnarian as Naib Nazim, with Raja Sitab Roy as his diwan. But soon new arrangements introduced by Clive necessitated even another change in the administration of Bihar. Samuel Middleton, the Chief of the Patna factory after Billiers, was appointed the Supervisor of Revenue collections in Bihar. He was to be assisted by Raja Dhiraj Narain and Raja Sitab Roy. The Kila was converted into Diwan's office where Middleton occupying the state Chair infront of a big masnad, with Dhiraj Narain seated on a cushion on one side and Sitab Roy on the other,[310] enacting the Moghul Nawabs, transacted business revenue and judicial. Thus, he wielded wide powers over the general administration. But Raja Dhiraj Narain could not remain long in office. On the complaint of Raja Sitab Roy an enquiry was held against him by Muhammad Reza Khan. Dhiraj Narain was removed from his office in Sept.,

1766 on the charge of irregularities in the revenue administration, and 'his revenues and jagirs were sequestered until the full balances due by him were liquidated, but a small pension was meanwhile reserved for his support."[311] Raja Sitab Roy was appointed, along with Naib Diwan, the Naib Nazim of Bihar. On the other hand, Middleton was also dismissed in early 1767, and Thomas Rumbold, a Madras Civilian, was imported by Clive to replace Middelton of Patna., Mr. Rumbold, though having an exciting time in Bihar, resigned his service of the Company in November, 1769, and was succeeded by James Alexander as Supervisor of Bihar.

Chiefs and Zamindars of Bihar not Ready to Accept the Verdict of Buxar

However, some prominent chiefs and zamindars of Bihar were yet not ready to accept the verdict of Buxar and the grant of Diwanee. They long remained rebellious and hostile to the new regime. Such a rebellious instance was first presented by the Zamindar of Seres and Kutumba, who even looted the government treasure. But the rebellion was crushed by Captain Goddard.[312]

The revolt of Hathwa Raj (Husepur Raj) proved to be more serious and enduring which stretched upto the Revolt of Raja Chait Singh of Benaras.[313] Maharaja Fateh Shahi, by his raids, harassed the Company for long and caused the loss of revenue to the tune of lakhs of rupees.[314]

Raja Jugal Kishore of Bettiah Raj also rebelled against the authority of the Company and did not pay the revenue.[315] However, Robert Barker was successful in his expedition against the Bettiah Raj which was brought under complete control.[316]

Anarchy under Dyarchy of Clive

Though country was brought under control but 'no civilised government,' as Sir Lecky has put it,' ever existed on the face of this earth which was more corrupt, more perfidious, and more rapacious than the Government of the East India Company from 1765 to 1772. The whole scheme of dual government inaugurated by Clive was unreal and anomalous which separated power from responsibility. As a matter a fact, it was a case of overall control without assumption of any responsibility for the good government of the provinces. The dyarchy has rightly been termed as anarchy by Prof. A.B. Kieth. In this double government, controlling authorities were corrupt to the extreme and the persons entrusted with the actual administration were weak and demoralised. 'Such a divided and complicated authority', observed Verelst writing on 16th December, 1769, 'gave rise to oppressions and intrigues unknown in any other period.[317]

Appointment of English Supervisors

As suggested by Verelst, 'Supervisors were appointed for the betterment of the situation.[318] Two supervisors- William Harwood for Bhagalpur and Rajmahal, and Ducarel for Purnea—were appointed in Bihar.[319] But the scheme did not deliver the goods. Supervisors, too, as Hastings had testified, proved corrupt and collected lacks in the districts they were stationed. The whole scheme was turned into a machinery for 'habitual extortion'.[320] As a safeguard against this, Revenue Councils at Patna and Murshidabad were constituted in Sept., 1769 and the office of the Naib Subah was abolished. However, Md. Reza Khan in Bengal and Sitab Roy in Bihar continued as Naib Diwans. The Council at Patna consisted of Alxender George Vansittart and Palk and Raja Sitab Roy.[321]

Distress Multiplied by Famine

All these patch works could not mitigate the sufferings of the people and evils of the system of government which is evident from the refreshing confessions of Richard Bechar, the Resident at the Durbar, in his famous letter of 24th May, 1769 to the Secret Committee of the Court of Directors: It must give pain to an Englishman to have reason to think that since the accession of the Company to the Diwanee the condition of the people of this country has been worse than it was before: and yet I am afraid the fact is undoubted.[322] Never before, observed Lecky, "had the natives experienced a tyranny which was at once so skilful, so searching, and so strong.[323] To add to the sufferings of the people there broke out a devastating famine in the provinces in 1769-70.[324] Depicting the miseries of the people Hunter wrote: Althrough the stifling summer of 1770, the people went on dying. The husbandmen sold their cattle, they sold their implements of agriculture, they devoured their seed-grain, they sold their sons and daughters, till at length no buyers of children could be found; they ate the leaves of trees and the grass of the field; and in June 1770, the Resident at Durbar affirmed that the living were feeding on the dead.[325] The suffering people could little expect from their merchant rulers. "But such is the little regard", wrote Ghulam Hussain with anguish, "which they (the English) show to the people of these kingdoms, and such their apathy and indifference for their welfare, that the people under their dominion groan every where, and are reduced to poverty and distress. O God? come to the assistance of your afflicted servants and deliver them from the oppression they suffer.[326] Under the circumstances, the East India Company was now preparing itself to throw off its hesitation to assume direct responsibilities for the government of Diwanee provinces. Professor A.B.Keith adds to the observation of Ghulam Hussain that while some of the Company's servants profiteered in necessities, the principle deputy added ten per cent to the assessment to make good, at the expense to the living, the losses involved in the wholesale depopulation.[327] Pathetic condition of the people in Bengal and Bihar had their echoes in England.

References

1. K.K. Datta, *Alivardi and His Times*, p. 136.
2. R.S.Whiteway, *The Rise of the Portuguese Power in India,* 1497-1550, pp. 7-8.
3. *Cambridge History of India*, Vol. V, p. 1.
4. Appendix Roteiro da Viagem, de Vasco da Gama J.J.A. Campos, *History of the Portuguese in Bengal*, p. 25.
5. *Ibid.*
6. Campos, Chapters III to V.
7. *Tarikh-i-Firozshahi*, pp. 45-46 and *Riaz-us-Salatin* p. 29
8. Dagh Register 1631-34 p.45, quoted in *Foster's Factory Record*, 1630 -33. p. 308.

9. Foster, *The English Factories in India*, 1618-1621, p. 197.

10. Report from Moghul governor, Kasim Khan, to the Emperor, Vide. Stewart, *The History of Bengal. p. 240.*

11. J.J.Campos, *Portuguese in Bengal*, pp.134-139, also Stewart, *The History of Bengal*, pp. 266-70.

12. Irvine's *Mannuci*, Vol. II, p. 83.

13. Ball's *Tavernier*, Vol. I, pp. 121-22.

14. Thomas Bowrey, *A Greographical Acount of Countries Round the Bay of Bengal* (1664-79) ed. R.C. Temple, Haklyut Society 1903, pp. 230-32.

15. Tavernier, Travels, Ed. V. Ball, Vol. II, pp. 258-263.

16. R.R.Diwakar, *Bihar through the Ages*, p. 568.

17. Aziza Hasan, Mints of the Mughal Empire', *Proceedings of.Indian History Congress*, Pt-I, 29th Session,1967.

18. Peter Mundy, *Travels of Peter Mundy*, II, p. 159, ed. R.C. Temple, London, 1914.

19. Ralf Fitch in *Early Travels*, Foster, Oxford, 1927, pp. 24-25.

20. Irvine's *Manucci*, Vol.II, p. 83.

21. Ray, pp. 21-22, and p. 38.

22. Stavorinus, *Voyage to the East Indies*, Vol. I, p. 512.

23. *Streynsham Master's Diaries*, edited by Temple, Vol. II, pp. 27-28.

24. J.B.Tavernier, *Travels in India* 1660-1667, edited by V. Ball, London, 1889, Vol. I, p. 122.

25. Ahmed Raza Khan, '*A brief survey of Trade and Commerce in Bihar During the 17th Century*'. Proceedings of the Indian History Cong., Hyderabad, 1778, pp. 473-75.

26. Sushil Chowdhary, *Trade and Com. Organ. in Bengal* (1650-1720), Cal. 1975.p. 170.

27. Francois Bernier, *Travels in the Moghul Empire*, ed. by Constable, p. 293 and 440.

28. Sushil Choudhry, op. cit., pp. 170-171.

29. John Marshal in India, (1668-72) ed. S.A. Khan, London,1627, p. 414, and Foster, English Factory in India, 1640-50, p. 38.

30. *Ibid.* p. 113.

31. C.R. Wilson, *Early Annals of the English in Bengal*, Vol. II, part-II, pp. 293-97.

32. S.C. Hill, *Bengal in 1756-57*, Vol. II, p. 258.

33. Letter to Court, 11th December,1741, Para 318.

34. Vide Appendix 'A' *The Dutch in Bengal and Bihar*, pp.163-67 by Dr. K.K.Datta.

35. J.C.Sinha, *Economic Annals of Bengal*, p. 22.

36. Memoires de Lespinay, pp.203-204, vide Cambridge Hist. of India Vol. V, *The French Factories in India*, pp. 70-71.

37. Vide J.C.Sinha, Economic Annals of Bengal, p. 12.

38. *Bengal Past and Present*, Vol.VII, p.122.

39. Captain Alexander Hamilton, *A New Account of the East Indies*, 1744, Vol. II, pp.12-13

40. Vide S.C. Hills, Three Frenchmen in Bengal, Ch.-I, p. 2.

41. J.C.Sinha, *Economic Annals*, p.17.

42. Rise of the French Power in India, *Calcutta Review*, 1866, pp.132-33.

43. Court to Bengal, 12 Dec., 1735-Peter Auber, II, p. 35.

44. Raye, *The Annals of the English Settlement in Bihar*, p. 154, foot note.

45. Patent Rolls, 43, Elizabeth, Pt. VI, Vide Cambridged Hist.,Vol. V, p. 77.

46. W.W. Hunter, *History of British India*, Vol. II, pp. 48-49.

47. Foster's English Factories, 1618-21, Vol. I, pp. VIII-IX, 37-40.

48. For details, W.W.Hunter, *History of British India*, Vol. II, Chapter II.

49. *Sir Thomas Roe's Journal*, Ch. IX.

50. Foster, *English Factories in India 1618-21*, p. 182

51. *Indian Antiquary*, Vol. XLIII, p. 83.

52. *Ibid*, p. 84.
53. Travels of Peter Mundy, Vol. II, pp. 151-56.
54. Stewart's, *History of Bengal, Shah Shuja's Nishan*, p.538; also Foster, *English Factories, 1655-60*, Appendix, and pp. 111-112.
55. Foster, *Englsih Factories*, 1655-60, pp. 142 and 189-90.
56. For details see Account of Patna by John Marshal, Streynsham Master's Diaries, Vol. II, p.89.
57. Irvine's Manucci, Vol. I, p. 96, also Ball's Taveneir, p. 122.
58. Streynsham, Master's Diaries, Vol. II, p. 89, also *Indian Antiquary* Vol. XLIII, p. 74.
59. Wilson's Annals, Vol. I, pp. 378-79.
60. *Court Minutes*, Jan. 27, 1658 and of March 17, 1668.
61. *Hughes Diary*, Vol. II, p. XIV.
62. C.R.Wilson Vol. I, pp. 45-46, 254-55, 291,392.
63. Sushil Choudhury, *op. cit.*, p.170.
64. Hedges, Vol. I, XVII, Vol. II, p. 46.
65. Elliot, Vol. VII, p. 248.
66. C.J. Hamilton, *op. cit.*, pp. 36-37.
67. Hunter, "*History of British India*", Vol.II, p. 304.
68. *Ibid*. also Hedges 'Diary, Vol. II, pp. 51-53, 68. *Beveridge, History of India*, Book-III, p. 377.
69. Ray, *op. cit.*, p. 94.
70. C.J. Hamilton, p. 56.
71. Raye, p. 94.
72. Eliphinstone-*Rise of Early British Power in the East*', p. 55. also Mill's History, Vol. I, p. 86.
73. *Bengal Past and Present*, Vol. V, p. 151.
74. Katheleen Blechnden, *Calcutta. Past and Present*, pp. 14-15 Thaker and Co., London, 1905.
75. Letter to Court, Aug., 15, 1702.
76. Raye, p. 122.
77. Calcutta Council Consultations, 14th April, 1707.

78. C.R. Wilson, *Early Annals of Entglish in Bengal*, Vol. I, p. 281 and Consultations, 30th June, 1707.
79. Consultations, vide C.R.Wilson, I, p. 293.
80. *Ibid.*
80. *Ibid.*, pp. 307-309.
81. *Ibid.*, pp. 3220-321.
82. Raye, plzy
83. C. R.Wilson, I, pp. 312-313
84. Raye-p. 127.
85. C.R.Wilson, Vol. II, p. 49.
86. *Ibid.*
87. *Ibid.*, Pt-I, p. LIX
88. *Ibid.*, pp. 141-152.
89. C.J. Hamilton, p.72.
90. Raye, p. 143.
91. C.J. Hamilton, p. 76, and *Stewart's Hist. of Bengal*, p. 402.
92. Raye, *The Annals of the Early English Settlements in Bihar*, p. 135; also C. R.Wilson, Vol. II, pt. I, p. LX.
93. *Stewart's History of Bengal*, pp. 394-95.
94. Raye, p. 142.
95. C.J.Hamilton, *The Trade Relations between England and India* (1600-1896), p. 72
96. K.K.Datta's *Alivardi and His Times*, p. 6.
97. Court to Bengal, 14th Feb.,1727, Aubers Account,
p. 28 (Vol. II).
98. Martin's *Eastern India*, Vol. I, p. 354.
99. Holwell's Interesting Historical Events, p. 68.
100. K.K. Datta's *Alivardi*, p. 7.
101. *Ibid.*, p. 9.
102. *Ibid.*, p. 9.
103. To Court from Bengal, Feb., 14, 1728, Wilson's *Fort William*, Vol. I, p. 124.

104. Bengal General Letters to Court, Dec., 24, 1939,

105. Wilson's Fort Willliam, Vol. I, p. 152.

106. Orme's History, Vol. II, p. 191.

107. Raye, pp.157-58.

108. K.K. Dutta, *The Dutch in Bengal and Bihar*, p.17 and also *Alivardi and His Times*, pp. 155-59, and also Raye-The Annals of the English Settlements in Bihar, pp. 158-60.

109. Raye, p. 102 and also Datta's *Alivardi*, pp. 157-60.

110. N.N. Raye, *Early English Settlements*, p. 187.

111. C.J. Hamilton, p. 20.

112. M. Jean Law. Vide, Hill's Bengal in 1756-57, Vol. III, p. 160.

113. K.K. Datta, *Alivardi and His Times*, p.128.

114. M.Jean Law, vide Hill, Vol. III, p. 160.

115. K.K. Datta's *Alivardi*, pp. 124-25.

116. Scrafton, p. 52, and Orme's Hindustan, Vol.II, pp. 45-46.

117. Dr. K.K. Datta, *Alivardi and His Times*, p. 115.

118. M.Jean Law, vide S.C. Hill's Bengal in 1756-57, Vol. III, pp. 160-61.

119. *Ibid.*, p. 161.

120. K.K. Datta, *Alivardi and His Times*, pp.129-31.

121. *Chatar Gulazar-i-Shujai, Elliot*, Vol. III. p. 210.

122. K.K. Datta, '*The Dutch in Bengal and Bihar*, p. 1 0, published by the University of Patna, 1948.

123. Jadunath Sarka, *History of Bengal*, Vol. II, p. 470.

124. Hill, Three Frenchmen in Bengal, p. 4.

125. *Ibid.*, p. 8

126. *Ibid.*

127. Dr. K.K. Datta, Alivardi and His Times, Preface.

128. Hill *Three Frenchmen in Bengal*, pp. 66-69.

129. M. Law quoted in Hill's Three Frenchmen in Bengal, p. 67.

130. *Ibid*, p. 69.

131. Orme, Vol. II, pp. 79-80.

132. S.C.Hill, *Bengal in 1756-57*, Vol. I, p. 5.

133. Siyar, Vol. II, p. 206.

134. *Ibid.*

135. For details Ibid, pp. 207-14, also J.N. Sarkar, *History of Bengal*, Vol. II, pp. 479-80.

136. *Muzaffarnamah*, fs. 57 a, 57 b.

137. Scrafton, *Reflections*, p. 61.

138. Hill,*Three Frenchmen in Bengal*, pp. 82-83.

139. Clive's Letter to the Secret Committee at Lond, 22 Feb., 1957 vide's *Hill's Bengal in 1756-57*, vol. II, p. 237-238, for details of the Treaty see C.U. Aitchison, A Collection of The Treaties, Engagements, and Sanads, etc. Vol. I, Suptt. Govt. Printing, Cal., 1909, Bengal No. LXI, pp. 181-184.

140. Hill's *Three Frenchmen*, pp. 83-84.

141. *Ibid.*, p. 87.

142. Hill's *Bengal in 1756-57*, Vol. I, p. CLXII.

143. Hill's *Bengal*, Vol. II, p. 307.

144. *Cambridge History*, Vol. V, p. 147.

145. M.Jean Law, vide Hill's *Three Frenchmen in Bengal*, pp. 84-86.

146. C.U. Aitchison, Treaties, *Engagements and Sanad*, Vol.I, Bengal No. LXIII, pp. 185-88.

147. Clive to Orme, vide *Cambridge History*. Vol. V. p, 151.

148. Hill's Bengal, Vol. II, p. 437.

149. K.Blechynden, Calcutta, *Past and Present*, Thacker and Co., London, Thacker, Slink and Co., Calcutta and Simla, 1905, p. 67.

150. Hill's *Three Frenchmen,* pp. 102-103.

151. N.N. Raye, p. 175.

152. Dastur-ul-Insha, *J.B.O.R.S.*, 1938.

153. Hill's *Three Frechmen*, p.104.

154. Hill's *Three Frenchmen*, p. 59.

155. Hill's *Bengal*, Vol. III, p. 210.

156. *Three Frenchmen*, pp. 107-108 also Siyar, Vol. II, p. 236.

157. *Ibid.*

158. *Three Frechmen*, p. 109.

159. *Ibid.*, p. 110.

160. Law, vide *Three Frenchmen*, p. 120.

161. Ives Voyages, pp. 169-70; Orme;'s Indostan, Vol. II, p. 193.

162. Vansistt's, *Narrative*, Appendix D, p. 557.

163. Siyar, Vol. II, p. 249.

164. Siyar, Vol. II, p. 254-56, and Clives Letter to Select Committee, 23rd Dec., 1757.

165. See Askari, H.S., The Bengal Revolution of 1757 and Raja Ram Narain, *Journal of Indian History*, Vol. XVIII, 1939.

166. Malcolm, Sir John, *Life of Robert Clive*, Vol. I, p. 333.

167. Orme's *Indostan*, Vol. II, pp. 191-192.

168. Bengal and Madras Papers, Vol. II, p. 69.

169. Orme's *Indostan*, Vol. II, p. 193.

170. A.C.Roy's *Mir Jafar*, p.111.

171. Siyar, Vol. II, p. 251.

172. 'The Bengal Revolution of 1757 and Raja Ram Narain' *Journal of Indian History*, Vol. XVIII, 1939.

173. Bengal and Madras Papers, Vol. II,Clives Corrrespondence Letter No. 220

174. Scrafton's *Reflections*, p. 109.

175. Bengal and Madras Papers, Vol. II, p. 105.

176. Orme's *Indostan*, Vol. II, p. 281.

177. Ibid, pp. 281-284.

178. Clive to Select Committee, 7 Feb., 1758, Malcolm's Clive, I, 409.

179. Broome's *Bengal Army*, p. 195. Ormes Indostan, vol. II, p. 278.

180. *Memoirs on the Revolution in Bengal*, p. 128.

181. Siyar, Vol, II, pp. 251-81.

182. Clive Letter to Court, 12th March, 1759.

183. Siyar, Vol, II, p. 290.

184. Calendar of Persian Correspondence, I, Nos., 202 and 239.

185. Broome's Bengal Army, pp. 258-269. and *Bengal Past and Present,* 1921, p. 74.

186. Council to the Court 22nd Oct.,1759, Fort William India Correspondence, Vol. II, p. 432.

187. Ironside's Narrative, Asiatic Annual Register, 1800, Siyar, Vol. II, pp. 327-66, A.C.Roy's *Mir Jafar,* pp. 162-65.

188. N.K.Singh, *History of Territorial Aristocracy in Bihar,* 1759-1793, Unpublished Thesis, Patna University, p. 185.

189. Siyar, Vol. II, p. 340, Muzaffarnamah, f.89.

190. *Ibid,* also Ironsides Narrrative.

191. *Ibid,* p. 23.

192. Muzaffarnamah, f. 70.

193. J.A.S.B.,1852, p. 117.

194. Broom's *Bengal Army,* pp. 320 -322.

195. A .C.Roy's *Mir Jafar,* p. 163.

196. Siyar, Vol. I, p. 357.

197. *Bengal Past and Present,* 1911, p. 191.

198. Vansittart's Narrative, pp. 25, 30, Siyar, Vol. II, pp. 365-66.

199. Bengal Past and Present, 1911, p. 188, Broome's Bengal Army, 322, Vansittart's Narrative, p. 32

200. Clive to the Secret Committee, 23rd Dec.,1757.

201. Vansittart's Narrative, Indian Reprint, p. 43, Proceedings of the Select Committee, 16th Sept., 1760.

202. Translator's Preface, p. 6, to the R.Cambray edition of Siyar-ul-Muttaherin, Vol. I.

203. S.B.Choudhuri's *Civil Disturbances during the British Rule in India*(1765-1857). The World Press, Cal., 1955.

204. Introduction to the Indian Reprint of Vansittart's Narrative, Ed. A.C. Banerjee and D.K. Ghosh, K. P. Bagchi and Co. Cal. pp. 10-11.

205. Vansittart's Narrative, A View of the State of the country, and the Company's Affairs described by Vansittart on his arrival p. 15.

206. C.U. Aitchison, Treaties, Engagements and Sanads, Vol. I, Bengal No. LXVI, pp. 214-217.

207. Introd. to the Ind. reprint of the 'Narrative'.

208. Siyar, Vol. II, p. 432.

209. *Narrative*, p. 16.

210. Firminger, *The Fifth Report*, Introduction, p. CXIV.

211. Letter from Meer Cossim, to the Governor, quoted in Vansittart's Narrative, pp. 482-484 .

212. Hill-*Three Frenchmen*, p. 123-fn. 1.

213. Vansittart's *Narrative*, p. 537.

214. Indian Reprint of the *Cambridge History of India*, Vol.V, p. 173.

215. Vansittart in his *Narrative*, p. 523.

216. Hill-*Three Frenchmen*, p. 122

217. Vansittart in his *Narrative*, p. 156.

218. Broome's *Bengal Army*, p. 322.

219. Hill's *Three Frenchmen*, p. 125.

220. *Ibid.*, p. 129.

221. Broome's, *Bengal Army*, p. 328.

222. Major Carnac's Letter to the Select Committee, Patna, 5th March 1761, Vansittart's *Narrative*, p. 82.

223. *Ibid.*

224. Cambridge History, Vol. V. pp.169-170.

225. Vansittart's *Narrative*, pp. 113-117, *Firminger*, p. CLVII.

226. Auber, Vol. I, p. 83

227. Coote's Journal Orme MSS, India, VIII, vide *Cambridge History of India*, Vol. V, p. 170.

228. Broome's *Bengal Army*, p. 332, *Muzaffarnamah*, f.74.

229. *Ibid.*

230. *Muzaffarnamah*, f.74.

231. *Ibid.*

232. Letter from Vansittart's *Narrative*, p. 116, also see p. 111, and p. 115,

233. Siyar, Vol. II, p. 416.

234. Broome's *Bengal Army*, p. 338.

235. Letters from the Nawab to Vansittart April 30, June, 15,16,1761, *Narrative*, pp. 88 -89.

236. Nawab's Letter to Vansittart, June 16, 1761, Narrative, pp. 92-97.

237. Vansittart's *Narrative*, pp. 80-97.

238. Letters from the Nawab to Vansittart, April 30, June, 16 and 17, 1761, *Narrative*, pp. 92-97.

239. Amytt in Vansittarts *Narrative*, pp. 163-165.

240. Select Committee's Leter of 9th Feb.

241. From the Select Committee to Colonel Coote, Apr. 21,1761 *Narrative*, p. 85.

242. *Ibid.*

243. *Cambridge History of India*, Vol. V, p.170, also see Letters of Instruction from the Select Committee to Colonel Coote, Apr. 28 and May 8, 1761, Narrative , pp. 85-86.

244. Letters from the Nawab to Vansittart, June 16 and 17, 1761. *Narrative*, pp. 92-97.

245. Letter from Vansittart to the Nawab, June 18,1761, C.P.C.I, p. 108.

246. Letter from Vansittart to Mir Qasim, Sep. 1,1761, Calendar of Persian Correspondence (C.P.C), I , p. 122.

247. Siyar, Vol. II, p. 419, *Muzaffarnamah*, f. 162 a.

248. Siyar, Vol. II, p. 493.

249. Vansittart's *Narrative*, p. 105.

250. N.N. Raye, p. 188, Vansittart's Narrative, pp. 149-155.

251. C.P.C.I. No.1761,1259, 1320.

252. Siyar, Vol. II, p. 431, also R.C.Mazumdar's *Maharaja Rajballabh*, p. 83.

253. Siyar, II, 493.

254. N.N.Raye, p. 199.

255. Siyar-ul-Mutakherin, Vol. II, p. 432.

256. Vansittart in his *Narrative*, p. 520

257. Major Grant in Third Report vide Thornton, Vol. I, p. 447.

258. Hill's *Three Frenchmen*, p. 123, fn.1.

259. Siyar, Vol. II, p. 421.

260. Amytt in Vansittart's *Narrative*, pp. 164-165.

261. *Ibid.*

262. Vansitstart in his *Narrative*, pp. 135, 148-49, 211. Verelst in his View, pp. 48, 215-217.

263. Letter from the Nawab to Vansittart in Vansittart's *Narrative* p. 148.

264. Verelst's View, p. 48.

265. Vansitart's *Narrative*, p. 148

266. Letter from Hastings to Vansittart 1 April, 1762, Narrative, pp. 182-184.

267. Introduction to the Indian Reprint of Vansittart's *Narrative*, p. XXV.

268. Vansittart's *Narrative*, p. 168.

269. Letter from Hastings to Governor dated Monghyr July 14, 1762 Narrative, p. 178.

270. *Ibid.*, 211

271. *Ibid*, pp. 221-225

272. *Narrative*, pp. 265.

273. *Cambridge History*, Vol. V. p. 173.

274. Vansittart's Narrative, p. 251, Council Meeting of 17th Jan., 1763.

275. Vansittart's *Narrative*, p. 366.

276. Vansittart in his *Narrative*, pp. 355, 362, 369, 394.

277. *Ibid*, p. 379.

278. *Ibid*, pp. 368, 375 & 376

279. *Ibid*, pp. 372-374.

280. Siyar, Vol. II. p. 473.

281. Mill. Vol. III, p. 239.

282. *Narrative*, p. 495

283. C.U. Aitchison, *Treaties, Enahements and Sanads*, Vol. I Bengal No. LXVII, pp. 217-221.

284. Broome's *Bengal Army*, p. 374; Siyar, Vol. II, p. 485.

285. Edward Thornton's *History of the British Empire in India*, Vol. I, p. 445.

286. Bengal Past and Present, Vol. V, pt. 10, p.105, also Elphinston, p. 399, Paper by Mir Cossem.

287. Siyar, Vol. II, pp. 493, 504 also Long's Selections, pp. 323-333.

288. Thornoton's Hist. I, p. 447; also 'The Patna Massacre' by H. Beveridge, *Calcutta Review,* LXXIX, Calcutta, 1884.

289. Mr. Fullarton's letter to the Board, vide Vansittart's *Narrative,* p. 517.

290. Vansittart in his *Narrative,* p. 517.

291. Siyar, Vol. II.p. 572.

292. Introduction to Vansittart's Narrative of the Indian Reprint, p. XLIV.

293. Vansittart in his Narrative, p. 520.

294. Broome's Bengal Army, p. 40.

295. J. C. Sinha, Preface to the *Economic Annals of Bengal*, Macmillan, London, 1927

296. C. U. Aitchison, A *Collection of Treaties, Engahements and Sanads*, etc. Vol. I, Supptt. Govt. Printing, Calcutta, 1909, Bengal, No. LXIX, pp. 222-225.

297. Introduction to the Indian Reprint of Vansittart's Narrative, p. XIV.

298. C. U. Aitchison, *Treaty of Allahabadad,* 16th Aug., 1765, Treatiesa & Sanads, Oudh No. XXXIV, pp. 89-91.'

299. Letters of 'Select Committee to Court of Directors, 30th Sep., 1975, vide Thornton, pp. 497-498 alxo Bolt's Considerations, p. 35.

300. C. U. Aitchison, *Treaties and Sanads Bengal* No. LXX, pp. 225-229.
301. *Ibid*, p. 228.
302. Siyar, Vol. III. p. 9.
303. Forrest's *The Life of Lord Clive,* II, p. 289.
304. C.U. Aitchison, *Treaties and Sanads, Bengal* No. LXXX, pp. 229-30.
305. *Ibid* Bengal No. LXXi, pp. 230-231.
306. Siyar, III, p. 9.
307. Thornton, *History of the British Empire in India*, Vol. I, p. 497.
308. Clive's Letter to the Court, 30th Sep. 1765 vide Bolt's Consideration, p. 36.
309. Firminger, *Fifth Report*, Vol. I, pp. CLVIII.
310. Thornton, *op.cit.*, p. 493, also N. Raye, pp. 260-62.
311. N.K. Sinha, Fort *William India House Correspondence*, V. pp. 22-23.
312. Siyar, Vol. III, p. 11.
313. Siyar, Vol. III, p. 17.
314. Siyar, III, pp. 17-22.
315. C.P.C. Vol. II, p. 260.
316. *Calcutta Review* 1807, July, pp. 35-36.
317. C.P. C. Vol. II, pp. 242-243.
318. Long, Selections from the Unpublished Records of the Govt., Vol. I, 411.
319. *Ibid.*, pp. 463-464.
320. Verelst's *A view of the English Government in Bengal*, p. 47.
321. Proceedings of the President and Select Commit., Aug., 16, 1769.
322. N. N. Raye-313.
323. S. B. Choudhuri, *Civil Disturbances* in India, p. 14.
324. Auber, Vol. I, p. 278.
325. Fourth Report, 1773, pp. 98 ff.

326. W.E. H. Lecky-A *History of England in 18 Century*, New Edi-, IV, 264.

327. N. K. Sinha, *The Economic History of Bengal, 1962*, Vol. II, pp. 48-50; also for details W.W. Hunter, *The Annals of Rural Bengal,* Indian Reprint, Delhi, 1975, Vol. I. pp. 19-43.

328. W. W. Hunters', *The Annals of Rural Bengal,* Indian Reprint, I, p. 26.

329. Siyar, III, 171.

330. A. B. Kieth - A *Constitutional History of India* (1600-1935), Methuen, 1936, p. 58.

CHAPTER 2
The Country Under Warren Hastings : Resistance by the Cross-Section of the People

The Company as Diwan and the Reorganization of Government

Pathos of the people of Bengal and Bihar groaning under the disastrous Double-Government had their echoes in England. Under the circumstances the Company was now compelled to prepare itself to throw off its hesitation in assuming the direct responsibilities for the Government of the Diwanee-provinces. In 1771, the Directors of the Company declared their historic determination to stand forth as Diwan and, by agency of the Company's servants, to take upon themselves the entire care and management of the revenue.[1] Mill marks the event as a revolution much greater probably than any previous conjuncture. He further observes : "It was an innovation by which the whole property of the country, and alongwith it the administration of justice, were placed upon a new foundation".[2] The Company also wisely sent Warren Hastings, a man of integrity and long Indian experience, to Bengal as its Governor, arming him with "full powers to make complete reformation of the notorious system of administration".[3]

In fact, as Lord Thurlow said in the House of Lords during Hastings' trial, he was empowered to destroy the whole fabric of the double-government.'[4]

Muhammad Reza Khan in Bengal and Raja Sitab Roy in Bihar divested of their posts as Naib-Diwan

Hastings assumed his office of the Governor of Bengal (Fort William) in Calcutta on 13th April, 1772, and next day he received the dispatch of the Directors to abolish the office of Naib Diwan. On 11th May, the decision of the Company to divest the Nawab Muhammad Reza Khan of his station of 'Naib-Diwan'[5] was notified. At the same time, Murshidabad-Council was directed to take over the charge of the Diwani and perform the duties in place of Muhammad Reza Khan". In the like manner, Raja Sitab Roy in Bihar was also divested of his post of Naib Diwan and George Vansittart, the Chief of the Council at Patna, was directed to take over the charge of Diwan.[6] Supervisors were continued in the districts with the title of Collectors. Both Muhammad Reza Khan and Raja Sitab Roy were summoned to Calcutta to face the prosecution on the charges of irregularities and embezzlement. 'After a very long and very exacting examination, destitute of any foundation, Raja Sitab Roy was acquitted with honour[7] and he was appointed to the high office of Roy-Reyan, the revenue farmer-general, of the province of Bihar.[8] But worn out by long and arduous trial at Calcutta Raja Sitab Roy died of illness soon after he returned to Azimabad (Patna).[9] To show his regrets on the sad episode Hastings proposed his epitaph: "He ever served the Company with a fidelity, integrity and ability which they can hardly expect to experience in any future officer of government, whom they may choose from the same class of people"[10]

Maharaja Kalyan Singh succeeds his Father

To honour the wishes and request of the deceased Raja Sitab Roy, the Governor even allowed his son, Kalyan Singh, who had ably helped his father with his sound knowledge of accounts and tact during former's trial, to succeed in all the offices held by his father;[11] and he was installed on the mashnad of Nizamut in Diwan Khana of the Killah with due honour.[12] He was allowed a stipend of Rs. 4, 166 per mensem,[13] and was provided with two naibs, Kheali Ram and Sadhu Ram, and Munsis and other staff.[14]

Changing fortunes of the Maharaja

If it would be unjust to accept the verdict of Ghulam Hussain[15] that Kalyan Singh was misfit for the high office, it is hard, in the light of facts, to accept judiciousness of the statement of scholar-poet, historian and administrator, Maharaja Kalyan Singh, that 'he regularly attended the Council on the days fixed for it and carried on all the work, both civil and political, conscientiously and economically and to the best of his power and abilities. In the evening he always held his Durbar in the Diwan-i-Khana and discussed affairs with the people and with the Aumils and Malguzars. He endeavoured to administer well, practised economy, never took a shell beyond what had been allotted to him, kept the English pleased with his work, tried to promote the interest of everyone, high or low, wounded the feeling of none to satisfy his own whims, was never guilty of embezzlement, and effected an increase in the Government money without ruining anyone on the charge of default'.[16] Owing to certain lapses on his part and mechanism of his naib, Kheali Ram, Maharaja Kalyan gradually began to have some difficulties with the English Chief at Patna and even lost the favour of the Governor-General.[17] Though he continued to hold the office of Roy-Royan of Subeh Bihar, he was desprived of the charge of Kotwali and faujdari, his territorial jurisdiction was also reduced by forming a separate collectorate of Sarkar Saran under Charles Graem. J. Reginald Hand Calls him a despotic Chief,[18] who exercised arbitrary powers over his subordinates. His allowances was also reduced from Rs. 50,000/- per annum to Rs. 18,000/- per annum.[19] The reduction was approved by the Court of Director.[20]

A Despotic Chief?

However, when Provincial Councils were abolished early in 1781, the Governor-General settled the Subeh Bihar for revenue farming with Maharaja Kalyan Singh for the annual rental of Rs. 29,21,107.[21] To reach the target of this increased amount Maharaja continued to be arbitrary in his dealings with the zamindars and Aumils, confirning them and confiscating their estates on default.[22] J.R. Hand even calls Maharaja Kalyan Singh 'A Despotic Chief'.[23] His relations with the Revenue Chief at Patna, Mr. Maxwell and his successors, remained any thing but cordial. He claimed to be an independent Chief directly under the Governor-General[24] and refused to pay kists of revenue to the Revenue Chief and insisted on depositing it directly into the

'Khalsa' at Calcutta. Ultimately, Committee of Revenue decided in April, 1782, that Raja Kalyan Singh should in future pay his 'kists' to the Revenue Chief at Patna, and not to the 'Khalsa' in Calcutta.[25]

Maharaja Kalyan Singh Falls in Heavy Arrears

Maharaja Kalyan Singh's settlement extended to an extensive area which included, Patna, Gaya, Shahabad and Tirhut, and so he had divided them with his Naib, Raja Kheali Ram of Benaras, who had the 'sublease of Siris, Cutumba, Chaynepur, and Sasaram, etc'.[26] But it was not possible for both of them to manage the collection of revenue for such an extensive area. Consequently, they had subleased them to sub-renters called 'Aumils' who were in most cases the old zamindars, but in many cases these 'aumils' were strangers with no local influence or prestige, and even ignorant of the people of the area. They collected rents with heavy hands, 'wrangled with zamindars and oppressed the raiyats'.[27] Even then most of them were in heavy arrears.[28] Roy-Rayan, the farmer-general of revenue, Maharaja Kalyan Singh, and his Naib, Raja Kheali Ram also fell in arrears. A letter, dated Ist June 1787 from the Committee of Revenue to Mr. Maxwell, the Revenue Chief at Patna indicates that Maharaja Kalyan Singh at that date was in arrears to the tune of Rs. 20,543. The Maharaja was called on to pay his arrears forthwith or 'coercive measures' would be adopted for forcing payment'. However, coercive measures could not be adopted against such a powerful Chief presently, owing to the political state of the country created by the revolt of Raja Chait Singh. Nevertheless, Raja Kalyan Singh's allowance was withheld in October, 1782 and some of the Jagirs were attached in order to realise the arrears of revenue, amounting to more than Rs. 6 lakhs. All his jewels and valuables were also sold to pay off the debt. Even then the debt could not be fully liquidated. Consequently, all his estates (Mokarrari Mahals) were taken by the Government for direct management, though he repeatedly urged for the waiving of the attachment. Under the circumstances, only means of his subsitence was the reduced allowance for him and for his dependents (being Rs. 500/- per month each for his wife and son).[29]

When all his prayers for relief were rejected, Maharaja Kalyan Singh personally went to Calcutta to represent his case and he had to stay there for nearly three decades but without any result. Exhausted and grieved he died in Calcutta in 1822.[30]

The Case of Raja Kheali Ram, the Naib

The case of Raja Kheali Ram was even worst as he did not enjoy the same status as Raja Kalyan Singh, and he had not the same security in personal property to offer for the discharge of his debt to the Company. The Committee of Revenue, therefore, in the letter of 14th November, 1781, directed Mr. Brooke, the Revenue Chief at Patna, to 'put him under restraint'. Raja Kheali Ram was arrested on the 21st November.[31] He was first confined in his own house, then in the Killah. In January, 1782, he was removed to 'Haveli-Begam'. All his property and jagirs were confiscated. Even then he was unable to liquidate the debt. Consequently, the Committee of Revenue in the letter of 29th August, 1782, directed the Revenue Chief at Patna to call on Kheali Ram's two sons - Roy Balgobind and Bakshiram — for payment, on failing, they were put under restraint. The final fate of the family is not known.[32]

Attempts of Warren Hastings to Consolidate the Power of the Company in Bihar : Resistance by the Cross-Section of the people

Resistance to the foreign rule had not been confined to Patna, Gaya, Shahabad and Saran, the western and northern regions of Bihar, but it also emerged from the tribal areas of the Tarai and jungle Mahals, comprising the modern divisions of Bhagalpur and Chhotanagpur, the south-east areas of the province; and to the extreme north-east in the District of Purnea. Whereas, on the one hand, Rajas, zamindars Ghatwals and Hillmen and their chiefs in the Jungle Tarai of Rajmahal and the tribal people and their chiefs of the Jungle Tracts of Chhotanagpur Plateau were not ready to acknowledge the English rule; on the other Sanyasees and fakirs by their organised raids challenged the English power from the north-east. Resistance to the foreign rule, it appears, had assumed, as if the universal character in Bihar, for almost all parts of the province rose against Company-rule at one time or other, in one form or other. The early English administrators had a tough time in suppressing the insurgent mood of these people; and to consolidate the power of the Company in these parts of Bihar, vigorous attempts were made by Warran Hastings to subdue the forces which were hostile to the Company.

Open-defiance by the Hill-Chiefs

Hill tracts of Jungle Tarai stretched from Rajmahal hills to Kharagpur hills, and from Colgong hills to Ramgurh hills which included the whole of modern Santhal Parganas, parts of Bhagalpur upto Kharagpur hills, Monghyr upto South Giddhour and upto, Kharakhdiha in Hazaribagh district. The inaccessible hilly tracts could not have been fully subjugated even by the mighty Moghuls. Captain Brooke had rightly observed that "the subjugation of the Jungle-Terri was not an enterprise for which the Moghuls had any fancy. The country was not suited to the operations of cavalry and the reduction of hill and forest tracts demanded a firm military skill and discipline which had Moghuls never possessed.[33] Many of the chief and zamindars of the area, naturally, had defying attitude against the power of the Company and upheld their virtual independence with the help of valliant hillmen (paharias) in their employ. Prominent among the refractory zamindars and chiefs of the Jungle Terai of Rajmahal hills were Jagannath Deo, zamindar of Lakshmipur and chief Ghatwal of the area, and Rani Sarbeshwari of Sultanabad and Ambar (Maheshpur Raj).[34]

Ghatwali Tenures were established by the Muslim rulers to guard the ghats or mountain passes from the Maratha incursions and other marauding hill tribes. Revenue letters of Bhagalpur Collector's Record Room (Sept. & Oct., 1774) inform us that Ghatwali system was allowed to continue in the disturbed areas of Jungle Terai. But as in the past, so in the present it did not fully serve the purpose for which it was intended, on the contrary, it created serious problems of law and order.[35] In addition to the Ghatwali Tenures, Warren Hastings appointed separate military administrator of the disturbed area of Jungle Terai who had a light Infantry of 800 strong under his command and was not under the authority of the Collector of Rajmahal and Bhagalpur.[36]

Jagannath Singh Deo, zamindar of Lakshmipur and chief Ghatwal of the area, revolted against the authority of the new English rulers. He along with other Ghatwals like Bisu Singh of Kakwara and Ummed Singh of Kharwar, prevented the collection of revenue and instigated other zamindars and farmers not to pay the rent.[37]

In the middle of 1773, Captain Brooke commenced an expedition against this rebellious zamindar and stormed his Fort of Tiur. The citadel which had recently been strongly strengthened and fortified held out till cannons were brought against it.[38] Jagannath Deo escaped into the hills and his other compatriots and zamindar were also expelled from the area by successful expeditions of Captain Brooke. However, Jagannath Deo again appeared on the scene with full force in early 1775. According to Major James Browne, the incharge of the military collectorship of the Jungle Terai after Captain Brooke: It was "the great insurrection in favour of Jagannath Deo and other expelled zamindars. The whole year passed in uninterrupted hostilities."[39] But Browne successfully crushed the rebellion and broke the 'confederacy'. Jagannath Deo alongwith other insurgents surrendered to the authority of the Company. Consequently, his son Rupnarain Deo was allowed to succeed his father in the zamindari of Lakshmipur in May, 1776.[40]

Rupnarain Deo could not long remain submissive and began to manifest hostile instance just after the death of his father in 1779. Enacting his father he stopped paying rents and even murdered two zamindars of Mandar who were loyal to the Company.[41] An attempt to arrest him failed as he escaped into the jungles of Beerbhum. But in the long run he found it futile to resist the English power and submitted to their authority in 1783. Subsequently, he was restored in his zamindari on his representation and pledge of loyalty.[42]

"Rebellious Rani Sarbeshwari of Sultanabad"

Another estate in the Jungle Terai whose proprietors did not readily submit to the new authority, were the zamindars of Ambar and Sultanabad (Maheshpur Raj) in the present Pakoor, subdivision of Santhal Parganas. Ambar and Sultanabad had a tradition of hostility towards the alien rulers and had always a ready party and support for all those hill-chiefs and their people, Ghatwals and zamindars, who were against the power of the Company. According to Captain Browne, the insurgency 'had existed for several years' in Ambar and Sultanabad.[43] Brooke,

Browne, and Cleveland, almost all the military administrators and Collectors, for the areas, had to undertake expeditions to subdue the rebellious Ambar and Sultanabad. Even a female successor to the zamindari, Rani Sarbeshwari, rebelled against the English in 1781.[44] But she could not hold for long against the power of the Company. She had to pay the price for disaffection. She was disposed of her zamindari and not permitted to reside at or near Sultanabad but was allowed a pension of Rs. 200/- per month which was further reduced to Rs. 150/-. She died in Bhagalpur Jail on 6th May, 1807.[45]

Thus the rebellious zamindars, chief and Ghatwals of the Jungle Terai were brought to submission. But the Hillmen of the area consumed much of the time, energy, and money before they were reconciled to the new regime and settled ways of life through a long-term plan.

Resistance by the Aboriginal 'Paharias' (Hillmen)

The problem of the Hillmen was the greatest and a peculiar problem which confronted the early English rulers in Bihar. The Hillmen or the Paharias, a race of aboriginals, were the earliest settlers in the area.[46] Since before the dawn of history they lived on their beloved hilltops 'surrounded by forests and rocky escarpment secure from intrusion or molestation.'[47] The Paharias did not go for regular labour, and lived on jungle food and meagre crops acquired through 'Jhuming' or Kurao.[48] They lived in a state of utmost barbarism[49] and did not conform to the settled ways of life. During the period of instability and disorder of the decline of the Muslim power they had become a race of bandits and dacoits', and were a menance for the travellers, merchants and people of the plains. Incursions of the hillmen had become common. At that time the country to the south and west was so unsettled owing to the inroads of the hill tribes, that the exact boundaries of the district could not be determined.[50] In their unlawful activities Paharias were encouraged and supported by the zamindars and Ghatwals of that area. John William Kaye quoting the early volumes of the Asiastic Researches mentioned: "It was a common practice for the zamindars on the skirts of the hills to invite the (hill) Chiefs in their vicinity with their adherents to descend and plunder the neighbouring zamindaree, for which and for the passage through their lands, the mountaineers divided their booty with them.[51] The fact is well confirmed by the then Collector of Bhagalpur, Augustus Cleveland, who wrote in 1783; "The hill people are generally employed for plundering by the Ghatwals and zamindari officers".[52] These ravages became more frequent, more violent and more systematic after the famines of 1770 as the low-country outposts manned by Ghatwals were abandoned due to famines. Even the government mail-runners were robbed and murdered between Rajmahal and Telliagurhy Pass. The situation had become so alarming that the low-country bordering on the hills was almost depopulated and travellers could not pass with safety between Bhaugulpore and Furruckabad.[53]

A Serious Problem

The problem of the Paharias and the disturbances in the Jungle Terai area became so serious that the administration of Warren Hastings had to raise a separate Battalion of Light Infantry of 800 strong for the protection of the low landers and the extirpation of the free booters so detrimental to the collection of revenues in these districts. At the end of 1773 a separate military collectorship was also formed for the disturbed area of the Jungle Terai under the charge of Captain Brooke, who had also the command of the Light Infantry. Captain Brooke was placed directly under the authority of the Board of Revenue and the Governor for the twin purposes of revenue and military operations.[54]

'Repression with Pacification'

Captain Brooke, as suggested by Warren Hastings, adopted the policy of repression with pacification. By his expeditions, he subdued the rebellious zamindars and Ghatwals like Jagannath Deo and many hill chiefs, thus, secured the frontier upon the old establishment. For the pacification of Paharias, he treated with sympathy and kindness the prisoners and their relations dependent on them. He also established villages at the foot of hills and induced them to become cultivators. But before he could establish things on a permanent footing he had to make over the charge to Captain James Browne in 1774.

James Browne picked up the thread left by Brooke and carried on the task with all seriousness. His jurisdiction and responsibilities increased manifold with the addition of the Jungle of Birbhum and Gidore (Gidhaur) in 1774 and in early 1775.[55]

Ambitious and Humane Plan of James Browne

Though Browne prepared an ambitious and humane plan[56] for the conciliation of the Paharias and for the future administration of the area; yet he could not execute them as most of the time he had been engaged in subduing the refractory Bhuians led by Jagannath Deo of Laxshmipur, and rebellious zamindar of Ambar and Sultanabad. His scheme envisaged the maintenance of the tribal system by division of the hills in Parganas or Tappas each under a hill chief called Sardar to be recognised through grants of Sanads to that effect by the Government[57] and assisted by naibs — Manjhis. In turn, Hill-Chiefs were to preserve the peace and order, to ensure the safety of roads and rivers in their respective Parganas. He also proposed to allot waste-lands at the foot of hills as Jagirs on small peshkush to the retired and invalid sepoys of the Company on the condition that they settle 'these with their families on the tenure of feudal services'.[58] These are known as Invalid Jagirs. By the time his scheme was approved by the Calcutta Council in 1778, Browne had to leave the Jungle Terai to join another assigment.[59] And the declaration of the Governor-General, Warren Hastings, to the effect that the Tract of the JungleTerai had been reduced to government proved to be premature. Even in December 1777 and January 1778, 44 villages were plundered and burnt. In May 1778, the hillmen actually carried off some of the Collector's tents within a few miles of Bhagalpur town.[60] Thus, though pioneering works were done by Brooke and Brawne for the pacification and submission of the Paharias, yet to bring the problem to a happy conclusion was reserved for Augustus Cleveland.

Augustus Cleveland; Beloved 'Jhilmili Saheb' of the Paharias

After joining the post of the Collector of Bhagalpur, and incharge of the disturbed area of Jungle Terai in 1779, Cleveland engaged himself with vigour and enthusiasm in pacifying and subjugating the Paharias.[61] His previous experience as the assistant to the collector at Rajmahal and Bhagalpur proved to be an extra advantage. He could well understand the vital issues that were at stake'. He was impressed by the simplicity, truthfulness and capabilities of the Paharias, and believed in their inherent goodness, and hoped that very soon all the Paharias would be induced to the settled ways of peace and civilization if given an opportunity. Cleveland, therefore, adopted a benevolent policy and sympathetic attitude towards the Hill-people. Taking advantage of the previous plan of Browne, Cleveland formulated comprehensive scheme. Writing to Warren Hastings from Sakari Gali Ghat on 21st November, 1780, he urged upon the Governor-General to employ the Paharias in a proposed corps of hill archers to provide with the means of subsistence to them because they committed illegal and inhuman acts only for that.[62] The Scheme involved an enormous disbursement of Rs. 29,440. So, Warren Hastings did not approve the plan but he sanctioned another scheme, which Cleveland proposed, for granting allowances of Rs. 10/- a month to all the Sardars of a Tappah and Rs. 5/- a month to their Naibs and Rs. 2/ - to a Manjhi or village headmen.[63]

The Hill-system and the Hill Assembly

There arose practical difficulties during the execution of the scheme, since many areas of the hillmen were beyond his jurisdiction. From the very beginning Cleveland had been urging to put the whole range of the hills under one authority.[64] Accordingly, he got Parganas Ambar and Sultanabad from the old district of Rajshahi and Tappah Belpatta from Birbhum transferred to his jurisdiction. The Paharias were also brought out from the jurisdiction of the ordinary courts. For all their civil and criminal cases they were to be tried by an Assembly of Hill-Chiefs, meeting twice a year, presided over by Cleveland himself. The system was incorporated in Regulation I of 1795.[65] He also removed the hill country and the belt of forest at its base from the control of the zamindars, and made them absolutely rent free. To provide employment to the Paharies, Cleveland also got his scheme of the Corps of Hill Archers, later on called Bhagalpur Hill-Rangers, sanctioned with the concurrence of Sir Eyre Coote in 1782. Cleveland took keen interest in the activities of the Bhagalpur Hill Rangers, and he was justifiably proud of its achievement. Writing on 16th August, 1799, J. Fombelle, the Magistrate of Bhagalpur said : "It affords protection to the district and serves as one of the strongest bonds of harmony between the Government and the Hill people".[66] For about three quarter of a century Hill Rangers were one of the most disciplined and gallant body of men, whom Captain Sherwil described in 1851, 'a fine body of soldiers as any in the regular army'.[67] To protect the people of the plains from occasional raids Cleveland executed the plan of Invalid Jagirs, initiated by Browne, more systematically and effectively.

Augustus Cleveland's mission, in the opinion of the Court of Directors," was attended with singular success in reclaiming the Hill people of that district from a state of utmost barbarism and the memory of that excellent officer ... held in reverence by the rude tribes ..... as well as by the inhabitants of the more civilized portion of the District'.[68] In fact, he was long remembered with respect and affection as 'Jhilmili Saheb' by the Paharias. He was amazingly successful in pacifying, subjugating and civilizing the Hill people. The secret of his success, writes P.C. Roy Choudhury, the author of the District Gazetteer of Santhal Paraganas, "appears to have been his personal influence and his real sympathy with the primitive people."[69] Explaining the way of his working Sir John Houlton wrote that he went about unarmed and unattended in the hills and villages, so recently feared as a race of savages. He had as much interviews with the Chiefs and people as was possible. He gave them presents and feasts, started schools and established many bazars below the hills and encouraged the hill people to bring their produce there for sale and barter.[70] These hectic exertions naturally told upon his health and he died on the high seas while going home for a change on 13th January, 1784,[71] at an early age of 29. Nevertheless, by his character and achievements, he has won an exalted place in the galaxy of able British Officers. His fame chiefly rests on his contribution to the most permanent and happy settlement with the hill people. In Bhagalpur two memorials one by the Company and other by the people—have been erlcted to perpetuate the affectionate memory of Augustus eleveland.[72] However, the Hill systems of Cleveland broke down by the first half of the 19th century owing to the indifference of his successors, with the exception of J. Fombelle, in the changed circumstances. Nevertheless, the creation of the non-regulation district of Santhal Parganas owes much to the Hill-system of Augustus Cleveland.

The Revolt of Raja Chait Singh 'Raised' the People 'Enmasse' in Bihar

The revolt of Raja Chait Singh of Benaras in August 1781 had wide repercussions on the province of Bihar. In fact, it proved to be 1857 in miniature which 'aimed at the expiration of the English'.[73] Consequent upon the revolt, the rising power of the English had to face serious troubles not only in Benaras Raj but also in the adjoining provinces. It did not remain confine to the city of Benaras and citadel of Ramnagar. Revolt raised a conflagration from Allahabad to Monghyr.[74] G.W. Hastings believed that Chait Singh had 'a plot agaisnt the English ready to his hand.'[75]

J. Reginald Hand, late Deputy-Collector of Shahabad (1886-90) after going through the records of the period, 1781-86, described the revolt of Raja Chait Singh, a political event of consequence in the context of early English administration of Bihar.[76] Bihar presented serious troubles even after the insurrection was suppressed in Benaras. It was because Raja Chait Singh was not alone and isolated in his attempt to overthrow the English yoke. People from Bihar came out for his active support and raised the standard of revolt in Bihar also. Many powerful Rajas, zamindars and Aumils in the district of Patna, Gaya, Shahabad and Saran rose against the Company-Raj. Standard bearers of revolt in Bihar were Raja Pitamber Singh of Tikari-Raj, Reza Kooli Khan, former Aumil of Sasaram, Raja Narain Singh, zamindar of Siris and Cutumba in Gaya, Raja Akbar Ali of Narhat and Samai, and Fateh Shahi of Hathwa Raj. Hussain Ali Khan, the renter of Arawal and Mussaurah, was 'employed as an emmissary by Chyte Singh who was 'propagating', their late misfortune. But soon he was taken into custody.[77]

The revolt of Raja Chait Singh burst suddenly on the English officials of Bihar. Europeans in general at Patna were so much alarmed that they planned to leave the city. However, they were dissuaded from doing so by Mrs. Hastings,[78] who had been left at Patna by the Governor-General on his way to Benaras. James

Lindsay Ross, who had assumed the Chiefship at Patna on the sudden death of Mr. Maxwell in early August, 1781, immediately took precautionary measures. He dispatched private 'Harcarahs' by different routes to the following gentlemen at their respective stations, Mr. Middleton at Lucknow, Col. Hannay at Gorukhpore, Col. Margan at Cawnpore, and Capt. William at Bagaha. He also issued necessary orders to Major Alexander Hardy, commanding the Patna Militia, to collect his people as many as he could sparing them from collections, in order to protect the city, secure the treasure and piece goods, and to suppress all tumults or apparent disturbance that might happen by the disaffection in the city.[79]

The situation was really alarming for the English, the banks of the river being lined with armed men who boarded and fired upon all boats indiscriminately. Several Europeans had very narrow escapes.[79] Concentration of troops by the rebels was made on a wide scale to harass the English.[80] The impact of the revolt was so widespread that even the Governor-General repeatedly advised his wife, beloved Marian, not to stay even at Bhagalpur but to proceed to Murshidabad or Calcutta, because she was not "absolutely safe at Baughulepur as he dreaded a surprise".[80] A letter of 28th August, 1781, written to the Council at Calcutta by Ross, the Revenue Chief at Patna, says : "Since the Revolt of Raja Chyte Singh on the 16th inst, every communications by Dak has been cut off from hence to Benaras, and so well has he concerted measures that we can obtain no intelligence whatever from that quarter".[81] The disruption of regular Dak is also confirmed by a letter of Warren Hastings to his wife, wherein he states: "Do not be uneasy if you do not receive frequent letters from me, three in four miscarry".[82]

Within a very short period, the revolt of Raja Chait Singh engulfed a large part of Bihar. On 29th of August, 1781. Mr. Graeme, the Collector of Saran informed Mr. Ross, the Revenue Chief of Patna, that there were disaffected people in his Division. He wrote : 'Reza Cooly Cawn, formerly the Aumil of Sasaram, is at this time with Raja Cheyt Singh. Many of the inhabitants of that District, and particularly the Oojains, a tribe of Rajput, are sincerely attached to him. Petambar Singh of the Tikcary Raj is most intimately connected with Cheyt Singh and his dependants are remarkable good soldiers. He has also a number of horsemen in his pay.[83]

Raja Narain Singh, the zamindar of Siris and Kutumba, also rose against the Company. He was also instrumental in fomenting troubles in Palamau.[84] Despite repeated requests he did not help Major Crawfurd's regiment at Sherghati.[85] Instead, he joined Bechu Singh, the Faujdar of Chait Singh, at Agroor pass with 1,500 matchlockmen, and harassed the English troops at many places and thus disputed their passage.[86] He pushed his way without molestation through Kaimur Hills to Bijoy Garh, apparently to join Raja Chait Singh there. Mr. Ross, the Chief at Patna forwarding the case against Narain Singh, described him as 'an arch traitor', who 'betrayed and showed every mark of disaffection to Major Crawfurd' while their 'affairs bore an unfavourable aspect'. He, most subtly, evaded supplying the Major with boats to cross the Sone on his march from Chitra'.[87] He had to pay the penalty for disaffection. He was deprived of his zamindari, and ultimately arrested by May, 1782, and sent to Dacca as a state prisoner on the 5th of March, 1786,[88] because he might disturb the peace of the district if 'received a footing in it'.[89] However, he was set free in 1790.[90] and restored in his zamindari in 1792.[91]

Raja Fateh Shahi of Hathwa Raj also joined the party of Raja Chait Singh alongwith other Rajas and zamindars of Bihar. A letter from Mr. Ross to Major Hardy of Patna Militia, informs us that 'one Fahte Shah was giving trouble in Saran at this period, while several zamindars and others in the jurisdiction of the Revenue Chief of Patna armed and clothed their dependents in the military accoutrements of the Company.[92]

Raja Akbar Ali Khan, described by J.R. Hand, as 'another traitor to the Government'[93] also rebelled during the revolt of Raja Chait Singh. He escaped from Patna where he had been confined for heavy arrears, and raised about 5,000 matchlockmen on reaching his zamindari.[94] Even a company of Ensign Downes of Patna Militia could not quell the insurrection or capture the rebels, who had taken up a strong position in the Gumeah pass to resist the advance of the English troops. Reinforcement of two companies of soldiers were sent under Capt. Powel from Danapore. Only then, Raja Akabr Ali Khan could be driven out of his zamindari.[95] He proceeded to the Kharagpur Raj in Bhagalpur Division where he tried unsuccessfully to raise the

Ghatwals against the Company.[96] Later on he escaped to Delhi. He met Warren Hastings in 1784, and was allowed to return to Bihar.[97] But he could not regain his former position. His zamindari, including Rajgir and Amartha, was given to Ali Ibrahim Khan.[98]

Anti-British feelings in Bihar were so widespread, distrust of Rajas and zamindars was so great at this time that Maharaja Kalyan Singh, the Roy Royan of the Company in Bihar, and his Naib, Raja Kheali Ram, were not allowed to raise body of troops to take the field against Raja Chait Singh.[99]

Consequent upon the revolt of Raja Chait Singh, Chotanagpur region long remained disturbed. Palamau zamindars such as Gajraj Roy and Saugand Roy, abetted and encouraged by Raja Narain Singh of Samai, harassed the English in many ways.[100] The zamindar of Narwada also raised the standard of rebellion and directed his retainers and raiyyats to withhold the payment of 'Kists' to the government. His followers also made an attack on the party of the Collector of Ramgarh who hurriedly escaped to safety to his headquarters.[101] The Nagabanshi Raja of Chutia Nagpur showed symptoms of disaffection. Raising of troops, evasion of payment of revenue Kists and his other activities smacked of disloyalty. Collector Dallas even foresaw danger in the 'refractory spirit of the inhabitants' of those hills.[102] He himself raised a 300 strong matchlockmen and requested for reinforcement of three to four companies of sepoys sufficient to crush the disaffection and to keep the inhabitants firm in their allegiance to the Government.[103]

It is in this background that the Dr. S.B. Choudhuri remarked in his monumental work that the revolt of Chait Singh gradually assumed the 'Character of a popular revolt'.[104] Though some of the leaders of the revolt in Bihar were 'seriously attached' with Raja Chait Singh, yet their open manifestation of discontent against the English rule must not be seen as 'a conspiracy on behalf of Chait Singh' rather it should be seen as a part of the anti-British movement to arrest or to overthrow the growing power of the Company as 'in the earlier years such resistance was naturally organised by the ruling Rajas and Nawabs, zamindars and other landed aristocracy.[105] They were political leaders in the society and they represented the people. The alleged aim, the expiration of the English, and the rise and progress of the revolt indicate that it was not merely a 'short lived-rising', but it had the support and sympathy of the people in general, in addition to the leading part played by Rajas, Nawabs, zamindars and Aumils. Infact, the people were 'raised enmasse'[106] to overthrow the English rule.

Sannyasi and Fakir Raiders

Resistance to the foreign rule, as if, was not supposed to be the sole responsibility and monopoly of the settled people, non-tribal and tribal, of the plains and plateau, as such nomadic Sannyasees and Fakirs also came out to contribute their share in their own way to resist the growth of alien rule. By their organised raids on factory, cutchehree and treasury of the government and its zamindars, they not only threatened government revenue[107] but also peace of mind of early English administrators. They had taken lessons and inspirations from the Maratha incursions[108] to harass the ruling power of dislike.

As soon as the Subah of Bengal felt the impact of English imperialists, Sannyasees and Fakirs became active. As early as 1760, Watt and Howitt returning from Burdwan and Kishengurh reported that the Naugurs (Naga Sannyasis) and Marhatta have advanced into those countries and commenced plundering which has obliged them to retire to Calcutta and will put a stop to the collection of tuncaws (revenue) in those countries'.[109] It was decided to send such a military force to those countries as may be necessary'.[110] Warren Hastings wrote in 1763: "Sometime ago a large body of Fakirs infesting the country about Bakergunge surrounded Mr. Kelly, my agent and put him in danger of life."

The Sannyasis entered Bihar in 1767. Thomas Rumbold, the English Chief, reported the matter to President and Select Committee on Apr. 20, 1767: "A body of 5000 Sinnasees entered the Sircar Saronge country; the phousdar sent two companies of sepoys after them, under the command of Sergeant who came up with them; the Sinnasees stood their ground and after the sepoys had fired away part of their ammunitions, fell on them killed and wounded near eighty and put the rest to flight".[111] This obliged the Patna Chief to send Capt. Wilding 'to rid the country of them as their stay strike terror into the country-people and greatly hurt the collection in that part.[112] In 1768, Raja Sitab Roy informed the Chief at Patna that the rebel zamindar of Hussepur Raj (Hathwa Raj) Fatehshahi, had waged a quarrelling war against the Company with the help of Naggis (Naga Sannyasis).[113] Consequently, Capt. Wilding again marched against them, dispersed them and took the fort of the Raja.[114] Purnea was frequently visited by Fakirs and Sannyasis where they entered from adjoining districts of Bengal. Ducarel, the Supervisor of Purnea, therefore, took precautionary measures, and 'stationed harcaras at the Ghats and passages of the Koosy river in Oct., 1770.[115] He also received intelligence to the effect that a body of 300 Fakirs 'armed with matchlocks and other offensive weapons were at Cundwah ghat and were preparing to cross the Koosy river. He, accordingly, directed Lt. Sinclair to march against them with the sepoys at Purnea. Lt. Sinclair with his 150 men captured the entire body of Fakirs and brought them to Purnea. But they were allowed to pass on representations of good faith[116] which proved to be false. The Supervisor of Dinajpur reported on 7th Dec., 1770 that the Fakirs coming from Purnea had changed their professed route, and were armed with 'personal arms, besides 4 camels loaded with rockets'.[117] Again in 1773, there was an alarm in Bihar due to the movement of Sannyasis. The Supervisor of Tirhut, writing from his headquarters at Darbhanga, on 15th March, to the Chief and Council of Revenue at Patna, informed ..." in ten days they (Sannyasis) will begin to assemble at a place called Janickpur (Janakpur in Nepal near Darbhanga) in commemoration of the birth and marriage of Sita which are on the same day of the year. They amount in number 20 to 30 thousand Sunnasses ... I should be glad that a sufficient force was sent for ten days.[118]

In fact, Sannyasis were trying to force their way through Purnea to Bengal. But they were frustrated in their attempts as Captain Brooke with his newly raised battalion of Light Infantry immediately rushed from Pirpainty near Rajmahal. Crossing the river he entered upon measures against the Sannyasis, wrote Warren Hastings, who were glad to escape as fast as they could out of the Company's possessions.[119]

Escaping from Purnea the Sannyasis moved westward and appeared in Champaran and Saran. On 7th April, 1773 the

Superintendent of Sarkar Saran reported to the Chief at Patna: 'The Sunnassis are moving in very large bodies along the borders of Champaran .... I have sent out all the sepoys that could possibly be spared from this side of the country under Captain Ashe to the assistance of Captain Hardy. But both the detachments when joined will be very inadequate to the force they are to oppose and it would be of great service if three or four companies more were to march from Patna with all possible expedition by the shortest road to Betteah... to revenge the insults which the Compnay's arms have recently suffered from them.[120] To answer the above request and as a means of promoting the plan of the Hon'ble Governor and Council for expelling the Sunnassies from these provinces' four companies of sepoys under captain Hay proceeded from Patna on 13th April to join the detachment at Betteah.[121]

Despite vigorous measures taken by Warren Hastings the Sannyasi and Fakirs could not be expelled completely from these provinces. They appeared now and then for next three decades. Rooke, the Chief of Purnea, reported to Committee of Revenue on the 15th Jan. 1783, that a body of Sannyasis were encamped in the north eastern portion of Purnea district and were daily guilty of the most violent depredations. On the approach of a detachment of two companies under Captain Williams the Sannyasies escaped to the Morung country.[122] Again in June, 1784, the Collectors of Bhagalpur informed the Supreme Council of Revenue in Calcutta: "The Renters of Rajmahal have sent me intelligence that Shaw Mudgnoo (Majnu Shah), noted Chief of Faqueers from the Morung hills, had appeared near Malda Factory, with seven hundred armed followers, several camels laden with some rockets, and other war like apparatus.... and that the whole district was in danger of being laid under contribution".[123] The Collector soon dispatched two hundred Hill Rangers with a small party from Sebundy corps against them. As a result Majnu Shah with his band of Fakirs made a hurried retreat.[124] However, Warren Hastings could not rid the provinces of the Sannyasi and Fakir-menace. Even in January, 1783 we hear the Fakirs plundering several places and making an attempt on one of the frontier posts but being 'repulsed' in Purnea.[125] Again in June 1794, the killing of sepoys and plunder of Ramgunj factory in Purnea is reported. In July also Y. Burges, Collector of Purnea apprehended, troubles from Sannyasis, and the collection 'fortuitous and uncertain', if some speedy stop was 'not put to the incursions'.[126] The Collector of Purnea also warned his superiors, such as Mr. Cowper, President and Member of the Board of Revenue, that 'unless Government adopts some decided measures to put an effectual stop to the incursions of those banditti or Fakeers, that the collections of the northern pergunnas will be rendered very uncertain.[127] Even in 1795 we hear of their raids on Purnea and Darbhanga.[128] It was only in the early years of 19th century that the activities of Sannyasis and Fakirs on an alarming scale ceased.

The Calcutta Council in 1773 described the Sannyasi and Fakir raiders as a set of lawless banditts. But it is in the fitness of things and proper perspective that we should not class them as such.[129] If we consider the origin, history and martial habits of the armed Sannyasis,[130] their employment in the armies of Marathas and Sikhs, [131] Ruhellas[132] and Rajputs of Jaipur, their bravery and faithfulness as a soldier,[133] times and target of their attack and plunder,[134] it will be very hard and improper to call them merely a set of lawless banditti (bandits). In fact, taking lessons and inspirations from the Maratha raids for harassing the ruling power of dislike, the nomadic bodies of Sannyasis and Fakirs came out also to resist the growth of alien rule in their own way. Though, they continued the profession of arms under some native princes for some time to come, but their raids ceased with the end of the 18th century when they found the Company-Raj 'a fait accompli'.

References

1. Firminger, Fifth Report , Vol. I., Introduction , p. CCXII.
2. Mill & Wilson - The History of British India, Vol. III, p.365.
3. Monckton Jones, Warren Hastings in Bengal, p. 145.
4. Vide Cambridge History, V. p. 207, Indian reprint.
5. Cambridge History, V. 414.
6. S.G. Mishra History of Bihar, (1740-1772), Munshiram Manohar Lal, Delhi 1970, pp. 162-171.

7. Siyar, Vol. III, pp. 47-48 also Kalyan Singh's Khulasat-ul-Tawarikh, ff 171B-175B.
8. Bengal Secret Committee Proceedings, 1773, p.p. 524-52.
9. Siyar, III, 48.
10. Monckton, Jones, Warren Hastings in Bengal, p. 199.
11. Siyar, III p. 67
12. Prof. S.H. Askari, Maharaja Kalyan Singh, Journal of Bihar & Orissa Research Society, 1940
13. J.R. Hand, Early, English Administration of Bihar, 1781-85, Calcutta, 1894, p. 5.
14. C.P.C., IV, pp. 228 & 236.
15. Siyar, III, pp. 67-68.
16. From Khula-satut-Tawarikh vide Prof. Askari, Maharaja Kalayan Singh, Journal of B & O. 1940.
17. C.P.C., Vol. V. p. 525.
18. Hand's Early English Ad. Chapter IV-A Despotic Chief, p. 40.
19. C.P.C., Vol. VII, P.
20. Letter from the Court, 5 Dec., 1787, Fort William India Hose Correspondence, Vol. X. pp. 546-547.
21. Hand, p. 31
22. Ibid, Hand, p. 5.
23. Hand, Chapter IV, p. 40.
24. J. F. W. James, Selections from the Correspondence of the Revenue Chief of Bihar, p.16.
25. Ibid, p. 22.
26. Hand, p.17,
27. Ibid, p. 31.
28. James, Selections from the Correspondence of the Revenue Chief, p. 20.
29. J.F.W. James - Selection from the Correspondence of the Revenue Chief of Bihar, pp. 15-21 & 33-38, also C.P.C ., Vol. VI, p. 206-10, & 448.

30. See for details Prof. Askari, Maharaja Kalya Singh, Journal of Bihar and Orissa Research Society, 1940, pp. 33-34.

31. Hand, *op. cit.,* p. 20.

32. For details see Hand, op. cit., pp. 17-22.

33. Vide Macpherson's Final Report on the Santhal Parganas Settlement, 1909-1910. p. 26.

34. K.K. Basu, Early Difficulties in Aministration in Bhagalpur, 1775-1805, "The Journal of Bihar Research Soc., Vol. 42, 1956.

35. Bhagalpur District Records, Vol. X,p. 288; Vol. ii, 127, Vol. III, 19.

36. D.G. Bhagalpur, P.C. Roychoudhury, pp. 51-52.

37. N.B. Ray, The New Light on the Hillmen Santhals of Jungle Terry, Bengal Past and Present, Vol., 73, pp. 52-53, 54.

38. *Ibid.*

39. Browne, Indian Tracts, Introduction, p. iii.

40. *Ibid.*

41. Ibid, p. IV, also F. Buchanan's Bhagalpur Report, pp. 522-524 and A.N. Singh, "A Study in some early British Sanads relating to Jungle terri" proceedings, Ind. Hist. Records Commission, 18th Session, p. 217.

42. Ibid, pp. 17-18, also Extract from the Proceedings of the Governor-General in Council, Revenue Deptt., Vol. 89. dated Ist April, 1785.

43. Brown, Indian Tract, Introduction, p. VI.

44. W.W. Hunter. A Statistical Account of Bengal, Vol. XIV, pp. 18-19.

45. Letter dated 7th May, 1806 to the Secretary to the Board of Revenue, Calcutta from P. Hamilton, Collector of Bhagalpur and Letter dated 15th March, 1821 Camp, Monghyr, from the Collector of Bhagalpur to the Sub-Secretary to the Board of Commissioner the provinces of Bihar & Benaras : also F. Buchanan, An Account of the District of Bhagalpur, pp. 551-52.

46. D. G. Santhal Parganas, P.C. Roychoudhury, p. 172.

47. Sir John Houlton, Bihar the Heart of India, Orient Longman, 1949, p. 83.

48. Ibid. p. 75, also D.G. Santhal Parganas and Bhagalpur.
49. J. W. Kaye, Ad. of the East India Co. Indian Reprint, p. 489 Kitab Mahal, p. 966.
50. Imperial Gazetteer of India by Byrne, p. 27.
51. J. W. Kaye, The Administration of the East India Company. Reprint Kitab Mahal, Allahabad, 1966, p. 490.
52. Cleveland to Warren Hastings 29th March, 1783, Bhagal District Records, Vol. II.
53. The Asiatic Researches, in J.W. Kaye's Administration of the Co. p. 490.
54. K.K. Datta, Edited - Old Zamindari Records of Bihar, Vol. II, pp. 27-29 also K.K. Basu Early Difficulties.
55. Browne, India Tracts, Introduction, pp. i-ii.
56. Browne, India Tracts, Ibid, pp. 62-68.
57. Ibid, also Proceedings of the Indian Historical Records Commission, 1940.
58. Ibid, p. 68.
59. Browne's Correspondence, Indian Record Series, ed. K.D. Bhargava, Introduction, p. iv.
60. Imperial Gazetteer of India by Byrne, pp. 27-28, also F.B. Bradely Birt, The Story of Indian Upland, p. 85.
61. Bradley Birt, pp. 86-90.
62. Letter dated Secreeagully, 21st April, 1780, from the Collector of Bhagalpur to the Governor-General, Bhagalpur Distt. Records Vol. II, p. 127.
63. Sutherlands's Report, 1818-19, para 41.
64. Letter from Cleveland, dated Sakarigali, 21st Nov., 1781, Vol. II.
65. W.B. Oldhum, Some Hisotircal and Ethnic Aspects of Burdwan Distt. 1894, also Selection from the Judicial Records of the Bhagalpur Distt. Office, ed. K.K. Datta, p. 130, pp. 242-247, Introduction, p. viii.
66. Selection From the Judicial Records of Bhagalpur, op. cit., p. 263.
67. Sherwill, Notes upon a Tour through the Rajmahal Hills, The Journal of Asiatic Society of Bengal, 1851.

68. J.W. Kaye Administration of the East India Company, p 489.

69. D.G., S.P. p. 68.

70. J. Houlton, Bihar the Heart of India, p. 74.

71. Busteed, Echoes from Cld Calcutta, p. 339.

72. Author's article, 'Memorials of Augustus Cleveland at Bhagalpur', Proceedings, Indian History Congress, Calicut Session, 1976.

73. The Letter of Col. Hannay from Fyzabad to the Governor-General, Forest's State papers, Vol. III pp. 1004-5.

74. J. Reginald Hand, Early English Adm. of Bihar, 1781-86, Bengal Secretariat Press, Cal., p 23.

75. G. W. Hastings, A. Vindication of Warren Hastings, p. 145.

76. Hand's Early English Administration, p.3.

77. Selection from the Correspondence of the Revenue Chief of Bihar, pp. 83-84.

78. Selection from the Correspondence of the Revenue Chief of Bihar, pp. 83-84.

79. Selections from the Correspondence of the Revenue Chief, p. 82.

80. Selections from the Revenue Chief, p. 78-80.

81. Ibid, J.L. Ross to the Council in Calcutta 20 Aug., 1781.

82. The Chronology of Modern India by Burgees, Edinburg, 1831, p. 248.

83. Letter of Warren Hastings from Chunar to his wife, Dr. H.E. Busteed, Echoes from Old Calcutta, W. Thacker & Co., London, 4th Ed. 1908. pp. 329-31.

84. Hand, Early English Admt. p. 6.

85. Busteed, Echoes from Old Calcutta, pp. 331.

86. Selection from the Correspondence of the Revenue Chief of Bihar-1781-1786, pp. 78-82.

87. Governor-General in Council (Rev. Deptt.) Proceedings, 7 June, 1782.

88. Hand, E.E. A., p. 10.

89. Ibid.

90. W.A. Brooke to Alexander Hardy, 5th March, 1786.
91. Ibid, for details see Hand, pp. 12-14.
92. Board of Rev. Proceedings, 21 July, 1796, Vol. 96, No. 12.
93. Ibid, 15 Aug., 1792, Vol. 142. No. 10.
94. Ibid, pp. 9-10 also J. L. Ross to the Council in Calcutta, 30 Aug., 1781.
95. Hand, p. 15
96. K. K. Datta, Ed. Old zamindari Record (Bihar), Vol. II, p. 15.
97. James, Selections from the Revenue Chief, pp. 30-31.
98. J. R. Hand, pp. 15-16.
99. Dr. Akhileshwar Kumar, A History of Bihar 1740-84, A thesis submitted to the Bhag. Univ. for Ph. D. degree, p. 371.
100. Bihar Distt. Gazet., Gaya, by P.C. Roy Choudhary, p. 42; also Firminger, 5th Report, Vol. II, pp. 441-43.
101. Rev. Deptt. Governor-General in Council, 9, Oct. 1781, Enclosure to copy no. 23, Original Consultations, No. 24.
102. Governor-General in Council (Rev. Deptt.) Proc. 7th June, 1982 Enclosures, Letter dt. 15 Apr. 1782 from Major James Crawfurd to the Committee of Rev., Ramgarh & No. 2 Maxwells Parwanah.
103. Governor-General in Council, Rev. Deptt. 6 Dec., 1781, Encl., Letter dt. 16 Nov., 1781 from G. Dallas, Acting Collector of Ramgarh to the Governor-General at Benaras.
104. Ibid.
105. Governor-General in Council (Rev. Deptt.) Proceedings, 12, Oct,. 1781, Letter from Dallas, dt. 25 Sept. 1781.
106. Dr. S.B. Choudhuri, Civil-Disturbances During the British Rule in India, 1765-1857 p. 203, also p. 56 & 76.
107. Foreward by late Dr. Rajendra Pd. to History of the Freedom Movement in Bihar by Dr. K. K. Datta Vol. I, p.i, also Dr. S. B. Choudhari, Civil Disturbance, p. 203.
108. Hand, E.E.A. p. 23.
109. Revenue General Letter to the Court, dated 18th Oct., 1774, also G.R. Gleig, Memoirs of Warren Hastings, I, 395.

110. J. N. Sarkar, Fall of the Mughal Empire, Vol. l, p. 169, Cal.,1932
111. Proceedigs of the Council, 21st Feb. 1760, Long's Selection, 206.
112. 25th Feb., Ibid.
113. Ibid No., 690.
114. Long's Selections, p. 576, No. 971.
115. Ibid.
116. W.W. Hunter Statistical Account of Bengal (Patna & Saran), Vol. XI, pp. 368-69.
117. C.P.C. Vol. II, pp. 202-203.
118. Letter from Supervisor of Purnea to the Controlling Council of Revenue at Murshidabad, dt. 25th & 26th Oct. 1770,
119. *Ibid.*
120. Letter from Supervisor of Dinajpur to the controlling Council of Revenue at Murshidabad.
121. Proceedings of the Controlling Council of Revenue at Patna, dated 22nd March, 1773.
122. Hastings to Sir George Colebrooke, dated 31st Mar., 1773.
123. Proceedings of the Controlling Council of Revenue at Patna, dated 12th Apr., 1773.
124. *Ibid.*
125. Letter from the Chief of Purnea to the Committee of Revenue, dated 15th Jan. 1783.
126. Letter from Charles Chapman, Collector of Bhagalpur, to the Council of Revenue, dt. 10th June, 1784. Revenue Deptt. Original Consultations, No. 20, dt. 20th July, 1784.
127. Letter from the Collector of Bhagalpur to the Council of Revenue, dt. 22nd June, 1784, Revenue Deptt. Original Consult., No. 21, dt. 20th July, 1784.
128. Revenue Deptt. Proc. No. 13, dt. 25th Jan., 1793, pp. 254-61.
129. Letter, dt. 27th July, 1794 from Y. Burges, Collector of Purnea to Capt. John Witherston, Commanding at Taujepore, Purnea Distt. Records, Vol. 10. pp. 18-19.
130. Letter, dt. 28th Jul, 1794, from the Collector of Purnea to W. Cowper, President & Member, Bd: of Rev., Fort William, Ibid, p. 16.

131. *Ibid*, pp. 128-30.
132. Bihar Through the Ages, ed. R.R. Divakar, p. 593.
133. For details the organisation of the Sannyasis of Vedanta, by J. N. Farquhar, Jrl. of the Royal Asia. Soc. of Britain & Ireland, July, 1924.
134. C.P.C., Vol. II. p. 5.
135. Siyar, Vol. II, p. 531-33.
136. For details Thomas Duer Broughton's Letters from a Maratha Camp, new edition, pp. 96-98
137. For details Sannyasi & Fakir Raiders in Bengal, J. M. Ghosh of Bengal Civil Service, Bengal Secteriat Book Depot, Calcutta.

CHAPTER 3
The Opposition in South Bihar : The Tribal Resistance

The tribal areas of the forest and hilly tracts stretching from Midnapur to Manbhum, Singhbhum, Barabhum, Dhalbhum and Chotanagpur upto Palamau, and present Santhal Parganas, violently reacted to the sudden imposition of the British rule. To consolidate their power in all parts of their territorial jurisdiction the new rulers brought new system and new peoples as their representatives even in secluded and secure areas, whose tribal people and their chiefs and Rajas had maintained their freedom, life style and administrative system throughout the ages. Even the greatest of the Great Mughals could not completely subjugate the region.[1] In the extension of the English power the people of the region saw real danger to their age-long-way of life, and as such they offered stiff resistance to the growing control of the English authority. We find a chain of organised resistance and rebellion throughout the Company rule by the tribal and non-tribal people led by their chiefs "who was dignified among his ryots with the title of the Raja."[2]

Mention may be made of several Chuar rebellions including the rebellion of 1799-1800, Munda and Urao rebellions of 1811, 1817, the Hos or Larka Kol's rebellion of 1821, the great Kol-Insurrection of 1831-32 and the Bhumij Revolt of 1832-33, and above all, the great Santhal 'Hul' (Revolt) of present Santhal Parganas in 1855-56.

Refractory Jungle Mahals

The forest covered hill tract of the region later to be known as the Jungle-Mahals and Dhalbhum in Midnapur Distt. came under the English Sway as dependencies of the zamindars of Midnapur,[3] when Mir. Qasim, under the treaty of 27th Sep., 1760, assigned the lands of Burdwan, Midnapur and Chittagong to the East India Company.[4] By the Grant of Diwani of Bengal, Bihar & Orissa in 1765, not only Company's earlier possessions were confirmed but also the whole of the extensive Chotanagpur plateau as a part of the Subah of Bihar[5] came under the English rule. The attempt to exert actual political control over the region began in early 1767 when the Company sent Lt. Fergusson to subdue the country west of Midnapur to subjection. The task proved to be uphill. Fergusson found none of those Jungle zamindars to have less than 2000 people in their parganas whose 'trade' was 'War'.[6] According to Edward Baber, the English Resident at Midnapur, the zamindars were refractory and the inhabitants unruly and ungovernable.[7] However, Fergusson, by his vigorous military operations, captured the fort of Jhargram' Chief[8], and secured the submission of the Zamindars of Ramgarh, Samkakutia (Lalgarh), Jambani, Jatbani, Ambikanagar, Manbhum, Singhbhum, Barabhum, Chhatana, Raipur and Phulkusum.[9] Though these jungle-zamindars had submitted before the superior military force, for years they evaded payment of revenue on one pretext or other. In fact, it was a nominal submission.[10]

The Company met with the most obstinate resistance from the zamindar of Ghatshila, better known as the Raja of Dhalbhum who was determined not to admit any 'Firinghee' into his country[11] and made all, preparations to forestall the English infiltration.[12] Nevertheless, the Raja of Dhalbhum could not withstand the onslaught of the superior military might of the English.[13] He was defeated and deposed and made a prisoner, and his nephew Jagannath Dhal in April 1767, was invested' with the zamindari of Ghatshila.[14]

But Jagannath Dhal proved to be as refractory and turbulent as his uncle had been.[15] Consequently, he was also deposed and his younger brother, Nimu Dhal, was ordered to be installed in his place in August[16], But instead of solving the problem it made the situation worse for the English.[17] The deposed Raja of Dhalbhum, Jagannath Dhal, carried out hostile operations and devastations on a wider scale with the help of turbulent and rebellions Chuars of Bhumijes and their Chiefs.[18] Chief among these Chuar Sardars were Subla Singh of Koilapal, Samangunjan of Dhadka, and Jagannath Pater of Dampara[19]. Jagannath Dhal harassed the English so much that Lt. Smith, who had ben sent to suppress the rebels, had to report that the Hon'ble Company can never receive an anna from this side (of) Sonbarnika (Subarnrekha) river ... till he (JagannathDhal) is (raja again), he will never cease destroying the country with fire and sword."[20] Thus the Company was compelled to restore Jagannath Dhal in his zamindari in 1777. The restored Raja agreed to pay a revenue of Rs. 2000/- for the 1st year, Rs. 3000/- for the second year, and Rs. 4000/- for the third year. In the year 1800 A.D. the estate was permanently settled at Rs. 4,267.[21] However, Chuars and their chiefs in the Jungle Mahals long remained hostile and rebellious. There were disturbances and depredations time and again in Jhalda, Patkum, Jharia, Tamar & Koilapal.[22] Ultimately the Company had to take stern measures and Major James Crawford was sent to suppress the rebellion and to take charge of the revenue collection.[23] For the time, Crawford was successful to a great extent in his mission. Mangal Shah, the tribal leader of Jhalda surrendered in March 1783,[24] and Sampal Singh, Jagirdar of Koilapal was captured and jailed in 1784.[25] Thus the disturbances were quelled. But again in 1789-90 Jhalda & Tamar were in flames. There was a wave of fresh disturbances in the Jungle Mahals in the wake of the Decennial and the Permanent Settlement in this tribal region. The Permanent Settlement, which according to Hunter, "tried to suddenly substitute contract for custom,[26] and the Cornwallis Code of 1793 adversely affected the people, the Paiks or Ghatwals, the Chiefs and the Rajas alike. The Paikan or Ghatwali (service) lands were resumed by the Govt. under Regulation I (Clause 4, Section 8) of 1793 as the Government itself had assumed the charge of the police Regulations XXII of 1793. This antagonised the great mass of under the Ghatwals and Paiks, the traditional police authority in the tribal areas. The Permanent Settlement resulted in the arrest and auction of the estates of many faulting chiefs and Rajas. These humiliated chiefs and Rajas naturally turned to be the enemy of the English. The Fifth Report of the House of Commons of 1812, has well scored the point: "Without sufficient attention to their peculiar character, this people had been included in the general system of internal administration. The immediate authority over them was given to police darogas, and by the operation of selling estates for revenue balances, many of the zamindars had been dispossessed. The effects of this violence on the habit of the people were felt by degrees. They sided with the discarded zamindars, condemned the authority of the police officers and were frequently guilty of great disorders."[27] In fact, change of their chiefs was wholly unacceptable to the tribal people, who were greatly attached to their chiefs and Rajas. Thus, the chiefs or Rajas, Ghatwals or Paiks and the people became one in opposing the new order. From 1795 to 1800 A.D. There were widespread disturbances in Midnapur (Karnagarh), Pachet, Raipur and Bishnupur when these estates were auctioned for arrears of revenue.[28]

The Chuar Disturbances (1799)

Disturbances and depredations proved to be more serious in dimension in the year 1799, for the year "is marked in the Midnapur Annals as the year of the great Chuar rebellion, ghastly with its tale of horrors and massacres. .... All the lawless tribes of the Jungle Mahals made common cause with the Paiks and carried slaughter and flame to the very doors of the Magistrate's cutcherry."[29] The whole of the Jungle Mahals, particularly Bishnupur, Midnapur (Karnagarh) and Raipur estates, were the worst affected areas by the Chuar ravages and rebellion from February 1799 to Feb. 1800 AD[30]. Battallions of regular troops proved unequal to the task of quelling the disturbances.[31] The Chuar raids were no less serious even by the beginning of 1800. According to Midnapur Collectorate Records on 16th Feb. 1800, the Chuars raided the zamindarelo of Kishan Churan Chatterjee and plundered the maujas of Cumorry, Inaitpur, Ghosepore, Ragennautpore and Aidipur."[32] Raja Durjan Singh, Zamindar of Raipur, Madhav Singh, the brother of the Raja of Barabhum, Raja Mohan Singh, Zamindar of Juriah, and Lachchman Singh of Dalma, were the chief leaders of Chuars.[33] In the wake of failure of even stern and punitive measures against these wide-spread disturbances and formidable resistance to the new system, J. Imhoff, the Collector of Midanpur, suggested the Govt. to frame separate regulations for the Jungle zamindars and their ryotts who were almost savages, their lands also should never be sold to realise the revenue as it only created disturbaces and greater loss to the Government...."[34] He also suggested to restore

Paikan (service) lands to the Paiks and Ghatwals; and police functions to the zamindar of the jungle Mahals.[35] Similar suggestions were made by the Special Commissioner of Ramgarh in his report on the disturbances in Pachet.[36] As was suggested by the Special Commissioner, Pachet Raja Garur Narayan was reinstated in his zamindari in May, 1799.[37] Further, Pachet and Chhatna were placed under Birbhum authorities for effective control over the country.[38] In the like manner, the sale of Raipur[40] and Bagmundi[39] estates were cancelled and restored to the former Rajas. The Jungle zamindars were also invested with police powers again under the Ghatwali or zamindari police system.[41] To bring the refractory jungle region under effective control and for the maintenance of the peace and the support of the General police of that part of the country', even more important measures were taken in 1805, when Regulation XVII was passed and all the 'Bun' or Jungle Mahals formerly placed under different districts were brought under one administrative unit, called the District of 'Jungle Mahals' with headquarter at Bankura under its own Magistrate[42]. The new District included following Jungle Mahals: Panchet, Bagmundi, Bagan Kodar, Taraf Baleapur, Katras, Hasla, Jhalda, Jharia, Jaipur, Mukundpur, Kismat nawagarh, Kismat Chutti, Torang, Tundi, Nagar Keari and Patkum from Birbhum District, Sainpahari, Shergarh and Bishnupur from the Burdwan District; Chhatra, Barabhum, Supur, Ambikanagar, Simlapal, and Belbidihi from the Midnapur District. However, Dhalbhum was left under Midnapur District.[43]

Rajas of Chotanagpur and Ramgarh

Chotanagpur came under the English sway with the Grant of Diwani i 1765. But the Company did not try to exercise political control over the extensive plateau immediately. The Bengal Govt. did not think it advisable "to take any immediate and strong measures against the different Rajas of Ramgarh and Palamau",[44] though they were creating troubles in matters of revenue collection. But this situation was not to continue for long. The revival of the Maratha menace prompted the Company to establish closer relations with the Chiefs and Rajas of Chotanagpur which would form an effective barrier to the incursions of the Marathas' and would give them the command of the passes into Deccan."[45]

The English penetration into Chotanagpur, till then a 'perfect terra incognita',[46] began with their campaign in 1769, through the district of Junglebury (Hazaribagh) under Capt. John Camac, against the different refractory chiefs and Rajas of Chotanagpur. Camac began well with the subjugation of Kharakdiha, recently annexed by Akbar Ali Khan, the Raja of the powerful estate of Narhat and Samai. Camac not only conquered Kharagdiha and Kendu, but also demanded arrears of revenue.[47]

After the conquest of Kharakdiha & Kendi, Camac embarked on his conquest of Palamau. The opportunity for invasion was provided by the long drawn family-fued for the chiefship of the Chero-Raj of Palamau between the two rival factions of the ruling family. Two candidates claiming to be the rightful Raja, one Gopal Rai, grandson of Jaikishun Rai (head of the younger branch of the family), to other Chitrajit Rai, grandson of the murdered ruling chief, Ranjit Rai, brought their suits to the British.[48] With a view to gain possession of the strategic Palamau fort and to secure the command of the passes on that side of Bihar, the Controlling Council of Revenue at Patna decided to support the cause of Gopal Rai against the hostile ruling Chief Chitrajit Rai.[49] Subsequently, Camac marched against the Palamau Raj. The invading English army received useful help from the Raja of Chotanagpur and Drig Narayan Singh, the Chief of Kunda.[50] Inspite of stubborn resistance offered by Chitrajit Rai and his Diwan Jainath Singh, Capt. J. Camac captured the fort of Palamau in Feb. 1771. Chitrajit Rai took shelter in Ramgarh-Raj and Jainath Singh in Sirguja. Gopal Rai was made Raja (feudatory chief) of Palamau on an annual tribute of Rs. 12,000/- for three years, and his supporter, Udwant Ram was appointed the Kanungo of the pargana.[51] But Palamau-Raj long remained disturbed on account of succession of minors (Gopal Rai's brother Basant Rai and then his step-brother (Churaman Rai) as Rajas and undue influence of Thakurai, pro-British managers of this estate. The unrest finally led to the Chero-insurrection of 1800 which was firmly suppressed by the English. Churaman Rai proved to be the last Chero-Raja. He was uncapable and an indolent pleasure-seeker. Consequently, the estate lapsed into heavy arrears of revenue and was put up to auction in 1814 and was purchased by the Govt. for Rs. 51,000. The Govt. in turn, granted it to Raja Ghanshyam Singh of Deo estate (in Gaya) on an annual revenue of Rs. 9,000/-[52] as a reward for his past services. This led to further agrarian troubles in 1817 and the estate was taken under Khas management in 1819.[53]

Raja of Chotanagpur Implores English Help

The Nagbanshi-Rajas of Chotanagpur tried to maintain, with great amount of success, their independent status throughout the Muslim-rule[54]. Though by the time the English came to rule over this region the power and prestige of the Chotanagpur Raja had completely been eclipsed by the Ramgarh Rajas, his former vassel;[55] and the chiefs and Rajas of Ramgarh and Palamau owed only nominal allegiance to him, yet the Raja of Chotanagpur was independent in his internal administration.[56] With a view to receive the English help against Kols of his southern border,[57] and the Raja of Ramgarh who was flourishing at the cost of his Raj, Dripnath Shahi, the Raja of Chotanagpur, presented himself before Captain Camac, who was on his march against Palamau, offered his allegiance and his aid against the Marathas.[58] He also promised to pay an annual tribute of Rs. 6,000/-.[59] Considering the valuable assistance received during the campaign of Palamau, and prospect of the advantages from the friendship with the Chotanagpur Raja against the Maratha incursions and against the refractory Raja of Ramgarh, Capt. Camac recommended his case to the Revenue Council at Patna.[60] Camac, on behalf of the Patna Council of Revenue, concluded an agreement with the Raja of Chotanagpur in 1772. The Raja was permitted to deposit his revenue of Rs. 12,000/- directly to the Company and not through the Raja of Ramgarh as had been the previous mode.[61] In view of the expiry of the last agreement, fresh settlement for the period from 1777-1788, was made with the Raja of Chotanagpur.[62] In 1789, the settlement was extended for another ten years and in 1799, the estate was permanently settled with the Raja of Chotanagpur.[63] However, it was 'looked upon rather as a tribute-paying chiefship and had 'never been held liable of sale of arrears of revenue."[64] Nevertheless, the Government began to interfere in internal affairs of the estate when it fell into arrears & disorder. Beginning with the maintenance of regular police thanas in 1809, the Raja of Chotanagpur was compelled to make over the complete control of the police to the Company authorities a decade later. The Raja's all attempt to oppose the growing English interference failed miserably.[66]

Rebellious Raja of Ramgarh

By the time the English tried to exercise political control over Chotanagpur, the Raja of Ramgarh had emerged as the most powerful Raja of the region. The Ramgarh Raj was thriving at the cost of neighbouring estates during those unsettled political conditions on the eve of British penetration into the area. Rulers of Ramgarh had annexed neighbouring territories yielding an annual revenue of Rs. 85,000/-[67] Following the martial tradition of the family, Mukund Singh, the 9th Raja of Ramgarh, did not submit to the authority of the Company and did not pay any heed to the summons of Camac for aid during latter's campaign against Palamau. Instead of helping the English, Raja Mukund Singh came out with open hostility to them by supporting with men and material Chitrajit Rai of Palamau. He even provided provision and protection to M.Law, the French fugitive and the defeated Raja of Palamau, Chitrajit Rai.[68] Moreover, he had been defaulting in payment of revenue. It was a hard nut for the Company to crack. Thus, the refractory and problematic Raja of Ramgarh had become an eye sore to Capt. Camac and to the Company, providing enough ground for invasion. With a view to gain time for his grand design to face the English challenge with the help of the defeated Raja of Palamau and the Marathas, Raja Mukund Singh apparently sent for settlement.[69] But Capt. Camac took an offensive to the designs of Mukund Singh with the help of Tej Singh, a claimant to the throne of Ramgarh Raj.[70] With reinforcement under Capt. Ewen from Patna, Camac invaded the Capital of Ramgarh Raj. Raja Mukund Singh lost heart and withdrew to a safe place without measuring strength against the Company's forces.[71] Subsequently, Tej Singh was installed with Ichak as his new capital first as Mustajir, and finally as the Raja of Ramgarh, for those refractory people knew no other form of Govt. excepting that their own Raja. However, his son was demanded as hostage and a garrison was placed in his country as measures of safety.[72] Raja Tej Singh also agreed to pay Rs. 15,000/- for the current year and Rs. 30,000/- next five years as annual revenue.[73] Ramgarh was made a sort of military Collectorate under Capt. Camac.

In 1780 Capt. Camac was succeeded by Chapman who was practically the first civilian administrator of Chotanagpur. The conquered provinces were formed into a new district called the Ramgarh Hill Tract which included Ramgarh, Kendi, Kunda and Kharakdiha. Present district of Ranchi was added to it as tributary. Chapman, as Judge and Magistrate & Collector of Revenue, backed and reinforced by a newly raised native infantry, the Ramgarh Battalion, stationed at Hazaribagh under an European Commander, held his court alternately at Sherghati (Gaya) and Chatra (Hazaribagh).[74]

The new district extended from Sherghati in Gaya to Pargana Chakai in Monghyr, from zamindari Raj of Pachet in Manbhum to Chotanagpur Raj and Palamau. "It was far too huge a district and too unexplored for a single magistrate to have any adequate knowledge of the vast mass of the population, which, in turn, was far too backward to appreciate all the regulations of a code framed for a more advanced community".[75] In 1800 A.D. the Collectorship of Ramgarh Hill Tract was abolished and merged with Bihar,[76] But it provided no solution to the problem. As late as May 1809, Major Roughsedge, commanding the Ramgarh Battalion, wrote to C.T. Seally, Magistrate of Ramgarh: "Scarcely an individual in the whole country had remained unchargeable with some act of arbitrary violence the origin of which is to be found in the notion only now destroyed of peculiar privileges and exemptions from the usual course of justice."[77] In fact, foreign rule and foreign elements or non-tribals (Dikkus) from Bengal and Bihar were the most distastable to the tribal people and they rose in rebellion several times. Rising of the Mundas & Uraos in 1811 may remarkably be mentioned here. All these disturbances were followed by administrative changes leading finally to the direct administration of the region by the Company.

The Kol-Rising-(1831-32)

The tribal people and their chiefs and Rajas of the Jungle Mahals and Chotanagpur, as we have noted earlier, reacted sharply to the establishment of the English rule. There were open manifestations of their violent reaction. With gradual extension of the British authority increased the fierceness of the resistance. The Kol-Rising of 1831-32, bursting forth the tribal passions, fears and frustrations, and engulfing the region 'from Chotanagpur to the frontiers of Oude' with a general commotion'[78], represents the first combined resistance (movement) of all the Kolarian tribals[79] and others of Chotanagpur on a wider scale.

Historical perspective - The British penetration into Singhbhum

The freedom loving Kols, particularly the Lurka-Kols or Hos of Singhbhum, had a long history of defying imposed outside authority. Naturally enough, in the Kol-rising of 1831-32 leading role was played by the Lurka (fighting) Kols who had 'held the country for a month'[80] during the insurrection. The Hos, 'physically and morally superior to other Kolarians'[81], and famous for their martial spirit, had successfully maintained their independence for generations, and had 'zealously guarded'[82] their country from all outside encroachments. And 'for the last fifty years' they 'had enjoyed perfect independence and had thrown off all the appearance of subordination to the Raja and other chieftains of Singhbhum'.[83]

The Raja of Singhbhum Implores English Aid

It was the Raja of Porahat whose ancestors claimed to be the Raja of Singhbhum, who called the British into the Kol-country. Though in the beginning he, too, had resisted the English attempt to penetrate into Singhbhum, yet under the changed circumstances during 1818-1820, he himself entreated the British help for the recognition of his paramountcy over the Raja of Saraikela and Thakur of Kharsawan, and for the reduction of his 'subjects in rebellion'[84]- the Hos.

On the 1st Feb. 1820, Raja Ghunshyam Singh of Porahat executed a 'Kuboolyat' (Agreement) whereby he agreed to be a feudal tributary of the British Govt. with an annual payment of 101 Sicca Rupees.[85] In return, he was granted the protection of the Honourable Company by a 'Pottah'.[86] Consequently, turning aside the claims of the Hos that they were never the subject to the Raja of Singhbhum, Major Roughsedge with a Battalion of Infantry, Cavalry and Artillery entered 'Kolhan' in 1820, and was later joined by Lt. Maillard. The British forces met with fierce resistance. The Lurka Kols, 'with a degree of rashness and hardihood scarcely credible, met the charge of the troops half way in open plain with battle-axe in hand'.[87]

Unwilling Submission of the Lurka-Kols and its Results

The refractory Lurka Kols not only ravaged the best part of the estate of Porahat and threatened Saraikela, but also put the English troops in a precarious position at a number of times.[88] Under the circumstances, the British Govt. had to undertake a major offensive led by a senior and more experienced military officer of the rank of Lt. Col. Rochards. A well planned and ruthless military operation[89] brought the turbulent tribals to submission in 1821. Thus, the Hos had to yield to an Agreement[90] in 1821 wherein they

(1) Acknowledge the authority of the British Govt.,

(2) I. agreed to pay their lawful chiefs and zamindars a fixed amount for each working plough,

II. to keep the roads through their Parganas open and safe for all description of travellers.

III. to allow persons of all castes to settle in their villages.

IV. and instead of taking to arms, to complain to the officer commanding the troops on their frontier, if oppressed by their chiefs and zamindars.

The Agreement of 1821 was intended to safeguard the interests of the tribals. But it failed miserably in its purpose. 'Though the stationing of troops on the frontier was admittedly made for the preservation of internal tranquillity of Singhbhum, it encouraged the ruling chief and his corrupt officers in their nefarious activities. Similarly, by allowing all castes to settle in the Kol-villages, a way was opened for the peaceful infiltration of non-tribal element into Singhbhum to the great chagrin of the Hos who resented the encroachments of outsiders on their lands.[@] Thus, this agreement paved the way for greater exploitation of the Kols in various ways which ultimately proved to be the main cause of the great Kol-uprising.

The Kols had to accept the agreement in 1821 under the threat of total annihilation. But they were still restive and in a mood of defiance. In fact, throughout the 20's of the 19th century they remained actively engaged in anti-British activities and open rebellions till their unrest merged with the general Kol-Insurrection of 1831-32.

The liquidation of the Powers and Prestige of the Maharaja of Chotanagpur and following evil Consequences

There was a general belief amongst the high English official's[92] that the rebellions of the Kols in 1831-32 had the blessings of the Raja of Chotanagpur. Willkinson and Dent, Joint Commissioners for the suppression of the Kol-rising, wrote in their report that there were some circumstances in the conduct of the Raja of Nagpur and the Kuar of Basia (Raja's brother) which gave the story an appearance of truth. There were reasons why the Raja should wish to get rid of their influence.[93] There was a gradual liquidation of the powers and prestige of the Raja of Chotanagpur.[94] Early in 1817, the Raja of Chotanagpur was deprived of his magesterial powers. Soon, his police powers were also transferred to the Superintendent of Police. The appointment, in 1819, of Major Roughsedge as the Political Agent to the Governor-General for the affairs of South Bihar was a major step in the same direction. In 1828, the Raja was prohibited from collecting sayer duties.[95] A tax on 'Handia' (rice-beer), the daily drink of the aboriginals, to their great chagrin, was also imposed. Simultaneous with gradual decline in the authority of the Raja of Chotanagpur, his tribal subjects were exposed to the evils of new system of administration.

Thus, the genesis of these tribal unrest can be traced to the very establishment of the English rule over the area and introduction of new Cornwallis system of administration with its complicated 'regulations' without taking into account the tribal systems, customs and interests. Though, 'Dikku' (non-tribal Hindu, Mulsims and Sikh) Mahajans (traders and money lenders), zamindars, 'Thikedars', police and other 'Amlas' (subordinate officers) were the immediate target of tribal wrath, it was ultimately directed against the British authority which permitted these foreign elements from the plains of Bengal and Bihar into their zealously guarded territory. It was not without reason that Mr. Metcalf, President of the Council in Calcutta, during the momentous period, observed. "I have no doubt, however much they have miscalculated, that they intend to expel the British

Govt. from their country and establish their independence".[96] If this was the mind of the Kols, they were fully justified, for as J.H. Hutton and rightly remarked, the establishment of the British authority in Chotanagpur 'led to a more general and more thorough 'victimization' of the tribal people of this area'.[97]

The Agrarian Discontent and the Hated Outsiders

The 'foreign settlers' as adventurous job-seekers, merchants, money-lenders, petty farmers and contractors, "seized the land, the very basis of the tribal society, and so inevitably set in motion the breakup of the tribal solidarity and the disintegration of village-community".[98]

The ignorance and neglect of the tribal rights and customs by the new rulers even led to their economic ruin.[99] Remarkably enough, the Kols—the Hos and the Mundas — had preserved their old system of village community under which a tribal leader called '**manki**' at the head of a group of villages was responsible for the rent of the villages either to the government or to the zamindar, and for the supervision of the work of the village headmen called '**mundas'** who were entrusted with the civil and police duties and represented the village community of their respective villages. But in suppression of this age old village-system, extensive lands were granted to the non-tribals by the local Rajas and chiefs.[100] The most of the grantees other than the relations of the ruling families were outsiders, whether priests, officials or traders. All alike sought, whenever possible, to dispossess the tribal land-owner within the villages.[101] The influx of these hated outsiders gave rise to the system of subletting two or three villages to small farmer or 'Thikedar'- 'a practice which eventually stifled all indigenous village organisation'. The 'Thikedar' was usually a Muslim and the 'Kols' bore that sort of hatred to him which the Irishman bears to the interloper who gets possession of his hut and craft'. The Hindus were mostly traders and money-lenders hated for their enormous profit and usurious interest.[102]

Exactions and Oppressions of the Native Officers

The Kols justifiably, also bore an animosity against the native officers who misused their powers and oppressed them in various ways. W.B.Blunt having previous experience of the area as a keen observing British Officer, wrote amidst the din of the insurrection: 'The most grievous oppressions and exactions have been practised by the native officers of the government especially the police Darogahs which alone amidst a people so poor, might well account for any general feeling of discontent."[103]

Wilkinson and Dent, Joint Commissioners for the suppression of the movement had well summed up the situation in their report: "The Kols throughout Nagpur had within the last few years had their rents increased by their 'elaqadars', 'Zamindar's and 'Thikedars' 35 per cent. They had made the roads throughout the 'parganas', on 'beggaries' (forced labour). The 'Mahajans' who advanced money and grains managed within a twelve month to get from them 70 per cent, and sometimes more. They disliked the tax upon liquor, which was fixed at four annas per house, but more than amount was levied very generally, besides a rupee 'salami' on almost every village and a 'khassi' or goat. The Kols were averse to undertake the cultivation of poppy, and we find a great disinclination on the part of their classes to carry it on.

The 'Thana' establishments were also complained of, and a 'Dak' establishment was kept up, the expense of which fall upon the Kols of those villages which were situated on the lines of roads traversed by the dak. Many people from below the 'ghat' have settled in Nagpur and it was one of the subjects of complaint amongst the Kols that within the last five years several of these settlers, to whom they had become deeply indebted, had pressed too hard for payment that many of the Kols had executed 'Sewak pattas', that is, they had sold their services till the debt was discharged, which was infact binding themselves to give their whole earning to the creditor, thus becoming his bondsman for life. The complaints against the 'thana amlas' were loud in our progress through the country..... The 'Mahtos', 'Pahans', or 'Elaqadars' of villages were required annually to register the names of the 'Kotwals' and 'Goraits' of their respective villages, on which occasion the 'Darogas' of thanas were in the habit of taking one rupee or more according to the size of the village under the denomination of 'Kotwali' or 'Gorait Likhai'"[104]

Taking this long list of oppressions and exactions still further, J.Thomson, Deputy Secretary to the Govt. of Bengal during the Kol-Insurrection, observed." When the oppressors wants a horse, the Kols must pay, when he desires a palki the Kols have to pay, and afterwards bear him therein. They must pay for his musicians, for his milchcows, for his pan. Does some one dies in his house, he taxes them (the Kols).... or does a death occur in the house of the Kol, the poor man must pay a fine. And this plundering, punishing, and robbing system goes on till the Kols run away."[105]

The Conflagration

Oppressed beyond forbearance, the Kols were now to revolt. The Flare up in 1831 was occasioned not only by agrarian discontent of the Kols but also indignities suffered by them at the hands of non-tribal 'Thikedars' (contractors) and local police 'amlahs'. A Sikh Thikedar not only dispossessed Singhrai and Bindrai Manki of Echagootoo of Hurnpur in Bandgaon of twelve villages but also dishonoured their women-folk. Bindarai Manki stated that the Moonshi and Jamadar of Chakkradharpur Thana carried off his two wives and ravished the younger one. The Singh (Sikh) of Surgaon had besides taken two of his sisters by force who were still in his (Sikhs) house.[106]

Surga Munda and others had similar complaints to the proper authorities which went unheard. Then, they 'invited all the Coles... To assemble at the village of Lankah in Tamer. After consultations at the Great Assemblage Bindrari Manki proclaimed. "The Pathans had taken our Hoormut (honour) and Sin (Sikh) our sisters and the Kuer Harnath Sahi had forcible deprived us of our estate of twelve villages, which had (been) given to the Sing (Sikh). We should commence to cut, plunder, murder and eat, conceiving that (by) committing such outrages our grievances would come to light, and if we had any master, notice would be taken of them and justice rendered."[107]

All the Kols-Hos, Dhangars, Mundas and Oraons—were now combined to avenge the wrong done to them. Arrows of war were 'circulated through the country like the fiery cross.' Soon plunder and murder of Dikus (non-tribals) spread over 'practically the whole of the present district of Ranchi and overflowed into Hazaribagh, the Tori pargana of Palamau, and the western portion of Manbhum'[108] Beginning with the murder of Jafar Ali, the Muhammadan 'Thikedar' and seducer of Surga's wife, and ten of his men, eight hundred to a thousand of 'Dikkus' were slaughtered or burnt in their houses.[109] Violence and pillage were universal and indiscriminate'.[110] Non-tribal villages were fired, roads were blocked and all passers by plunderd. At times the number of rebels swelled upto six or seven thousand strong, and the British forces engaged in quelling the rebellion had to suffer serious losses.[111] It was not without valiant fights with reckless bravery[112] on the part of the Kols and ruthless and extensive military operations with usual British vandalism[113] that the Kols submitted before the mighty Government by March-April, 1832.[114] However, the Lurka Kols of Bamanghaty and South-eastern Singhbhum remained refractory till the campaigns of 1836-37 after which the entire district was finally annexed by the British Govt.

The Bhumij-Revolt (1832-33)

Immediately after the Kol-Insurrection there broke out the Bhumij Revolt, also known as Ganga Narain's Hangama', in the tribal areas of Jungle Mahals and Dhalbhum of old Midnapur district. Causes of discontent of the tribal people and their semi-tribal chiefs, similar to those which were responsible for the outbreak of the former—the Kol-Insurrection,[115] also led to the latter — the Bhumij rebellion of 1832-33. In fact, it should be seen as 'a natural contravention of the earlier resistance to the British system'.[116]

The Bhumij Revolt was 'born out of frustration and anger, frustration with new system of Government and laws (which ignored tribal customs), and anger at the people who either enforced them (like police 'daroga') or took undue advantage of them (like the 'amlas' of the government, the diwans of the Zamindars, the money-lenders and others).[117] The evils of the new administration affected the local chiefs and the people alike. Mr. Dent observed in his report. "Disaffection with the administration of law of debtor and creditor appears to have been rife at this time in Barabhum and the sale of ancestral holdings for debt was particularly objected to as something entirely opposed to the customs of the aboriginal tenantry. Nor were indebtedness and its consequences confined to the tenantry, but we are told that almost all the zamindars, the members of their families holding maintenance and other grants, the Sardar Ghatwals, and the bigger intermediate holders, generally were in embarrassed circumstances. General improvidence seems to have been the order of the day and much of the land had already at this time passed more or less permanently to money-lending outsiders. The state of things disclosed was not unlike that already prevailed in Chotanagpur proper'.[118] Thus, there was general disaffection and unrest which was fanned into flame by a gifted and popular leader like Ganga Narain. Though Ganga Narain had much to do with his personal grievances and family feuds, yet 'with his emergence as the supreme leader the revolt took a more political and general aspect'.[119]

Ganga Narain was a disappointed claimant[120] to the Barabhum Raj. He had been deprived not only of many of his 'Tarafs' (fiscal divisions) inherited by him as the son of the late 'Hakeem' (younger brother of the Raja so - called locally), but also of the very means of daily subsistence, reducing him to beggary, by Madhav, 'the Diwan and half-brother of the ruling Raja, Gangagobind. Madhav had also usurped all the powers of the Raja and had become the symbol of tyranny, oppressions and evils because of his usurious money-lending business and oppressive and ignoble methods of amassing wealth, misusing his power as Diwan.[121]

Naturally enough, the disturbance started with the murder of Madhav by Ganga Narain and other Bhumij Sardars[122] on 26th April, 1832. Next target of attack was the Munshif's cutchery at Barabazar. The Bhumijes and their chiefs had serious grievances and revulsion against the Munshif who, it was alleged, used to favour[123] the Diwan and other 'mahajans' in money-suits and issue all decrees against them (the Bhumijes). The Munshif's cutchery, police thana, and salt-daroga's cutchery were burnt, peons were killed, and the Bazar was plundered.[124] Soon, 'nearly every Bhumij, whether Ghatwal or Ryot, had joined Ganga Narain who announced his determination to clear the country of Police Thanas upto the great Benares Road'.[125] Russel, Magistrate and Collector of the Jungle Mahals, failed in his attempt to win over the Ghatwals and his camp with detachment of the 50th N.I. at Barabazar was itself attacked[126] by the insurgents led by Ganga Narain on 12th-13th May, 1832. Though, reinforced by detachments of 25th, 31st, 33rd , and 48th regiments, the Govt. troops had to withdraw in the first week of June, 1832, due to inclement climate and hostile situation. Encouraged by his success Ganga Narain assumed the title of

'Rajah', received revenue and disposed of the lands, the property and even the lives.[127]

The most part of June, 1832, had been the period of inactivity, the Government authorities being busy with preparing the plan to contain the insurrection and Ganga Narain with the marriage of his daughter and Bhumij Kols with their ploughing and sowing. But the disturbances flared up again at the end of the Month when Ganga Narain with 1,000 of his followers, and Tulsi Digwar and Berah Singh with 500 of their tribal men threatened the Thana of Patkum, the Daroga of which place fled to Kharsawan in Singhbhum. Soon Lurko-Kols of Singhbhum under their leader Bindarai Manki also joined the Bhumij Kols of the Jungle Mahals,. At the end of July, Ganga Narain, with the help of Bahadur Singh of Koilapal created havoc in parganas Puncha, Ambikanagar, Manbhum, Supur and Raipur. In fact, Ganga Narain's forces traversed the whole eastern flank of the Jungle Mahals from Puncha to Phulkusum unopposed.[128]

Ganga Narain alongwith the men of his lieutenant Raghunath Singh, pushed on southward to Dampara in Midnapur district. Later on when opposed by govt. troops, he moved out to Pachet Pargana, threatening even the palace of the loyal Raja of Keshargarh. The Govt. started the general offensive against the rebels by mid-August. A cordon was made positioning troops at Bankura, Puncha and Keshargarh in the north, and from Silda to Dhalbhum in the south. The Commissioner of Burdwan with a detachment of the 50th N.I. himself reached Keshargarh on the 13th August to supervise the operations.[129] Crossing the river Kasai Commissioner Braddon had first encounter with Ganga Narain on the 19th which resulted in the defeat of the latter.[130] The Govt. forces soon began to recover itself. However, parties of insurgents under Raghunath Singh, Bahadur Singh, Anand Digwar, Jirpa Naya and Ganga Narain himself remained active in a wider area upto November, 1832. Hence the Government had to undertake three-pronged scouring operations by regiments of the 24th, 50th & 34th N.I. forming three columns[131] against the insurgents in early December, which continued throughout the month. Through vigorous drives insurgents were driven to the Dalma Hills. And from January, 1833, concerted attacks were made upon the Dalma Hills by all the field force of the Jungle Mahals.[132] Smaller parties were formed from different columns and every day hills were ravaged, arrals (temporary huts) were burnt, grain taken from hidden stores, women and children captured.[133] Hardpressed by these intensive operations many Bhumij Sardars and Manjhis (like Gardi Munda) began to surrender in the Dhalbhum area and many more were won over by Captain Wilkinson through timely bribes.[134] Ganga Narain escaping capture many a times and 'deserted by almost all of his followers of whom some were killed, and may had submitted or been taken prisoner, fled to Singhbhum and endeavoured to rouse the Coles (Lurka Kols) to join him,[135] but failed in his attempt and was killed by men of Thakur Chetan Singh of Kharsawan at Thana Hindusahar in early February, 1833. Thakur Chetan Singh sent with pleasure his head to Captain Wilkinson.[136] With the death of Ganga Narain the insurrection virtually came to an end. Seen as a military campaign, it was a minor affair but in devastation and destruction, it was a full scale war.[137] Ganga Narain's successful assertion of power for a considerable period and widespread insurrection supported by, with a few-exception, all the local Chiefs and tribal people, was indicative of the popular character[138] of the insurrection.

The Result

As was but natural, the Kol and the Bhumij revolts of 1831-33 were successfully suppressed by the powerful British arms, but the sacrifices and sufferings of the tribal people and their leaders did not go in vain. The Government had to recognize the peculiar problems, special position and privileges of the tribal people and their Chiefs of the Jungle Mahals and Chotanagpur. The preamble of the Regulation XIII of the 2nd December, 1833, says : "Whereas consideration connected with the present state of certain tracts of country now included in the district of Ramghur, Jungle Mahals, and Midnapur, the nature of the disturbances which presently prevailed in various parts of those districts, and the character of the inhabitants, have rendered it expedient to separate these tracts from those districts and place them under an officer to be denomical Agent to the Governor-General; and whereas it is necessary to provide special rules for the administration of civil and criminal justice, and for the superintendence of police, land revenue, custom, abkarry, stamps, and all their local civil duties and whereas it becomes expedient with reference to the proposed arrangements to abolish the Dewanny Adawlat of Zillahs Ramghur and Jungle Mahals.[139] Thus, the withdrawal of the complex Cornwallis regulations from the area, and formation in its place the non-regulation administrative unit of the South West Frontier Agency was the direct outcome of these tribal outbursts. After a good deal of deliberations and consultations by the end of the year 1833, the South West Frontier Agency was created under Regulation XIII of 1833; and with Captain Thomas Wilkinson at its appex as the Agent to the Governor-General, and assisted by two senior and two junior Assistants,[140] was inaugurated on the 15th January, 1834. The arrangement was approved by the Court of Directors.[141] Abolishing the old districts of the Jungle Mahals and Ramgarh, three new districts, viz., Manbhum, Lohardagga and Hazaribagh,[142] were formed to which the district of Singhbhum including the entire Kolhan', was incorporated in 1837.[143] The jurisdiction of the South West Frontier Agency extended to the whole of Chotanagpur proper, Palamau, Kharakdiha, Ramgarh, Kunda, the Jungle Mahals excluding Bishunpur, Senpahari and Shergarh, portion of the district of Midnapur including the Paragana Dhalbhum and Ghatsheela.[144] However, subsequently in 1854, the Legislative Council of India, amending the Regulation XIII of 1833 of Bengal Council, passed the Act XX, and transformed the South West Frontier Agency into the Division of Chotanagpur with a Commissioner[145] at its head.

The Santhal Insurrection of 1855-56

Formidable Santhal 'Hul' or the Insurrections of 1855-56, represents a typical example of tribal resistance and 'their yearning for independence, and for recognition as lords of the soil'. The principal theatre of this 'entirely unforeseen calamity', the District of Santhal Paraganas, was then divided between old districts of Murshidabad, Bhagalpur and Birbhum. The Rebellion chiefly proceeded from 'the inefficiency of administration', and economic grievances of excitable but peace-loving aboriginal Santhals.

Economic Background

The Santhals, described to be industrious and hard working, frank and manly, peaceable and in-offensive, simple and unlettered people,[146] were even more 'skilful' clearers of the jungles and reclaimers of the soil'.[147] In the wake of the

Permanent Settlement and excessive demands of zamindars, the Santhals had to leave their original homes and lands which they had cleared, reclaimed and tilled for centuries. Driven from pillar to post in the districts of Cuttack, Manbhum, Dhalbhum, Birbhum, Bankura, Midnapur and Chotanagpur,[148] they finally came to settle in the Jungle-Terri area skirting the Rajmahal Hills.[149] This tract of the country known as 'Damin-i-koh' had already been carved out as the government Estate for another primitive people, the Paharias or the Hillmen[150]. However, the new industrious emigrants were welcome and encouraged to settle by the English which 'a generation ago had been the masses of dense jungle, the haunt of tigers and wild elephants'.[151] By 1851, the district was studded with Santhal villages.

Usurious Traders and Money Lenders

With increase in cultivated lands and its fertility, there emerged new factors to disturb the peace of peace-loving Santhals. In few years, there appeared on the scene 'moira' and 'Diku' - non-tribal Bengalees and upcountry Hindus—as money lenders and traders. In 1851, in Barhait 'the capital town of the hills', alone there were fifty families of Bengali traders who took from the thriftless Santhals their produce at a price far below its true value.[152] The Santhal was ignorant and honest, the trading Hindu keen and unscrupulous who cheated the poor Santhal in every transaction.[153] Through these dishonest means these traders and money lenders soon became great 'Mahajans', who lent money to the improvident Santhals at excessive interest 'ranging from 50 to 500 per cent.[154] Many of the Santhals after losing all their lands and properties became prey to a 'pernicious system' of 'Kamiauti', prevailing throughout the district under which a man borrowing money had to pledge his own person to pay off the debt. In the hands of unscrupulous Mahajan this became "little better than slavery".[155] The master neither expected nor wished for the repayment of debt, and took care, by working his slave every hour of the day, to leave him no leisure for earning a 'peculium' with which to pay his liberty. "The only inheritance, he had to leave, was the debt".[156]

With increasing disaffection the unfortunate bounded Santhal after 1854 contrasted his lot with that of his brethren who in a few months came back from the Railroad construction sites, with their girdles full of coin, and their women covered with jwellery just like Hindus. 'Freedom had became a great issue to be tried'.[157]

Oppressions of Rajas and Zamindars

The troubles of the Santhals were aggravated further by the Rajas and Zamindars, like the Rajas of Maheshpur and Pakur, who granted leases of Santhal villages to non—Santhal Bengali zamindars and money—lenders.[158] Greedy zamindars living near the border of the 'Damin' had begun for sometime to cast a wishful eye on Santhal lands, claiming their proprietorship and demanding rent which took the form of exactions.[159]

Inefficiency of Administration

Sir W.W. Hunter rightly believed that 'the wrongs of the Santhals proceeded chiefly from the 'inefficiency of administration' which being 'cheap and practical', had only time to look at its revenues, that rose from £ 668 in 1838 to £ 6803 in 1854, giving nothing in return.[160] The government cared little for the people, being almost indifferent to what the aboriginals thought, felt or did. Since 1837 Damin-i-koh was under the fiscal and general management of a Superintendent, Mr. Potent, subordinated to the Commissioner of Bhagalpur, and in-criminal matters, under the Magistrate of Bhagalpur. He had no independent authority to deal with civil and criminal cases. There was only one Resident Magistrate at Deoghar. Higher officials rarely visited the Damin.

Inaccessible and Costly Courts

To the wild Santhals justice was far off and very difficult to access at Bhagalpur courts.[161] This was resented even more by the Santhals who could appreciate non but the simplest mode of adjusting a disputed demand and were utterly unable to contend for their rights with any hope of success under a complicated legal system.[162] While the natives of the 'Damin', the Paharias (hillmen), had been given the benefit of exemption from the ordinary courts of law under Regulation of 1827, Santhals were not given the same facility. With the result that for justice Santhals had to go a long way to the distant courts at Bhagalpur and other places at enormous cost which they could not afford. Even if they could, they were not always sure of success because of the frauds practised on them by the court 'Amlas', 'Mukhtars', peons, and Barkandazes.[163] Thus the Santhal had no sufficient protection against the crafty Bengali and the machinery of the Civil courts was employed only as an instrument to revert the chains of servitude.[164]

Base and Corrupt Police

Moreover, base and corrupt police, instead of giving protection to grieved Santhals, sided with the oppressors and were making unlawful gains.[165]

Illegal Exactions by the Revenue Officials

There were illegal exactions by the Amlas (subordinate staff) of the revenue Deptt. A contemporary Calcutta Review mentioned: 'where authorised to receive some six rupees on behalf of the Sircar (Govt.), they will lay some six other rupees for their private benefit; or where a rent of four annas for a plot and all it contained was fixed in the settlement, they take a rupee more for a sapling bamboo', clump, or a solitary fruit tree thereon.[166]

Oppressions and Indignities by the Europeans on the Railroad

As if to test the forebearance of sentimental Santhals, the English Officers engaged in the construction of Railways oppressed them in various ways and insulted their women-folk. There were cases of 'forced abduction of two Santhal women, and even murder and some unjust acts of oppression as taking kids, fowls, etc., without payment on the part of the Europeans employed on the line of railroad.[167]

W.G. Tayler, Assistant Commissioner at Srikand (near Tinpahar) while writing to the Deputy Commissioner at Dumka, had well summed up the situation : "Zamindars or more properly speaking zamindari retainers, as gomasta, surbarkar, peons and other mahajans and their mustajirs' or agents, the police, revenue and court amlas have exercised a combined system of extortions, oppressive exactions, forcible dispossession of property, abuse and personal violence, and a variety of petty tyrannies upon timid and yielding Santhals, usurious interest on loans of money ranging from 50 to 500 per cent, false measures at the haut and market, wilful and uncharitable trespass by the rich by means of their untethered cattle, tattoos, ponies and even elephant, on the growing crops of the poorer race; and such like illegalities have been prevalent. Even a demand by individuals from the Santhals of security for good conduct is a thing not unknown, embarrassing pledges for debt also formed another move of oppression.[168]"

Harsh conduct of the Superintendent, Mr. Potent, was also said to be the cause of the Santhal unrest. However, he was strongly defended by the Commissioner of Bhagalpur.[169]

Sense of Insecurity and Unrest

Complaints were carried to the authorities, but without any other palpable effect than to lead the Santhals to conclude that there was no redress for the wrongs he had suffered and no remedy for the evils from which he saught protection.[170] Thus the Santhals were left with no alternative but to redress their grievances themselves. Analysing well this state of mind of the Santhals, Sir W.W. Hunter wrote : 'During the cold weather of 1854-55 the Santhals appeared to be in a strange, restless state of mind.' Inspite of 'excellent crop' high prices for their grain, and high wages for their labour,[171] 'the race swayed restlessly about. The truth was that, the rich Santhals had determined to be no longer the dupes of Hindus who intercepted their high prices, the poorer agriculturists had determined to be no longer their serfs, and day labourers had determined to no longer to be slaves'.[172]

Four Brothers

To a people in this frame of mind leaders are seldom wanting', The leadership was provided by two brothers—Sidhu and Kanhu, and later joined by two of their less forward brothers - Chand and Bhairab of a village Bhagnadihi near Barhait, the capital of all the Santhal villages and towns. The two brothers were men of strong personal character and brooded over the wrongs of the race. They claimed to have seen apparitions of their Thakur and to have been favoured with scraps of paper which alongwith 'Sal' tree branch were distributed through the country as a sign to rouse the clans.[173]

On the 30th of June, 1855, 10,000 Santhals representing 400 villages assembled at Bhagnadihi. At the assemblage the 'Divine Order' to put an end to the 'Zhulum of officers and deceit of the

Mahajans', was announced by the two brothers. Finally to take possession of the country and to set up the government of their own, was declared to be the aim. Letters were addressed to the Government, to the Commissioner, to Collector and Magistrate of Birbhum, to the Darogas of Thanas Dighee and Rajmahal, and to several zamindars and others. Sidhu and Kanhu were proclaimed to be their Soobahs or Governors.[174]

The Santhal take to Arms

Letters remained unanswered. The Santhals were exasperated. They took to arms, and began plundering and killing the Mahajans. On the 7th July when the Daroga of Thana Dighee or Borio Bazar tried to disperse them, he was immediately slain alongwith nine others. The rebels next proceeded to Barhait Bazar where they plundered the rich mahajans and then in parties marched into different directions.[175] The outbreak now took a formidable form. Armed chiefly with axes and poisoned arrows, large bodies of these half reclaimed and savages carried fire and sword into scores of happy villages, attacked every outlying European Bungalow, murdered with equal readiness English planters and railway servants, native police officers, tradesmen, peasants, their wives and children, and even swarmed upto the larger European stations in the districts of Birbhum, Rajmahal and Bhagalpur.[176] 'Nevertheless', Hunter rightly wrote, 'their proceedings retained a certain air of rude justice'. Leaders had revelation enjoining immediate slaughter of oppressors, but protection to all other classes.[177]

The authorities at Bhagalpur, at first did not believe it, but when by the 8th of July, the news of violent outbreaks was confirmed, they began to take steps for the defence of important stations and security of postal communication,[178] Executive authorities in the neighbouring places in Bihar and Bengal were asked to give their help. Zamindars were directed to pool their resources for the suppression of the rebellion. Reinforcements were requested from Dinapur and Berhampur.[179] A detachment of Hill Rangers under Major F.W. Burroughs was sent from Bhagalpur, in the direction of disturbances. But on reaching Colgong he had to make a halt on the 11th July due to the presence of a large number of insurgents in the neighbourhood. When advanced further, Major Burroughs was defeated severely by the Santhals who stood their ground firmly', near Painty (Pirpainti) in the afternoon of the 16th July, 1855. The English loss included their Sergeant Major, some native officer, about 25 sepoys and an indigo planter. The English party had to retire to Colgong via Pirpainty.[180] Victorious Santhals declared the end of the English rule and the commencement of the rule of their 'Soobah' (Governor).[181] In fact, the insurgents, by that time, had established their full control over the area between Borio and Colgong, and were moving towards Rajmahal and Bhagalpur destroying railway works and postal communication. There was not at that time 1200 troops within 80 miles of the rebels. For a time the Santhals held possession of the country from Colgong to Palso on the Ganges and nearly to Birbhum and Raniganj on the west.[182]

The insurgents were also active on the Murshidabad border on the north of the Damin-i-koh and alongwith the south bank of the Ganges from Colgong to Rajmahal. To the west of Rajmahal they ravaged the country in the face of the troops.[183] A party of Santhal rebels under Gocho Manjhi was proceeding towards Pakur plundering on their way Lakhsmipur, Littipara, Hiranpur and Sangrampur where they were joined by some low caste Hindus like 'Teli, Gwala, and Lohar'.[184] The main body of the insurgents under the leadership of four brothers also joined Gocha Manjhi at Pakur. In Pakur they plundered the town and the palace. Rani Kshemsundari had already taken to flight with her valuables. Killing tyrannical amlas and mahajans, the insurgents proceeded to the borders of Murshidabad District. Despite hotly pursued by the British troops of the 7th N.I. dispatched from Berhampur, they looted the palace of the Raja of Maheshpur on the 15th of July. Near Maharajpur two English ladies, namely Mrs. Thomas & Miss. Pell, and one English gentleman named Mr. Hernshaw alongwith his two sons were also killed.[184] However, at this time the rebels were surprised by the English forces in which 200 Santhals were killed or wounded. Three of the Brother leaders, Sidhu, Kanhu and Bhairab were themselves wounded, but not mortally.[186]

In the meantime, in response to the Bhagalpur Commissioner's request Major Shuckburgh with the entire Regiment of the 40th Native Infantry from Danapur arrived Bhagalpur on the 17th July; and soon afterwards, stating that the outbreak had 'assumed all the characteristics of rebellion', proclaimed Martial Law calling out 'the destruction of the rebels found in arms', and offered high rewards for the capture of rebel leaders[186] But Martial Law was annulled and rewards were reduced to half by the Govt. About the 25th July the reduction of the insurrection was entrusted to military authorities under Major General Lloyd, though subjected to some extent to civil control.[187] 'Even this half measures, according to Hunter, 'gave a new vigour to the action of the military'. Detachment after detachment hurried to the field of action. Zamindars and Rajas sent their armed retainers. His Higness of Murshidabad sent a splendid train of elephants at his personal expense.[189]

Full Scale War Against the Half Armed Santhals

Thus started a full scale war against the half armed and half reclaimed savages. But 'it was not a war', said a Major 'They did not understand yielding. As long as their national drums beat, the whole party would stand, and allow themselves to be shot down. Their arrows often killed our men, and some had to fire on them as long as they stood'.[190]

Troops of the 7th Native Infantry from Berhampur defeated a large number of Santhals near Tarai river west of Pakur. The detachment under Mr. Togood inflicted defeat on the rebels at Raghunathpur. They stormed Berhait, the stronghold of the insurgents, on the 24th July and burnt Bhagnadihi, the home village of the four brother-leaders. Soon afterwards, Sidhu was given upto the Bhagalpur troops 'through treacher.'[191] Villages after villages were burnt or destroyed. The detachment of the 40th Native Infantry under captain Sherwill destroyed 12 Santhal villages, major Shuckburgh 15, Lt. Gordon 2 and Lt. Rubie six villages.[192] Even then valiant Santhals could not be subdued. As such to carry out the measures for the entire suppression of the insurrection,' a special Commissioner Mr. A.C. Bidwell, was appointed. A Proclamation, calling the insurgents to surrender on terms, was issued, but it was rejected by them. The rebels under arms were still estimated to exceed 30,000".[193]

Second Wave of Insurrection and Material Law

In fact, there was a fresh wave of outbreaks in the month of September in parts of Birbhum and Bhagalpur; and by the end of that month the whole country from Deoghar to the south-western border of the district was in their hands. In one direction an army of Santhals moved through the district three thousand strong, and in another, there number amounted to seven thousand.[194] Under the circumstances some drastic action was needed, and the Govt. proclaimed Martial Law on the 10th November, 1855. The Proclamation stated:

'It is hereby proclaimed and notified, that the Lientenant-Governor of Bengal in the exercise of the authority given to him by Regulation X of 1804, and with the assent and concurrence of the President in Council, does hereby establish Martial Law in the following districts, that is to say: so much of the district of Bhagalpur as lies on the right bank of the river Ganges; so much of the district of Murshidabad as lies on the right bank of the river Bhagirathi; the district of Birbhum'.

It further declared that "all persons who, after the date of this Proclamation, shall be taken in arms in open hostility (to the British Government) or shall be taken in the act of opposing by force of arms the authority of the same, or shall be taken in the actual commission of any overt act of rebellion against the State (within the disturbed districts) shall be tried by Court Martial....... and the sentence of such court will be liable under section 3, Regulation X of 1804, to the immediate punishment of death".[195]

Final Suppression

Armed with proclamation, a vigorous campaign under favourable weather was organised. A large force now 'swept through the country'. The Santhals were unable to offer resistance or break through the cordon of out-posts, in some places twelve to fourteen thousand strong. Weaken by disease and hunger, they were driven out of the open country to the thick jungles. In six weeks nothing remained but to sweep the jungles clear of straggler.[196] By the end of December, 1855, the insurrection was officially declared to have been entirely suppressed, and the operation of the Martial Law was suspended on the 3rd January 1856.[197] However, sporadic disturbances in Hazaribagh and elsewhere continued till the capture and execution of the rebel leader Kanhu at the end of February 1856. Other leaders also met the same fate. A large number of Santhals were captured, tried and sentenced to various terms of imprisonment.[198] According to Balfour's Encyclopaedia "half their number perished"[199] till the final suppression of the insurrection.

The Result—A separate non-Regulation District of Santhal Parganas

Thus, was suppressed the great Santhal 'Hul' of 1855-56. Marked as it was 'by some of the worst features of elemental tribal passion', and suppressed as it was with most inhuman barbarities', the Santhal Insurrection did not go invain. Blood and sacrifices of thousands of Santhals resulted in the recognition of their special position. Enquiry was made into their grievances. The investigation, well conducted by Sir Ashley Eden Specially deputed for the purpose, was followed by Acts, XXXVII of 1855 & X of 1857. A separate non-regulations-District,known as the District of Santhal Parganas, out of the Domin-i-koh and other areas principally inhabited by the Santhal tribe, and making it independent of the jurisdiction of the regular courts, was formed. A Deputy Commissioner was placed in-charge, with four Assistants, all vested with civil as well as criminal jurisdiction, and the Commissioner of Bhagalpur as the Commissioner of Santhal Parganas.201

Refereces

1. Gokhale's Manbhum Settlement Report, I, Para 35, also J.C. Price's Notes on the History of Midnapur, 1876, I, p. 68.

2. H. Coupl and, Bengal District Gazetteers, Manbhum, 1911, p. 55.

3. J. C. Price, Notes on the History of Midnapur, I.p. 29.

4. C.U. Aitchison, Collection of Treaties, Engagements and Sanads, Vol. I, Bengal No. LXVI, pp. 214-217.

5. Ibid, Bengal, No. LXX, pp. 2221-229.

6. Firminger, Midnapur Distt. Records, I, no. 139.

7. Ibid. IV. no. 163. also. J.C. Price, Notes on the History of Midnapur Vol. I, pp. 155-156.

8. Ibid. I, no. 120.

9. Ibid, nos. 125-126, 129-130.

10. Ibid, nos. 139-150, also J.C. Jha, The Bhumij Revolt pp. 3-4.

11. S.B. Choudhury, Civil Disturbances, p. 54.

12. Ibid. no. 127, also J.C. Price, Notes on the History of Midnapur Vol. I, pp. 47-48.

13. Midnapur Dist. Records, Nos. 129, 159, and 171.

14. Ibid, no. 235.

15. Ibid, nos. 359, 3, 2.

16. Ibid, nos. 374, 376 and 379.

17. Ibid, nos. 447, 503, 510, 512 also nos. 335, 339.

18. Ibid, IV, no. 70.

19. Ibid, iii, no. 339.

20. (a) Bengal Rev., Consult No. 20, 27th March, 1794, para 7.

(b) J. Reid, Dhalbhum Settlement Report, para 10.

(c) L.S.S.O. 'Malley, Bengal Dist. Gazetteers : Singhbhum, Seraikela and Kharsawan, 1910, pp. 30-31.

21. Midnapur Dist. Records, ii, nos. 499-533.

22. Hunter, Bengal MS Records I, no. 269, also Home Misc, no. 207, p. 432.

23. Ibid, no. 403.

24. Ibid nos. 677-678.

25. Bengal MS. Records, i. 89.

26. Quoted in D.G. Midnapur, 196.

27. D. Gs of Bankura, pp. 31-37, Midnapur, pp. 38-44, Manbhum 55, also N.L. Chatterjee, Jungle Mahals under Lord Wellesly in BPP LXXIII (Sl. No. 137).

28. J. C. Price, The Chuar Rebellion of 1799, quoted in Midnapur Distt. Gazetteer, p. 43.

29. Huter, Bengal MS records, Nos. 7890-93, 7953, 7956, 8024-28, 8073-74, 8660, 8892, also D.G. Bankura, p. 37.

30. Bengal Criminal Judicial Consultation of 11 July 1799 (128/42); also Bengal Revenue Consul. 18 of Feb. 1799 (53/60).

31. Report of the Regl. Reocrds Survey Committ, for West Bengal, 1949-56, p. 61.

32. N. L. Chatterjee, Jungle Mahals under Lord Wellesley in BPP, LXXIII (Sl. No. 137).

33. Imhoff to the Bd. of Revenue, 4 March, 1799, para 5, Bengal Revenue Consul. 33, of 15 March, 1799 (54/1).

34. Ibid, also Beng. Rev. Cons. 20 of May 3, 1799 (54/37).

35. Ramgarh Spl. Comm. to Govt. Beng. Rev, Cons. 20 of 20 May' 99 (54/3).

36. Beng. Rev. Cons. I of 21 June 1799 (54/3).

37. Beng. Cr. Judl. Cons. 12 of 19 Sept. 1799 (128/43) and 6 of 10 Oct.'99.

38. Beng. Rev. Cons. 1 & 2 of 16 Oct. 1800 (54/13) Beng. Cr. Judl. Cons. 12 of 26 Feb., 1801 (128/52).

39. Beng. Rev. Cos. 20 of 25 Mar. '99 (54/1).

40. N.L. Chatterjee, Jungle Mahals under Lord Wellesley in BPP, LXXIII, Sl. No. 137.

41. Beng. Cr. Judl. Cons., 16 of 25 July 1805 (129/14)

42. Beng. Cr. Judl. Cons. 16 of 13 Dec., 1805 (129/18)

43. Letter dated 4 Aug., 1769 from Thomas S. Rumbold, Revenue Chief at Patna to the Council at Calcutta, Vide Report of the Select Committee, 1769, p. 432.

44. T.S. Macpherson and M.G. Hallet, Bihar and Orissa Gazetteers, Ranchi, 1917, pp. 27-28.

45. The region so described by Broome, vide C.E. A. W. Oldham, 'Routes Old & New From Lower Bengal', Beng. Past and Present, Vol. XXVIII (July-Dec.). 1924, pp. 29-30.

46. Minutes of Consultation of the Proceedings of the Controlling Council of Revenue at Patna, Nos. ; 4690-92, Sept. 16, 1771, Patna Archives.

47. Dr. J. N. Sarkar, Palamau Jagirdars', The Jrl. of Bihar, Res. Soc. Vol. XLI, part IV.

48. From the Revenue Chief to J. Camac, L.C. 72-73, No. 37, Proceedigs of the Controlling Council of Revenue at Patna, 16 Jan. 1771.

49. E.Lister, Bihar & Orissa District Gazetteers : Hazaribagh, 1917, pp. 63-64.

50. E. Lister, Beng. Distt. Gazetteers: Palamau, 1907, p. 267.

51. J. N. Sarkar, 'Palamau Jagirdars', Journal of Bihar Research Society, Vol. XLI, part IV.
52. Ibid.
53. S.C. Roy, Munda & Their Country, 1912, pp. 151-161, also. H. Blochman, 'Notes from the Muhammadan Historians on Chitianagpur, Pachet and Palamau', Jrl,. of Asiatic Soc. of Bengal, Vol. XL, part I, 1871, pp. 112-113.
54. J. Reid, Final Report on the Survey & Settlement Operations in the District of Ranchi, 1902-1910, p. 14.
55. Ibid.
56. Sir John Houlton, Bihar the Heart of India, 1949, pp. 131-33.
57. Bradley Birt, Chotanagpur, A Little Known Province of the Empire, 1903, p. 17.
58. T. S. Mecpherson & M.G. Hallett, Bihar & Orissa Gazetteers, Ranchi, 1917, pp. 27-28.
59. Capt. Camac to the Revenue Chief at Patna 9, July, 1771, vide Minutes of Cons. Controlling Council of Revenue, Patna 3 Aug., 1771, 345-55.
60. Bradley Birt, p. 18.
61. S. C. Roy, 'The Mundas & Their country', The City Book Soc., Calcutta, 1912, Append. XXI.
62. Ibid, pp. Append. XXII.
63. Baden-Powell, The Land System of British India, Vol. I, Book II, p. 494.
64. Bihar Through the Ages, p. 603.
65. Capt. Camac to Joseph Jeckyll, Chief of the Council of Revenue at Patna, 18 Aug., 1771, vide Minutes of Cons. Controllig Council of Revenue, Patna, 489-501, 27 Aug. 1771.
66. Ibid.
67. Minutes of Consultations, Controlling Council of Revenue, Patna, 1771, pp. 671-77.
68. Camac to Revenue Chief, 17 Oct., 1772, Ibid, 22 Oct., 1772, pp. 1641-1645.

69. Camac to the Reven. Chief, 28 Oct. 1772, Nov. 5, 1772, pp. 1665-77.

70. Camac to Reven. chief, 2 January, 1773, Ibid, Feb.8, 1773, p. 1830-39.

71. Camac to Rev. Chief, 21 July, 1773, Ibid, 29 Jul. , 1773, pp. 2175-87.

72. Bradley Birt, Chotanagpur, p. 18.

73. Ibid, p. 19.

74. Board of Revenue to the Collector of Ramgarh, Bd. of Rev. Proceeding, Fort, William, 15th Apr. 1800, West Bengal Secretariat Archives.

75. J. D. Sifton, Final Report on the Survey & Settlement Oper. in the district of Hazaribagh (1908-1915), p. 21.

76. Editorial, The Indian Gazette, Feb. 9, 1832.

77. H. H. Risley, The Tribes & Caste of Bengal, 1819, Vol. I, p., 319, also W.W. Hunter, A Statistical Account of Bengal, XVII, 1877, p. 36, and E.T. Dalton, An Introduction to a Descriptive Ethnology of Bengal, 1878, 1878,p.152.

78. Southerland's Minute of March 27, 1832, Bengal Judicial Criminal Consultations, No. 44, Apr. 27, 1832, Vol. 572 (West Bengal State Archives.

79. S. B. Choudhury, Civil disturbances During the British Rule, p. 97.

80. L.S.S. O'Malley, Bengal Distt. Gazetteers, Singhbhum, Saraikela and Kharsewan. pp. 31-33.

81. Major Roughsedge to Metcalf, Secretary to Govt., May 9, 1820 political Agents, South West Frontier 'Agency Dispatch. Apr. 20, 1820 to June 1821, Central Record Room, Patna Secretariat.

82. Ibid.

83. C. U. Aitchison, Treaties & Engagements etc. Vol. I, Bengal-Chotanagpru-Singhbhum, 'Porahat, No. CXLIX, p. 370.

84. Ibid.

85. D.G. Singbhum, pp. 32-33.

86. For details C.P. Singh, The Ho Tribe of Singhbhum, Classical Publication, Delhi, 1978, pp. 66-78.

87. For details of the Plan & Campaign, Ibid, pp. 79-83.

88. Aitchison, Treaties, etc. Bengal-Chotanagpur Lurka Kols, No. CLV. p. 381.

89. C.P. Singh, the Ho-Tribe, p. 86.

90. Blunt's Minute on the Kol-Insurrection, dt. 27th Apr. 1832. Bengal Judicial Criminal Proceedings, No. 17, dt. 19th June, 1832, West Bengal State Archives.

91. Special Commissioners Report, vide Ranchi Settlement Report by J. Ried, pp. 24-26.

92. S. C. Roy, The Munda & their country, 1912, p. 190, also P.C. Roychaudhury, 1857 in Bihar (Chotanagpur & Santhal Parganas) Patna, 1959, p. 127.

93. Board of Revenue Letter to the Court of Directors, dated 26th June, 1828, para 126 (W.B.S.A.)

94. Vide J. Ch. Jha, The Kol-Insurrection of Chotanagpur, Calcutta, 1964, p. 139.

95. J. H. Hutton in L.S.S.O. Malley edited Primitive Tribes in Modern India and the West, 1941, Chap. XVI, p. 419.

96. Ibid, p. 430.

97. Ibid, p. 438.

98. D.G. Singhbhum, p. 35, also S.B. Choudhury, Civil Disturbances, p. 99.

99. J.C Jha, The Kol-Insurrection, p. 150.

100. Ibid, p. 153.

101. Blunt's Minute of Apr. 4, 1832, para 12, 1363, Collection 54227 Board's Collections.

102. Special Commissioners' Report vide J. Ried, Ranchi Settlement Report, pp. 24-26.

103. Vide Calcutta Review, Vol. XLIX No. XCVII (97), The Kols-Insurrection of 1832 etc. pp. 119-120.

104. Ibid.

105. W.W. Hunter, Statistical Account of Bengal, Vol. XVI, Distt of Lohardagga. p. 452.

106. D.G. Singhbhum, p. 36.
107. Mill, IX-X, 234, also S.B. Choudhary, Civil Disturbances, p. 99.
108. Thornton, History of India, V. p. 202.
109. Ibid, pp. 202-203 also Hunter, Statistical Account, op. cit. p. 454.
110. S.B.Choudhary, Civil Disturbances, p. 100, also. Hundter, Statistical Account, pp. 452-454.
111. Ibid.
112. Joint Commissioners Report dated April, 13 & April 26, 1832. Op. cit.
113. Similar causes were responsible for the tribal unrest of Santhals in 1855-56.
114. J.C. Jha, The Bhumij Revolt, Munshiram Manohar Lal, Delhi, 1967, p. 114.
115. Ibid, p. 185.
116. Vide D.G. Manbhum pp. 64-65.
117. J.C. Jha, The Bhumij Revolt. p. 186.
118. For details see Ibid, pp. 116-122.
119. Russel, Magistrate of Jungle Mahals to Braddon, Commissioner of Burdwan, 11th May, 1832, Boards, Collections, Vol. 1501, Collection 58887; and Martin, Assist, to the Magistrate of Jungle Mahals, the Commissioner of Burdwan, 5th June, 1832, para 6, B.C. 1501/58887; also Bradden to Govt. 12th June, 1832, Ibid; Dent to Govt., 4th Sept. 1833, paras 11 & 12.
120. W. Dent, Joint Commissioner, Chotanagpur to Govt. 4th Sept. 1833, para 12, B.C. 1501/58886.
121. Ibid, para 22, also Braddon to Govt., 12th June, 1832, Op. cit.
122. Russel to Govt. 5th May, 1832, B.C. 1501/58887 also An Officer of the 50th N.I., 13th May, 1832, India Gazettec, 19th May, 1832.
123. Dent to Govt., 14th Sep. 1832, Op. cit. para 14.
124. An Officer, of the 50th N.I. from Barabazar 14th May, 1832 India Gazettel, 19th May, 1832.
125. India Gazette, 14th June, 1832.
126. For details J.C. Jha, The Bhumij Revolt. p. 80-83.

127. Braddon to Govt. 15th Aug. 1832, B.C. 1501/58887.

128. Braddon to Govt. 22nd Aug., 1832 Ibid.

129. Dent to Govt. 21st Nov., 1832, B.C. 1501/58888.

130. For Details see J.C. Jha, The Bhumij Revolt, pp. 90-97.

131. Wilkinson to Major Benson, Private Secretary to Lord William Bentinck.

132. Bhumij Revolt, p. 100.

133. An Officer taking part in the fighting quoted in Bhumij Revolt, ft. 5, p. 101.

134. Thakur Chetan Singh to Wilkinson, 7th Feb. 1833, B.C. 1502/58889.

135. Wilson, Mill's History of British India, 1858, Vol. IX, pp. 237-238.

136. Ibid, also S.B. Choudhary, Civil Disturbances, pp. 101-102; and for a detailed discussion of the nature, see, J.C. Jha, The Bhumij Revolt, Chapter IV.

137. Judicial Criminal Proceedings dated Fort William, the 2nd December, 1833, para I, p. 99. (West Bengal state Archieves).

138. Ibid, paras II-IV, pp. 99-101.

139. From the Court of Directors to the Govt. of Bengal, dated, 16th, Sept, 1835, India & Bengal Dispatches, Vol. VI, pp. 376-378.

140. Ibid.

141. H. Rickets, Reports on the District of Singhbhum, Selections from the Records of the Bengal Govt. No. XVI, (1864), p. 63.

142. Ibid, para III, pp. 100-101, also D.G. Manbhum, pp. 65-67.

143. Judicial Criminal Proceedings dated Fort William, 14th Sep. 1854, paras I & II, p. 94.

144. From the Court of Directors to the Governor-General in Council, dated, London the 1st October, 1856, Judicial Deptt. No. 42 of 1856.

145. Sir George Campbell, Cit. Abhay Charan Das, the Indian Ryot,

146. Ibid.

147. Buchanan Report, Bhagalpur, 1810-11.

148. See Ante, Hillmen's Resistance.

149. Sir John Houlton, Bihar, the Heart of India, p. 75.

150. Journal of the Asiatic Society of Bengal, 1851, p. 564, 574,-76.

151. W.W. Hunter, Annals, of Rural Bengal Vol. I, pp. 228-29.

152. Calcutta Review, vol. XXV, March, 1856.

153. Houlton, Sir John, Bihar the Heart of India, p. 75 also Bradely Birt. The Story of an Indian Uplan d, p. 175.

154. Hunter, Annals, pp. 232-34.

155. Ibid, pp. 234-235.

156. Letters from G.W. Taylor, Asstt. Commissioner, Sreekand near Teen Pahar, to Mr. A.R. Thomson, Deputy Commissioiner, Dumka, dated 16th February 1856, Pakur Records also, see K.K. Datta, The Santhal Insurrection, Cal. 1940. p.7.

157. Calcutta Review, Op. Cit. pp. 238-40.

158. Annals, pp. 231, 337-38, 254.

159. Buckland, Bengal under Lt. Governors, I, p. 111.

160. From the Court of 'Directors to the Governor-General in Council, Ist Oct. 1856, Op. cit.

161. K. K. Datta, Santhal Insurrection, p. 4.

162. Buckland, I, p. 12.

163. Tayler, Asstt. Commr. Sreekand to Thomson Dy. Commr., Dumka, 16th February 1856, Op. cit.

164. Calcutta Review, XXV, March, 1856.

165. Ibid.

166. G.W. Tayler, Asstt, Commissioner at Srikand, to A.R. Thomson, Deputy Commissioner, Dumka, 16th Feb. 1856, Op. cit.

167. From G. F. Brown, Commr. of Bhagalpur to A.C. Bidwell, Special Commr. for the suppression of the Insurrection, dated 1st Oct. 1855, Bhagalpur Commr's Correspondence, Vol. 687, 1855.

168. Summary of causes and events, from the court of Directors to the Governor-General in Council, 1st Oct. 1856, Op. cit.

169. This refers to the extensive work carried on for the construction of the Railways.

170. Hunter, Annals, p. 236.

171. Buckland, I.p. 12.

172. Calcutta Review, March 1856, also K.K. Datta, Santhal Insurrection, pp. 14-16.

173. K. K. Datta, Santhal Insurrection, pp. 16-19.

174. L. J. Trotter, History of British Empire in India, Vol. I, p. 369, for details pp. 368-74.

175. Hunter, Annals, p. 240.

176. Letter from G.F. Brown, Commissioner of Bhagalpur to the Govt. of Bengal, dated 9th July 1855, Op. cit.

177. Ibid.

178. Letter dated the 17th July, 1855, from Commissioner of Bhagalpur to Major General Lloyd, Dinapur.

179. Letter, dated 17th July, 1855, from Commissioner of Bhagalpur to the Govt. of Bengal.

180. Buckland, I. p. 13.

181. Ibid.

182. From Commissioner of Bhagalpur to the Govt. of Bengal, dated 28th July, 1855.

183. K.K. Datta, Santhal Insurrection, pp. 35-36.

184. Buckland, I.p. 13.

185. Letter dated 18th July, 1855 from the Commissioner of Bhagalpur to the Govt. of Bengal.

186. Buckland I.p. 13.

187. Hunter, Annals p; 246.

188. Personal Narrative of Major Jervis, vide Annals, pp. 247-48.

189. Buckland, I.p. 14.

190. Calcutta Review, Op. cit.

191. Buckland, pp. 13-14.

192. S.S. O' Malley, revised S.C. Mukherjee, 1938, D.G. Santhal Parag, 86.

193. Buckland, I, pp. 14-15.

194. Ibid.
195. Hunter, Annals, p. 252, also O'Malley, D.G. Santhal Parganas.
196. For details see Datta, Santhal Insurr., pp. 67-68.
197. Balfour's Encyclopedia of India, III, p. 527.
198. R.C. Majumdar, British Paramountcy and Indian Renaissance, Vol. IX, chapter XIV, pp. 457-58.
199. Buckland, I. p. 16.

CHAPTER 4
The Wahabi Movement : The Muslim Resistance

History of Modern India is incomplete without a reference to the Wahabi Movement. In fact, it forms an inseparable and glorious chapter of its history.

'It has to be admitted that of all the movements which the British rule in India called into existence, the Wahabi Movement was the most remorselessly anti-British'[1]; and the progress and sustenance of the movement owed substantially to Bihar in general and Patna in particular. For about half a century Patna remained the chief Wahabi Centre in India.

Genesis and Development of the Movement

The establishment of the British rule in India was resented by the Muslims most,[2] for they were the ruling race who had been dislodged from the seat of authority. This loss of political power affected not only the Muslim ruling houses and nobility but also the Muslim masses. Dethroned from the rulers to be ruled, they in turn now had to experience the inherent basic hardships imposed by new conquerors. The burden was great, sources of affliction were many and varied-political, economic, social and religious. It was not without open fights, rebellions, and revolts that the Muslim rulers gave in. After the failure of their princes and governors to resist the growing power of the English, the people came forward to shak off the alien rule. To make this political struggle broad based, people's leaders wisely thought to unfurl the green banner of 'Jehad'. Hence we find religious movements with political overtones being organised, and at times plots and conspiracies being hatched. It is in this background that there rose the formidable Wahabi Movement and conspiracies, including that of Patna in 1845-46.

The disintegration of the Mughal Empire in India was followed by degeneration in polity, society and religion. Rising to the occasion reformers and thinkers in all the major communities came out with reform programmes. The Wahabi Movement in India originally started as a socio-religious movement to reform the Muslim society and religion, was transformed into a 'religio-political creed' even during the life time of its founder, Sayed Ahmad "Barelvi" (1786-1831).

Salient Features of Wahabism in India

The most important point to be borne in mind is that the Wahabi Movement in India, though having some similarities, is quite different[3] from the Wahabi Movement launched by Abdul Wahab of Najd (1707-1792) in Arabia. Hence, the term Wahabi here is a misnomer. In fact, the so called Wahabis in India, the followers of Syed Ahmad of Rae Bareli, called themselves 'Unitarians', but they were so called (Wahabis) derisiously or derisively by their opponents, particularly the English.

Socio-religious Character of the Movement

In its socio-religious aspects, as advocated by Syed Ahmad,[4] Wahabism stood for reforming and restoring Islam to its pristine glory discarding all pernicious innovations that had crept into the Muslim society and religion in India.[5]

Economic Under-current of the Movement

In it is economic aspects, the Wahabis were on the side of the helpless peasantry whom they helped to resist the tyranny and oppressions of landed proprietors. The Baraset disturbances of 1831 and Farazai disturbances of 1841 have a bearing on the point.[6] In Bihar, the leaders opposed the resumption of different, kinds of land free tenures.[7] The severity of resumption laws causing economic afflictions and social dislocation, wrote Hunter, gave birth to panic and hatred.[8]

Political Aspect of the Movement

More remarkable is the political aspect[9] of the Wahabi Movement which subsequently even obscured its socio-religious character.[10] It was the 'ambition'[11] of Syed Ahmad, as Bellew put it, 'to establish the Empire of Islam and to rid the Indian Peninsula of its infidel people - the British and the Sikhs. To raise a fighting force for the contemplated struggle, regular military training of the followers by the Supremo was started early from Bareli itself. Syed Ahmad even sought the help of Hindu Chiefs like Raja Hindu Rao, brother in-law of Maharaja Daulat Rao Sindhia of Gwalior, in driving out of India those alien people from distant lands' who coming as 'traders and vendors of goods' had become' the rulers of territories and times', and had attained the rank of sovereignty.[12]

Patna Achieves the Rare Distinction as the First Organised Centre of the Wahabis

Syed Ahmad (1786-1831) of Rae-Bareli, under the influence of, and with the permission of his preceptor Shah Abdul Aziz (1746-1824) of Delhi, in about 1820, began to preach about and organise his order of 'Tariqa-i- Muhammadia', better known as the Wahabi movement, to promote his ideas of socio-religious reform and achieve his political mission of freeing the country from the 'infidels'. Endowed with rare qualities of a preacher and leader, he soon won a large number of zealous followers through his missionary tours in the United provinces and Delhi.[13] But it proved to be a turning point in the history of the Wahabi movement as well as in the history and fortunes of the renowned Muslim family of Sadiqpur, Patna, when one of its member, Wilayat Ali, while studying at Lucknow[14] met and became disciple of Syed Ahmed. Subsequently, after the return of Syed Ahmad from Haj in 1822, all the members of Wilayat Ali's family including his brother Enayat Ali, were initiated into Wahabi creed.[15] Not only the families of Wilayat Ali, Shah Muhammad Hussain, Elahi Bux and Mazhar Ali of Panta City[6] became disciples of Syed Ahmad, but nearly the whole Muslim brotherhood of Patna and neighbouring places joined the Wahabi order. This overwhelming large and enthusiastic following necessitated a regular system of organisation at Patna. Accordingly, four 'Khalifas' or spiritual vice-regents, namely Shah Muhammad Hussain, Wilayat Ali, Enayat Ali and Farhat Hussain were appointed.[16] Then, as O'Kinealy wrote in the Calcutta Review, 'a general meeting of his (Syed Ahmad's) Caliphs was held, and a permanent arrangement was made to forward supplies of men and money to support the long contemplated struggle.[17]

Thus, rightly remarked Prof. Q. Ahmad, Patna had the rare distinction of being chosen as the first organised centre of the Wahabis. During the subsequent years Patna-Wahabis amply justified the confidence shown in them by Syed Ahmad, and played a dominating role in the history of the movement.[18]

'Hijrat' of Syed Ahmad to the Frontier

On the establishment of the British power and consequent loss of independence by the country, India had become Dar-ul-Harb (enemy territory). In pursuance of his doctrine of 'Hijrat' Syed Ahmad with a large number of followers proceeded early in 1826[19] to an independent area in North West Frontier Provinces and Afghanistan wherefrom he could wage a holy war — 'Jihad' — against the Sikh and the English 'infidels'. Wilayat Ali and his brothers, Enayat Ali and Talib Ali, accompanied the 'Apostle' on this great journey, and established a character for themselves on the Frontier as fanatical firebrands.[20]

The establishment of the Wahabi colonies on the 'Frontier' by the 'Hindustani Fanatics', their intermittent fortunes and misfortunes are exciting tales in themselves. For our present purpose it will suffice to mention that the Patna Maulvies served the cause with zeal, sincerity and success whether as preachers, envoys at courts or fighters at the field. After their short but successful stay in Afghanistan and in the Frontier Provinces, Wilayat Ali and Enayat Ali were deputed by Syed Ahmad to India for missionary and organisational work.[21]

Wilayat Ali in the Deccan

Wilayat Ali through his missionary tours in the Central Provinces, Bombay and Deccan successfully won considerable number of supporters to the Wahabi cause. In Hyderabad his efforts were so fruitful that even Nawab Muwariz-ud-daula, the younger brother of the Nizam, became his disciple and active Wahabi conspirator[13] and women cast off their jewels for 'Jihad'.[22]

Enayat Ali in Bengal

In Eastern Bengal, Enayat Ali was even more successful in his 'mission', particularly in procuring recruits and money for transmitting to the North west.[23]

Enayat Ali also sowed the seeds of future Panchayati system, boycott and civil disobedience to the Government, a policy to be adopted on national scale by the Congress and Gandhi. Emphasising on this notable aspect of Enayat Ali's work, O'Kinealy wrote: 'those who were not in a position to abandon this country and join in Jihad were recommended to resist passively and refrain from all intercourse with their Kafir rulers to form as it were, a power within the Government and totally opposed to it. Assistance should not be demanded from the infidels, their courts... should be avoided and complaints between brother and brother should be decided by the local leaders.[24]

Shah Muhammad Hussain in Bihar

In Bihar, Shah Muhammad Hussain put the organisation on sound footing and opened new branches at several places.[25]

Writing about the missionary zeal and selfless devotion of Patna Caliphs, Hunter observed, "Indefatigable as missionaries careless of themselves, blameless in their lives, supremely devoted to the overthrow of the English Infidels, admirably skilful in organising a permanent system for supplying money and recruits, the Patna Caliphs standforth as the types and examples of the sect. Much of their teaching was faultless and it had been given to them to stir up thousands of their countrymen to a purer life and truer conception of the Almighty. "[26]

Giving details of the Wahabi headquarters in Sadiqpur, Patna, the central propaganda', as he called it, Sir W.W. Hunter wrote[27] that the Friday lectures in the Sadiqpur mosque were different to those in the other mosques in the city. They were vehement harangues, exposing the inefficiency of work without faith, warning the hearers of the great spiritual danger and urging them to cultivate inward life. Around the Mosque were the dwelling houses of the priest with a small college for the students of the reformed theology where youths of high promise were received and trained, a hospice for pious travellers.

Misfortune Overcome

While the two brothers were thus engaged in preaching and organising, they heard the news of defeat and death of Syed Ahmad at the battle of Balakote in 1831. It was at this time that death occurred also of their father , Fateh Ali at Patna.[30] this brought the two brothers together at Patna to decide the future course of action, The death of Syed Ahmad was a great blow to the movement , but it must be said to the credit of the Patna "Khalifas" that they not only kept it alive but made it even more vigorous in a few year's time. To remove the immediate danger of dispendency among the followers, Wilayat Ali propagated the idea of 'disappearance' and 'resurrection' of Syed Ahmad.[31] At the same time they engaged themselves whole and soul in reorganising the movement in Bengal and Bihar and continued to send men and money to the Wahabi camp at Sittana.

Fresh Troubles and the Movement Revived

At the 'Frontier', in the meantime, Wahabis had gathered at Sittana under Maulvi Qasim of Panipat. The part of party then shifted to Takhtaband in Bonair.[32] However, Syed Ahmad's Khalifas in India selected Maulvi Nastr-ud-din of Delhi, nephew of Abdul Aziz, as their military commander to carry on the Jihad. [33] But more trobles were in store for the Wahabis. The Wahabi forces under Nasir-ud-din were severely defeated at Ghazari while defending the citadel for Dost Muhammad, the Afghan ruler. And, there rose a difference in the Wahabi camp on the issue of 'resurrection of Syed Ahmad. It was on this issue that Zainul Abedin of Hyderabad, a Khalifa of Wilayat Ali, who had come from the Eastern Bengal with a considerable number of volunteers, defected and returned to Calcutta explaining the 'fraud' all along the way.[34] It was a great crisis. 'Again the fanantical cause seemed ruined,. But the missionary zeal of the Patna Caliphs and the immense picuniary resources at their command once more raised the sacred banner from the dust. They covered India with their missionaries and brought about one of the 'greatest religious revivals that has ever taken place'.[35]

Taking advantage of the death of Ranjit Singh and consequent political convulsions the Wahabi forces under Enayat Ali and later joined by Wilayat Ali, within a few years established their dominion over a large extent of territory along the left bank of the Indus, stretching from Hurreepore to Kagan and from Sittana to Kashmir."[36] But the Wahabi Raj at the Frontier proved to be short lived. The entry of the British on the scene, and subsequent establishment of their sway over Punjab completely changed the situation. The Wahabis now came into direct conflict with the English. And, they (Wahabis) were no match either for the British power or diplomacy. There followed the natural result. With their gradually reducing number (about 500), Ali Brothers had to surrender before the English forces at Haripur early in 1847. Wilayat Ali and Enayat Ali were sent to Patna and bound down on bails of their good conduct and not to leave the city for four years.[37]

The Anti-British Plot of Patna (1845)

In the meantime, while the English fortunes were balanced on the bank of the Sutlej,[38] and all the resources of the Company's Government were being drawn to the North Western Frontier[39], there was uneartherd at Patna a well organised conspiracy (1845-46) to temper with the loyalty of the sepoys and to assail the English authority. 'It was incident', observed Kaye, 'which in quiet times might have made itself heard all over the country, but which lost in the din of battle (with the Sikhs) in that momentous winter, gave only a local sound'.[40]

The Magistrate of Patna, on the 26th December, 1845, informed the Govt. of a widespread conspiracy 'to temper with the allegiance of the native officers and sepoys of the Danapur Regimental Centre.[41] In fact, the conspirators had successfully managed to plant mutiny in the Native Infantry Regiment No. 1 of Major Rowcroft at Danapur, through Mushi Peer Bux and Pandit Durga Prasad of the same Regiment. Rahut Ali, an influential zamindar of Neora, Khwaja Hasan Ali of Patna, and Saif Ali, came out to be the principal figures in the plot, who distributed money even promising six months salary in advance to the native officers and sepoys of the Regiment.[42] However, the plot was divulged by Jamadar Motee Mishra to Major Rowcroft on the 18th December, 1846, and was confirmed next day when, as instructed by his Major, promised money was received by Motee Mishra for the detachment of the Regiment proceeding to Gaya. But it was only on the 24th that the Major arrested Munshi Peer Bux and reported the matter to the Officiating Magistrate of Patna. The Magistrate not only arrested Rahat Ali and intercepted all his letters, but also announced reward of 600 rupees to anyone giving the clue of the plot and a reward of 200 rupees for the apprehension of the supposed Moghul (Saif Ali).[43]

The arrests of the leaders and search of their houses revealed a widespread conspiracy. Attempts had also been made to temper with the Regiments at Hazaribagh, Dorunda (Ranchi) and Sugauli (Champaran). The 66th Native Infantry had already been corrupted.[44] Baquar Ali, the 'Kotegust' (patrol) Darogah of Patna city was engaged in winning over the 7th Irregular cavalry at Sugauli[45].

The Organisers of the Plot?

Contemporary English officials, like William Tayler, Commissioner of Patna from 1855 to August, 1857, believed 'that the conspiracy of 1846, was but a branch of a more general plot', in which the Mohamedans of Patna and the neighbouring districts were concerned and that the object of that conspiracy was the destruction of the English, the overthrow of the British Government, and the re-establishment of Mohamedan dynasty.'[46]

Likewise, Colonel Malleson attributed this conspiracy of successfully 'corrupting some of the native officers and sepoys stationed at Dinapur 'to the Mahomedan nobility'[47] of Patna, 'a city which was the headquarter of the two notorious, viceregents of this great Prophet (Syed Ahmed).[48]

The Commissioner of Patna reported to the Government of Bengal that the emissaries had been sent to every division of the Army from Sutledge to Calcutta.... To the Mohammadans they ... held the hope of restoration of the family of Timoor to the throne of Delhi, and to the Hindus the fear of conversion to Christianity'.[49]

A Wahabi Conspiracy?

Amongst modern scholars Qeyamuddin Ahmad convincingly puts forward the claims of the Wahabis as the chief organiser of the conspiracy.[50] To drive the point home, Prof. Q. Ahmad says that the Wahabis were the first to realise the key position of the Indian Army in their struggle with the English, and they tried to nuetralise the effectiveness by sapping the loyalties, of as many units as possible. Where simple preaching and appeal to patriotism failed the more sure, if more sordid, approach of monetary inducement was also tried.[51] The strategy of infiltrating in the Army units was standardised by the

Wahabis from a very early date.'[52] To substantiate his contention, he gives details of the different recorded instances of their (Wahabis) tempering with the Army units, including that of Danapur.[53] Q. Ahmad further points out that in the Patna conspiracy case all the principal organisers, like Khwaja Hasan, Rahut Ali, Saif Ali and others were either 'Wahabis' or closely related to the 'Wahabs'. In his concluding remarks he observes: 'In view of all these significant points ..... it is clear that the Wahabis were the main organisers of the conspiracy of 1845.[54]

General Anti-British Combination

Dr. K. K. Datta, eminent historian from, and on modern Bihar, views it as a secret anti-British alliance in which a large number of influential persons, bankers, Amlahs (native officers), Rajas and Zamindars, both Hindu and Muslims, were involved.[55] And, its genesis and development, according to Dr. Datta, can be traced in the deep seated discontent of the people against the new rulers for its administrative, social, economic, religious and educational policies, the severity of the resumption laws, particularly resumption of lands endowed to religious institutions[56]. In 1829 there was staged a big demonstration led by Rahut Ali and Mir Abdullah before the office of Resumption Officer, Mr. Elliot. Growing activities of Christian missionaries, encouragement given to the spread of English education, new messing system in the Jails, followed by serious disturbances in many of them, were some of the causes of discontent; and which were considered by some people as a positive interference on the part of the Government in their religious observances and social customs. To defend their religion both Hindus and Muslims of Bihar combined together and their leaders held a secret convention' at Harihar Chhatra on the occasion of Sonepure Fair in Khwaja Hasan's tent'. A plan was chalked out and for its successful execution, co-operation or atleast the acquiescence of the sepoy in it, was felt necessary.' It was also decided to obtain help from the Rajah of Nepal and the king of Delhi, and to raise a force of their own.[57] Dr. Datta further writes that Babu Kunwar Singh of Jagdishpure appears to have played a very significant role in this anti-British combination. He had come over to Patna during the 'Jail disturbances', and was in communication with

Rahut Ali. He is said to have gone to Nepal to represent its Rajah' the acts of oppression committed by the Europeans in Hindustan. Kunwar Singh had also been assigned the task of raising a suitable force for the contemplated struggle. Accordingly, he was organising a military force in Shahabad.[58]

The guilt of Baboo Mod Narayan of Tikari and Munshi Cheragh Ali, his Diwan, was proved. Khwaja Hidayat Ali, Principal Sadar Amin of Gaya, Ashruff Hussain, Maulvi Neaz Ali, Principal Sadar Amin in Tirhut, and other Amlahs who had signed the "Mazharunama" (Public petition) were all in the know of it. The Magistrate of Patna had been privately informed that the Rajah of Nepal, all the Rajas in these territories, all the principal zamindars in the surrounding districts, the most powerful merchants and bankers were in the league. "There might be some exaggeration in this information,' concludes Dr. Datta, "but there is no doubt that the plot was widespread."[59]

We, in the light of facts, may safely conclude that the Mohammuddan nobility with immense Wahabi connections planned the plot and skilfully utilised the local causes of discontent and anti-British elements to make the conspiracy widespread.

The Organisers Remained Unpunished

It is interesting to note that virtually all the principal organisers of the plot remained unchastied.[60] Rahut Ali and Khwaja Hasan were released due to mechanism of Munshi Peer Bux of Danapur Regimental centre and chief prosecution witness who had earlier turned an approver and was pardoned. Saif Ali could not be traced out. Though Magistrates of Shahabad, and Patna[61] were convinced of the complicity of Kunwar Singh in the plot, yet no action was taken against him due to political considerations[62], for the arrest of Baboo Kunwar Singh was very likely to be followed by a general rising of the people.'[63] Baqur Ali, the Kotegust Darogah of Patna City, Barqatullah, the Govt. pleader and Neaz Ali, the Qazi, were removed from their respective posts. Pandit Durga Prasad and Bhukkan Khan Jamadar of Danapur Regimental Centre, were lightly punished as "it was not necessary to strike terror into the minds of an army hovering on the brink of general mutiny.'[64]

The Wahabis During the Revolt of 1857 and After

Supported well by the Patna Centre with men amd supplies,[65] the Wahabis under Wilayat Ali, and after his death in November, 1852, under Enayat Ali, till his death in 1858, were actively, engaged in anti-British activities at the 'Frontier'.[66] They (Wahabis) as a group in Bihar did not take active part in the Great Revolt as a matter of well-defined policy,[67] writes Prof. Ahmad, as a chief Wahabi Centre inside the country had only been assigned the organisational work, and had a vital role in 'collection and transmission of men and materials to the Frontier, propagation and circulation of anti-British literature, and infiltration among Army units',[68] and they continued to function as such without participating in the great uprising. Had the Wahabis', pleads Prof. Ahmad, 'come out in open opposition in Bihar they too would have surely been suppressed and the (Wahabi) Movement would have come to an end much earlier than when it did. By keeping low the Wahabis survived the violent storm of 1857-59".[69] Thus, he has tried to justify the Wahabi policy (of non-participation) during the Revolt. But the soundness of the policy has rightly been doubted by the two great scholars[70] of the Great Movement.

The Wahabi Leaders Arrested

However, it would not be out of place to mention that William Tayler, the redoubtable Commissioner of Patna during the parts of the momentous year of 1857, was apprehensive of 'the numerous and fanatical Sect of Wahabis'.[71] Prominent amongst these were three men, Shah Muhammad Hussain, Ahmadullah and Waizul Haq. "To seize these men openly', writes Malleson, 'would have provoked the outbreak which Mr. Tayler, was careful to avoid. But it was necessary for the public peace that they should be secured. Mr. Tayler, therefore, requested their presence, and the presence of others, to consult on the state of affairs. When the conference was over he allowed the others to depart, but detained the three men, informing them that in the then existing state of affairs it was necessary that they should remain under supervision'.[72] Thus, treacherously, on the 19th

June, 1857, Tayler 'took possession of these leading men as hostages for the good conduct of their whole brotherhood'.[73]

With their improved situation in India, the British forces under Sir Sidney Cotton destroyed the Wahabi Settlement in Sittana during April-May, 1858.[74] Nevertheless, undeterred by heavy odds and sacrificing everything, their lives and fortunes, homes and hearths[75], a chain of Sadiqpur (Patna) Maulvies at the head of zealous Wahabis continued their heroic struggle against the mighty English Infidels even after the Great Revolt of 1857-58.[76] In fact, 'fanatical' Wahabis, till they were completely stamped out, were a permanent sources of danger to the British rule in India.[77]

The popular basis of the Wahabi Movement, Dr. S.B. Choudhury has rightly remarked, "stands vindicated by its well knit and integrated organisation drawing recruits and supplies from the whole expanse of the country extending from Dacca to Peshawar'.[78] To this we may add that without a popular base the Movement could not have sustained for such a long time in a situation so hostile, and against an enemy so powerful.

References

1. S. B. Choudhary, Civil Disturbances, 51.
2. Ibid-pp. 50-51; also W.W. Hunter, Our Indian Mussalmans, London, 1871.
3. R. C. Majumdar, ed. British Paramountcy & Indian Renaissance, I, pp. 883-84.
4. Sirat-i-Mustaqim, Compiled by Shah Ismail & Abdul Hai, pp. 75-115.
5. For details-Q. Ahmad, The Wahabi Movement in India, Calcutta, 1966, pp. 6-9, 15-16.
6. S. B. Choudhary, Civil Disturbances during the British rule in India, Calcutta, 1955, pp. 50, 95-97, also Thortan, History of India, London, 1843, Vol. V, pp, 179-187.
7. Sir W.W. Hunter, Our Indian Mussalmans, London, 1871, pp. 182-84.
8. For details K.K. Datta Biography of Kunwar Singh and Amar Singh, Patna, 1957, pp. 63, 91-92.
9. Hunter Indian Mussalmans, p. 68.

10. S.H. Askari, Political Significance of the Movement of Syed Ahamd Barelvi, IHRC, Vol. XXXI, 1955, pp. 174-181.
11. R. C. Majumdar ed. British Paramountecy and Indian Renaissance, Part I, pp. 883-84.
12. H.W. Bellew, A. General Report on the Yusufzais, Lahore, 1864. p. 84.
13. Syed Ahmad's Letter from the Frontier to Raja Hindu Rao, Unnamed collection of Syed Ahmad's Letters, Patna Univ. Library M.S. Copy, pp. 102-103, also Q. Ahmad, Wahabi Movement, Appendix VIII. Lahore, 1952.
14. Q. Ahmad, Wahabi Movement, pp. 27-28, & 38-39.
15. For details Abdul Rahim, Tazkira-i-Sadqa, 2nd Ed. Allahabad 1904, New Ed. 1964.
16. Sirat-i-Syed Ahmad Shahid, p. 218.
17. Tazkira-i-Sadqa pp. 41-42; also selections from the Records of the Govt. of Bengal, Vol. XLII, pp. 32-34.
18. J. A. O'Kinealy, Cal. Review, 1870, Vol. 51, pp. 82-83.
19. Q. Ahmad, Wahabi Movement, pp. 31-32.
20. Mehr, U.P. 282.
21. Hunter, Indian Mussalmans, p. 22.
22. Ibid, also pp. 101-102.
23. N. C. Choudhury, The Wahabi Conspiracy in Hyderabad, 1839-40. Proceedings Indian History Congress, Vol. XIX, 1956.
24. Hunter, Indian Mussalmans, p. 52.
25. Govt. of Bengal, Judicial Deptt. Consultation, dated 29th May, 1943, Nos. 21.24.
26. Calcutta Review, Vol. 51, 1870, p. 393.
27. For an account of Wahabi Organisation See R.C. Majumdar, British Paramountcy and Indian Renaissance, I, pp. 996-99.
28. Hunter, Indian Mussalmans, p. 68.
29. Calcutta Review, Vol. XL, 1864, pp. 130-131.
30. Qeyamuddin Ahmad, p. 102.
31. R. C. Majumdar, British Paramountcy & Indian Renaissance, I, pp. 888-89, also for critical exam. Hunter, Indian Mussalmans, pp. 46-48, 61-64, & the Calcutta Review, vol. 51, pp. 186, 392.
32. Calcutta Review, 1870, p. 186.

33. Foreign (Secret) Proceedings, dt., July 10, 1839, No. 21.
34. Calcutta Review, 1870, pp. 187-191.
35. Hunter, Indian Mussalmans, pp. 49-50.
36. Calcutta Review, Vol. 51, p. 381.
37. Ibid, also Hazara Gazetteers, Urdu, 1908, 135, and Bellew, Op. cit. p. 95.
38. Malleson, The Mutiny of the Bengal Army, p. 174.
39. Sir J. Kaye, History of the Sepoy War, Vol. I, p. 6.
40. Ibid, p. 303-304.
41. Letter from E.S. Lillie, officiating Magistrate of Patna to the Secretary to the Govt. of Bengal, dt. 26th Dec. 1845, Patna Commissioner's Confidential File, 1845-46.
42. Deposition of Peer Bux involved in the conspiracy under Act V of 1840, on 7th March, 1846.
43. Letter from J. E. S. Lillie, officiating Magistrate of Patna, to the Govt. dt. 26th December, 1845, *op. cit.*
44. Statement of Peer Bux, as Encl. to the letter no. 43C from the Officiating Magistrate of Patna to the Secretary to the Govt. of Bengal, dt. 20th January, 1846, *op. cit.*
45. Letter from the Ofg. Magistrate to the Govt. No. 16, dated 14th Jan. 1846.
46. William Tayler, Our Crisis, Calcutta, 1858, p. 5.
47. The Mutiny of the Bengal Army, p. 174.
48. G. B. Malleron, History of the Indian Mutiny, vol. I, p. 550, also p. 547.
49. Letter from the Commissioner of Patna to Secretary to the Govt. of Bengal, dated 8th Jan, 1846, p. 1002.
50. For details see Q. Ahmad, Wahabi Movement, pp. 164-68.
51. In the Patna Conspiracy of 1845 money was extensively distributed among the Indian troops.
52. Ibid, pp. 157-58.
53. Ibid, pp. 160-64.
54. For details Ibid, pp. 164-68.
55. K. K. Datta, Biography of Kunwar Singh & Amar Singh, Patna, 1957, pp. 62-63.

56. Ibid and pp. 91-92; also Hunter, Indian Mussalmans, 182-84
57. Ibid. pp. 63-64.
58. Ibid. p. 66.
59. Ibid. p. 67
60. For details, Q. Ahmad, Wahabi Movement, pp. 163-64; Kaye, History of the Sepoy War, Vol. I, p. 308-9 Datta, Biography 66-69.
61. Letter from Elphinston Jackson, officiating Magistrate of Shahabad to the Secretary to the Govt. of Bengal, dt. 3rd Jan. 1846 and Letter from the Officiating Magistrate of Patna to the Secretary to the Govt. of Bengal, dt. 27th Dec. 1845.
62. Letter from the Govt. of Bengal to the Magistrate of Patna, dated 28th January, 1846.
63. Letter from Jackson, Magistrate of Shahabad to the Govt. of Bengal, dated 22nd January, 1848.
64. Kaye, History of the Sepoy War, Vol. I, p. 309.
65. Report of T. E. Ravenshaw, Magistrate of Patna to the Commissioner of Patna, dated 9th, 1865.
66. For a short account see Hunter, Indian Mossalmans, pp. 22-24.
67. For a detailed discussion on the subject see Q. Ahmad, Wahabi Movement, Chapter VII; also R.C. Majumdar, British Paramountcy, I, p. 891.
68. Ibid. p. 217.
69. Ibid. p. 226.
70. S. N. Sen, Eighteen Fifty Seven, Delhi, 1957, p. 248; and R. C. Majumdar, The Sepoy Mutiny and the Indian Revolt of 1857, Calcutta, 1957, p. 37.
71. Letter from William Tayler, Commissioner of Patna, to the Secretary to the Govt. of Bengal, No. 623, dated 17th July, 1857.
72. Col. G. B. Malleson, History of the Indian Mutiny, London, 1878, pp. 52-53.
73. G.W. Forrest, A History of the Indian Mutiny, Vol. III, pp. 400-402; also William Tayler, Our Crisis, pp. 26-36.
74. For details W.H. Pagat & A.H. Mason, Records of Expeditions Against Tribes of N.W. Frontier since the Annexation of Punjab, London, 1884, pp. 90-97.

75. For details, Q. Ahmad, Wahabi Movement, Chapter VIII.
76. For further studies Ibid, Ch. IX.
77. Hunter, Indian Mussalmans, p. 35, for details pp. 25-39.
78. S. B. Choudhary, Civil Disturbances, p. 50.

CHAPTER 5
A Century of the English Administration

Anarchy Under 'Dyarchy' of Clive

The battle of Plassey in 1757 made the English Kingmakers in Bengal, and that of Buxar in 1764 the King itself. Mir Jafar and Mir Qasim made them zamindars of a limited tract of the country; and after the battle of Buxar, the Moghul Emperor, Shah Alam II, raised them to the office of the 'Diwan' of the three provinces of Bengal, Bihar and Orissa. Thus the 'Company-Bahadur' received the 'Diwani', the right to collect and reimburse the revenues, and to administer the civil-justice of the three provinces from the titular Emperor; and by arrangements and engagements with successive Nawabs of Bengal, they also got the 'Nizamat', the military control and administration of criminal justice and police. The merchant-sovereigns, as they had now become, did not realise the 'obvious moral' of assuming the direct responsibility for the good government of the people of the provinces, and left the actual administration in the hands of the old machinery of the Nawab, undertaking only the superintendence of the collection and disposal of the revenues. This 'dyarchy' established by Clive proved an anarchy. The writer-turned administrators of the Company were concerned to 'attain easy fortunes and to leave a land for which they had no affection'. The people of the provinces experienced such skilful, searching and strong tyrannies which were unknown and unparalleled in the history of the world. The people were beggared and starved, their sufferings multiplied by the devastating famine of 1769-70, and the Company reached on the verge of bankruptcy. Hence, while the Company in 1772 decided to standforth themselves as

'Diwan', and sent Warren Hastings to Bengal as its Governor with specific instructions to abolish the 'double-government' and 'to make a complete reformation' in every branch of government;[1] the British Parliament in 1773, enacting the Regulating Act, and suspending the collection of 'Crime-tax' from the Company, acquiesced in the political role of a private trading Company.

The Machinery of Merchants as the Machinery of Government : Administrative Reforms of Warren Hastings

Since the assumption of office in 1772 A.D. as the Governor of Bengal Warren Hastings gave all consuming thought, besides, to the consolidation of the power of the Company, 'to make a complete reformation' in every branch of Government. The task before him was not easy one, considering particularly the circumstances and limitations under which he had to work. Changing the whole outlook of the mercantile rulers, he had to 'transform the Company of merchants, factors and clerks into the machinery of government',[2] and to make a government out of the confused heap of undigested materials as wild as chaos itself.[3] to which the country powers and people might look with respect and confidence. Moreover, he had to adopt 'the Directors' Regulations to the manners and understanding of the people, and Exigencies of the Country, adhering ..... to the ancient Usages and Institutions.[4] Thus, the structure of government which Warren Hastings raised was naturally bound to be defective and imperfect. But he laid the foundation on which was subsequently erected the grand edifice of the Anglo-Indian Administration. Since Bihar was a sub province of Bengal, the organisation of administration introduced by Warren Hastings affected Bihar as much as it affected Bengal.

Direct Assumption of 'Diwani' : Revenue the First Object of Government

For the merchant-rulers 'the revenue' was 'beyond all question the first object of Government'.[5] But the Dual-Government had resulted in serious disorders in their revenue administration. The Company's government had been allegedly defrauded of its just demands and the raiyats had been oppressed to the extreme.[6] To remedy the situation, the

Company stoodforth in the character of Diwan and directed its servants to take upon themselves the entire care and management of the revenue.[7] Naturally enough, Warren Hastings began with the revenue administration and had to devote much of his time and energy to the intricate problem of the mode and machinery of revenue collection. Though a good organiser, Warren Hastings, unfortunately, was not equally good at the complicated matters of revenue. The result was 'unfortunate'[8] and 'a ghastlry failure'[9] as far as revenue administration was concerned. However, Warren Hastings began well. Immediately after the arrival of the famous dispatch, Muhammad Reza Khan in Bengal and Raja Sitab Roy in Bihar were divested of the office of Naib-Diwans. The entire revenue administration was placed under the direct control of the President and Council who formed a Board or Committee of Revenue for the purpose, and were assisted by an Indian officer styled as 'Rai-rain'. The 'Khalsa' or the Treasury was removed from Murshidabad to Calcutta.[10]

Revenue-Farmers and European Supervisors as Collectors in the Distt.

Land were farmed out to the highest bidders, known as revenue-farmers, many of whom were not hereditary zamindars. This farming was for a period of five years beginning with April 10, 1772. The 'supervisors' now styled as 'Collectors' placed in different districts were entrusted with the task of revenue collection with the help of native 'Diwans.' This was intended to 'bring a British central control and a joint British and native agency in the district into the direct contact of the people'.[11] Immediate charge of supervision and settlement for Bihar was entrusted to the controlling Council of Revenue at Patna.[12] In 1774 European Collectors were recalled from the districts by the orders of the Directors and their place was taken by the native 'Diwans' or 'Amils'. To control and supervise the work of collection six Provincial Councils - each consisting of a chief and four others as members, all senior servants of the Company, at Calcutta, Burdwan, Dacca, Murshidabad, Dinajpur and Patna—were constituted.[13] Changes necessitated by the Directors' orders were for the worse. The Provincial Council of Revenue from Patna in its report of 16th March

1774 sent in a moving description of the distress in their province.[14]

The Regulating Act of 1773 (13th of Gerge III, C 63) made Warren Hastings the Governor-General of Bengal and changed the structure of his Council, majority being hostile to him. The Act also empowered the Governor-General-in-Council to make and to issue such rules, ordinances and regulations which were expedient for the good order and civil government of the settlement. However, the evils of the quinquennial settlement and auction system which were proving more and more disastrous year after year, were a matter of grave concern for the Governor-General and his Council. Philip Francis, a Member of the Council observed: "The greater part of the zamindars were ruined and dispossessed of the management of their lands'.[15] He recommended the perpetual settlement of lands with zamindars and emphasised his point again and again.[16] Many other proposals were also put forward.[17] A Commission known as the Amini Commission was also appointed in November, 1776, to procure material for the settlement of different districts.[18] But nothing definite came out of it; and on the expiry of quinquennial settlement in April, 1777, the system of auction was modified and lands begun to be let out annually, preferably to hereditary zamindars.[19] At the same time zamindars were warned that failure to meet obligations might result in the sale or transfer of zamindari.[20] In fact, owing to the high assessment, defaults were frequent and sales numerous.

However, a new scheme was in offing. Being free from the hostile majority in the Council,[21] and taking advantage of the Amini Commission Report, rightly acclaimed as the most valuable document in the early revenue history of Bengal,[22] early in 1781, the Governor-General opted a new plan for the revenue administration of Bengal and Bihar.[23] The new scheme aimed at complete centralization and saving. Warren Hastings himself said: "By this plan we hope to bring the whole administration of revenue to Calcutta, without any intermediate charge or agency, and to effect a saving of lacs to the Company and to the zamindars and ryots'.[24] Accordingly, all the Provincial Councils were abolished and all powers were vested in the new Committee of Revenue at Calcutta consisting of Senior servants of the Company, assisted by an Indian Diwan. European

Collectors were reappointed but were divested of any real power and were subject to the minute control of the Committee of Revenue.[25]

Affairs of Bihar Directly Under Warren Hastings

Under the scheme of 1781, the affairs of Bihar were directly under the control of Warren Hastings, Edward Wheeler and Richard Brusell, after whose resignation Mcpherson took his place in October, 1781.[26] William Maxwell became the Revenue Chief at Patna and after his death in August, 1781, Roses took charge of the office. But Brooke succeeded to the permanent office of the Revenue Chief at Patna extended over Sircar Bihar, Sarcar Shahabad, Sircar Tirhut, Havilly Azimabad (Patna) and Havilly Rohtas to which was added parganas of Siris and Cutumba, Churikiya, Sasaram and Chayenpur.[27]

The System of 1781 Breaks Down

The new scheme also proved equally and wholly inefficient.[28] It neither gave relief to the raiyats from the oppressions of zamindars, nor-zamindars from disgrace and ruin. Shore even ventured to pronounce: 'With respect to the Committee of Revenue, it is morally impossible for them to execute the business they are entrusted with'.[29]

High assessment and rigorous collection resulted in the oppression of raiyats and defaulting of revenue farmers, renters and sub-renters. William Rooke, the Collector of Purnea, reported on 13 March, 1783, that a certain farmer had repeatedly flogged those who preferred any complaint to him and setting aside their 'pattahs', exacted enormous increase from them.[30] Even after enormous exactations and oppressions revenue farmers fell in arrears.[31] Beginning from Maharaja Kalyan Singh, the farmer-General of Subeh Bihar and his naib Raja Kheali Ram, many zamindars, Aumils, and Malguzars were in heavy arrears for which they were deposed, confined and disgraced. Even their effects and valuables were attached. Maharaja Kalyan Singh and Kheali Ram were not the lone unfortunates, many other met the same fate. Cases of Raja Narain Singh, zamindar and Aumil of Siris and Cutumba, Raja Bikramjit Singh, Aumil of Sircar Shahabad, Raja Mitrajit Singh of Tikari, Raja Bhup Narain Singh of Jagdishpur, and Raja Akbar Ali of Narhat and Samoy, are glaring examples.[32] All these disaffected Rajas and Zamindars proved a ready gun-powder for extending the revolt of Raja Chait Singh of Benaras to Bihar.

In fact, "the system of 1781 had broken down".[33] Evils of the farming system combined with failure of rains caused a great scarcity in 1783 in Bihar. John Shore was sent from Calcutta to enquire into the causes of famine in Bihar and to adopt ameliorative measures, besides making settlement of land revenue. He took certain measures. It was on his recommendation that a big granary at Patna, known as Golghar and standing till this day, was built.[34] However, his revenue scheme for the province was merely a rearrangement of leases under the farming system on a three year's settlement.[35]

The dominant motive of the commercial government, in its early phases had been to collect the revenue as rigorously as possible and as much as possible. Based on the same profit policy, the defective and ever changing revenue administration of Warren Hastings ruined the princes and people, and zamindars and raiyats alike. Warren Hastings failed miserably in his revenue reforms. One of the charges in the impeachment of Hastings related to the arbitrary settlement of the land revenues.[36]

Administration of Justice

In contrast to his failures in revenue reforms, Warren Hastigs was more successful in organizing the administration of justice which had completely broken down with the decline of Moghul power, particularly after the battle of Plassey. His long experience in India had convinced him that 'if only original principles were observed the indigenous courts might well serve the purpose of Company's Government. At the same time recent developments of Zamindari-system had necessitated the reconstitution of the districts and establishment of regular courts of justice. For the 1772 reform, plans and procedures were provided by the General Regulations for the Administration of justice which were approved by the Governor-General-in-Council on 21 August, 1772.[37]

For the purpose of judicial as well as revenue administration, districts were constituted into Collectorships in the Diwani provinces of Bengal, Bihar and Orissa. In Bihar, Saran,

Champaran, Tirhut, Rohtas, Ramgarh, Monghyr, Bhagalpur, Rajmahal and Purnea were formed into such collectorships. In each collectorship two courts of law-Mofussil-Diwani Adalat, for Civil cases, and Mofussil Faujdari Adalat for criminal cases were created.[38] District Mofussil Diwani Adalats were to be presided over by the European Collector who held his Diwani Court twice a week and heard cases upto Rs. 500.[39] Criminal courts remained under the charge of the Nawab's officers. In Mofussil Faujdari Adalats of districts a Qazi and a Mufti assisted by two Maulavies were to try the criminal cases. But the European Collector was ordered to exercise a sort of general superintendence over their procedure, "so as to see that all necessary evidences are summarised and examined; that due weight is allowed to their testimony, and that the decision passed is fair and impartial according to the proofs exhibited in the course of the trial".[40] District Faujdari Adalats could award corporal punishment, fines, labour on roads, but they were not empowered to award capital punishment.[41]

Two superior courts of appeal and supervision for civil and criminal cases, namely, Sadar Diwani Adalat and Sadar Nizamat Adalat—were provided at Calcutta.[42] Sadar Diwani Adalat was presided over by the President and two members of his Council and assisted by Diwan of the Khalsa, the head Qanungo and others. Sadar Nizamat Adalat was held by Daroga-Adalat, a Chief Qazi, a head Mufti and three qualified Maulavies and was supervised by President himself till 1775 when the Court was transferred to Murshidabad.[43]

Muhammadan Judges were enlisted as regular judicial officers payable by Government, and 'the oppressive exactions under the head of fines and fees which had fed the revenue of the law officers, under the Moghal management were abolished.[44]

Changes in revenue administration in 1775 necessitated changes in administration of justice. European Collectors were to oversee revenue administration as well as Civil Justice. Six Provincial Council of Revenue at Calcutta, Burdwan, Murshidabad, Dacca, Dinajpur and Patna were established and a civil Court was attached to each of the six Provincial Councils for appeal from the Mufussil Courts, though final appeal still lay with the Governor-General-in-Council which acted as the Sadar Adalat. Sadar Nizamat Adalat was transferred from Calcutta to Murshidabad and placed under Muhammad Reza Khan.[45] Mohammad Reza Khan, with the approval of the Governor-General-in-Council, introduced a new scheme of Criminal Justice and police. Under this scheme 23 Faujdari Adalats were established, of which five were in Bihar, one each at Bhagalpur, Rajmahal, Kharagpur, Patna and Purnea.[46]

While Warren Hastings was engaged in improving the indigenous system of the administration of justice, the British Parliament by the Regulating Act of 1773, provided for a Supreme Court of judicature at Calcutta consisting of a Chief Justice and three other judges with full powers to exercise all civil, criminal, admiralty and ecclesiastical jurisdiction.[47] Ill defined powers and jurisdiction of the Supreme Court led to serious troubles which were removed by the Amending Act of 1781.[48]

Warren Hastings effected further changes in the administration of justice in April 1780. Improving on the Regulations of 1772 and 1775, Provincial Councils were deprived of judicial powers and six District Courts (Diwani Adalat) established within the jurisdiction of Provincial Councils and presided over by a covenanted servant of the Company, were invested with those powers. After the abolition of Provincial Councils in 1781, number of sub-district courts were increased to 18, of which 7 were in Bihar. They were located at Tajpur, Raghunathpur, Darbhanga, Lauriya, Patna, Chapra and Bhagalpur.[49] Convenanted servants of the Company presiding over these districts Courts exercised only the powers of judge and magistrate, and not of revenue collection. Thus was effected separation of civil justice from revenue collections. But in the four frontier districts, two in Bengal i.e. Islamabad (Chittagong), Rangpur, and two in Bihar i.e., Chatra (Hazaribagh) and Bhagalpur, for local reasons, the powers of Judge-Magistrate, and Collector were vested in the same person, but with a provision that the judicial authority should be considered distinct from and independent of revenue functions.[50]

Hastings professed to retain indigenous system of law and justice. But in reality he was responsible for many innovations. These related to subjects like the position of the judges, the jurisdiction of the courts, the procedure to be followed, barring fresh proceeding when a matter was already decided, invalidity of arbitration awards, abolition of certain judicial fees, creation of certain new offences, changes in punishments in which definite principles of English Law can be discerned.[51] Taking much from Shore's Minute of Feb.10, 1790, as a fail verdict on the administration of justice of Warren Hastings, Kaye observed: "As much had been done, as under all circumstances could have been reasonably expected ..... and imperfect as were these initial efforts, it is still apparent that the system which Warren Hastings introduced and the practice which he enforced, were great improvement upon those of Moghuls".[52]

Police Reforms

In the field of criminal administration and police, Warren Hastings, in the beginning, tried to follow the Moghul system and it was because of this that under his administration of justice criminal courts were left under the charge of Nawab's men. Mufussil Faujdari Adalats and Sadar Nizamat Adalat were presided over by Muhammadan Judges, with supervision respectively of European Collectors and the President in Council. In 1774 Warren Hastings planned to restore faujdari system by the establishment of fourteen thana as each under a faujdar.[53] In the wake of change in revenue administration in 1775, Nizamat was transferred from Calcutta to Murshidabad and Reza Khan was recalled as Naib Nazim. Early in 1776, Md. Reza Khan, with the approval of the Governor-General-in-Council, introduced a comprehensive scheme for police and criminal administration.[54] Under this scheme Faujdari thana as under Faujdar at important district towns with a number of inferior police 'Chaukies' under Thanadars were established. Bhagalpur, Rajmahal, Purnea and Patna were each provided with faujdari thana in Bihar. Whereas Patna was given 8 'Chaukies' and Purnea four, Sarkars of Saran, Champaran, Tirhut, Hazipur, Shahabad, Rohtas, Bihar and Munger were given one each.[55] But this Faujdari system of Md. Reza Khan proved a total failure owing chiefly to its inheret weakness and changed circumstances. Faujdars were quite weak before a hostile agent of the Company and quite corrupt under the corrupting influence of the time. According to contemporary historian Ghulam Hussain, Faujdars were incapable of performing the business expected of them, and their institution originally set up for the care of the subject had perverted into a scene of extortion and tyranny.[56] Consequently, Warren Hastings' revenue and judicial reforms in, 1780, were followed by police reforms in April, 1781.

On 6th April, 1781, the office of Faujdar and Thanadar were abolished and European judges of the Civil Courts were empowered to act as 'magistrate' also. In this new capacity they were to maintain law and order, apprehend criminals, and commit them to the Faujdari Adalats of their respective district.[57] The zamindars were also enjoined to perform their traditional duty of police work and to erect thanas in such places as shall be pointed out to them by the Magistrates.[58] To coordiniate the works of the Magistrates and Zamindars the post of the Remembrance of Criminal Courts was established.[59]

Although a successor to the Mughal Faujdar in the discharge of police and executive functions, the English Magistrate thus came to differ from the basic military character of his predecessor. Unlike a Faujdar, the English-Magistrate was essentially a civil functionary with no powers to command any fauj or military contingent. However, the reforms of 1781-82 made no provision for a local control as in the Mughal system.[60]

Fiscal Reforms

Hastings also took certain measures for fiscal and economic reforms for the growth of internal trade and commerce. He abolished the notorious 'dustuk' system and a uniform but reduced duty of 2 1/2 per cent on all goods, belonging either to the European or Indian merchants, was imposed. However, the Company retained the monopolies of Salt, Tobacco and Opium.[61] Rahadarry duty levied by Zamindars were declared illegal and only five central custom houses at Calcutta, Murshidabad, Hughli, Dacca and Patna, were maintained.[62] But J. Reginald Hand, after going through the correspondence of the period in Bihar, informs us that there were two custom houses in Bihar, one at Patna, and the other on the frontier at Chausa.[63] Hand gives us further interesting information that import duty levied by Government on all grains imported into the province of Bihar, was suspended from the 16th October, 1783 to 31st June, 1784, and reimposed on 1st July, 1784.[64] Economic reforms of Warren Hastings included the currency reforms. For maintaining uniform standard in weight and finance for the Sicca rupees, he closed the Patna Mint alongwith others to have only one Mint at Calcutta. Copper coins of four denominations were also issued. But it led to serious troubles due to over valuation. Hastings also proposed to issue paper currency which could not be given effect to. On the whole Hastings was 'singularly unsuccessful in all his currency reforms.[65]

Thus Hastings made 'strenuous and loyal endeavours',[66] but the fact remains uncontested that the whole system of government over which he presided was corrupt and full of abuses.[67] In conclusion, we may quote Romesh Dutta: From a man so gifted with powers of organisation and so rich in the knowledge of the country and its people, a high degree of administrative success would naturally be expected. Yet if the success of a government be judged by the happiness it confers on the people, the administration of Hastings was a ghastly failure.[68] Though the administration of Warren Hastings witnessed the consolidation of the British power and influences, it 'left behind it a dark trail of misery, insurrections and famines'.[69]

The Firm Foundation of the English Administration and Exclusion of the Natives : Administrative Changes in Bihar under Cornwallis and Subsequent Governors General

Pitt's India Act, Resignation of Warren Hastings and Macpherson as the Acting Governor-General

Affairs in India, particularly after the loss of American colonies engaged the attention of British Statesmen and thinkers. The vast territorial acquisitions of the East India Company yielding enormous annual revenue were sufficient to influence these people of a mercantile nation. Under the same consideration, Adam Smith thus denounced the working of the East India Company as a trader sovereign: "If the trading spirit of the East India Company renders them very bad sovereigns, the spirit of sovereignty seems to have rendered them equally bad traders.[70] The anxiety was expressed even in Westminster Hall. Dundas's proposed Bill on India, and Fox's India Bill were great denunciation of and stricture on the misrule of Warren Hastings and of his masters. Pitt's India Act of 1784[71] reflected the same criticism. Warren Hastings, though indignantly, understood the implications and resigned his office in early February, 1785. Delivering over the charge of his government to Mcpherson, he left for home. Pitt's India Act of 1784 (Act 24th, George III) placed the administration of the East India Company under the control of the Crown through the Board of control and compelled some reforms.

Changes Under Macpherson

John Macpherson, the acting Governor-General of Bengal (8th February 1785 to 12th Sept., 1786), as instructed by the Directors of the Company in their letter of 11th April, 1785[72] took some measures of economy effecting retrenchment in the civil service and military establishments. He also introduced certain reforms in revenue administration aiming at decentralization. "The division of the province into districts is the back bone of the whole system of reforms".[73] The office of provincial Diwans was abolished and districts were made fiscal units under the English Collectors who were made responsible for making the settlement and collection of revenues. As ordered by the Directors in their letter of 21st Sept., 1785,[74] further changes were made in the Central administration of revenue. By June 1786 the Committee of Revenue was reorganised as the Board of Revenue[75] which was empowered to control and advice the Collectors and sanction their settlements. The President of the Board of Revenue was to be a members of the Governor-General's Council. In July the office of the Chief Sheristadar was instituted to keep the revenue records bringing them from Kanungos to the government control, a measure long overdue, and no less calculated to protect the great body of people from the oppressions than to secure the full legal rights of the sovereign'.[76]

Amending Act of 1786 and Cornwallis as Governor-General

Nevertheless, the short administration of Macpherson was as corrupt as the previous one. Writing to Henry Dundas about the 'late Government', Lord Cornwallis remarked that 'the grossest frauds were daily committed before their faces'.[77] Sir John Shore was even more critical and he observed : "Never before was any administration so thoroughly despicable as his;

evasion was substituted for decision, caution and hesitation instead of action".[78] So, search was on for an upright and honest man of action as the Governor-General who could bring the government out of chaos and corruption and establish an orderly system of administration in India. Marquis Cornwallis was such 'an English nobleman of good parts, unsullied character, and extensive influence",[79] whose 'probity in financial matters was so high that it probably transcended that of all other politicians of his day.[80] But he had declined the offer till the Pitt's India Act was amended. Hence, the Amending Act of 1786[81] was passed to combine in his person both the office of the Governor-General and the Commander-in-Chief, and to empower him to override his Council.[82]

Cornwallis assumes Charge and Lays down the Firm Foundation of English Administration based on Racial Superiority and Class Exclusiveness

Lord Corwallis assumed the charge of his high office on 12th September, 1786. Though an English nobleman of high rank and high character, he had little knowledge and no experience of the Indian affairs. As such he brought a fresh mind to his new assignment having no regard at all for the past traditions or current usages in the Presidency.[83] Consequently, the Governor-Generalship of Lord Cornwallis was a period of momentous administrative changes which affected wholly the life and polity not only of the provinces of Bengal, Bihar and Orissa, but the whole of India. By his striking reforms, on the one hand he laid down the foundation of future administration and constitution of India, and on the other, 'brought India a stage nearer to incorporation in the overseas Empire of Britain.[84] At the same time 'it set in motion forces which ultimately led to the emergence of new India.[85]

Lord Cornwallis picked up the scattered fragments of government and reduced them to 'one comprehensive system'.[86] He sought to reform every branch of administration and to remove rampant corruption and abuses in the Company's government. In this sense early years of his administration have well been described 'as a period of remedy and seed time'. However, all his measures benefited more his country and the Company and less the native people. It was because they were limited in purpose. Though he had to work for 'the creation of an efficient administrative machinery' but such a machinery 'which would provide peace and dispense justice, repair the Company's finances ruined by corruption and misgovernment and achieve the ultimate aim of realising a regular surplus of revenue sufficient to purchase the annual investment of India piece goods and China trade'. And, above all, in establishing the system of administration in India, Cornwallis was guided by the 'aristocracy of the European model'. Cornwallis' distrust and low opinion of Indians grown out of his sense of racial superiority led to the Europeanisation of higher services whether military, civil or judicial. As a 'fundamental principle of the English to make the whole of Indian nation subservient in every possible ways, remarked Shore, 'the Indians were excluded from every honour, dignity or office'. But it was an unfortunate practice begun by Cornwallis, confirmed by the Charter Act of 1793, and followed by the subsequent Governors-General to the great detriment of Indians. Marshman candidly described it as an impolitic system which closed against Indian prospect of legitimate and honourable ambition.[87] To remove corruption and to purify the services, Cornwallis enhanced the salaries of the covenanted servants of the Company[88], which in course of time became and highest paid civil servants in the world with the heaviest burden on Indian Exchequer.

Reforms in the Deptt. of Commerce

As Cornwallis was determined to root out the corruption from the Company's administration, it was but natural that abuses in the commercial department of the Company engaged his attention first. His reforms in this field, though intended chiefly to promote the prosperity of the Company by substitution of the Agency-System in place of contract-system, a deviation approved by the Directors,[89] had indirect bearings on the people of the provinces, particularly on the manufacturers, weavers, and traders. The Commercial Residents, under the control of the Board of the Trade, were authorised to make 'investment' directly and they were to receive adequate commission on the 'investment passing through their heads.[90]

It was expected that under this system there would be no oppression on the native manufacturers. Under a Regulation passed on 23rd July, 1787 and confirmed by Regulation XXXI of 1793, the weavers were not to be prevented from undertaking the works other than that of the Company, provided they supplied goods for advances taken. Cornwallis, indeed, looked to the (Commercial) resident for the protection of Indian workers. They were also to set as useful barriers to the oppression of Zamindars and other revenue farmers, as they were in direct touch of the people.[91] But subsequent history of the province proved contrary to the wish of the Governor-General.[92]

Reforms in the Administration of Justice, Police and Revenue

Far more important, permanent and somewhat controversial, were those reforms which Cornwallis effected in the domain of the administration of justice, police and revenue.

Criminal Justice and Police

Under the new administrative scheme of Cornwallis introduced on 27th June, 1787, the Collector became all powerful, for the functions of revenue collection and management were re-united with the administration of justice. Excepting Dacca, Murshidabad and Patna, all the district courts were placed under the Collectors. The Collectors were made both Judge and Magistrate and were empowered to 'hear and determine' without any reference to the 'faujdari' (or native criminal) courts, all complaints or prosecution brought before him for petty offences, such as abusive language or calmuny, inconsiderable assaults or affrays, and to punish the same, when proved, by corporal punishment, and imprisonments than that above specified, he was to commit the offender to the nearest criminal courts. The Magistrate could even arrest the Zamindars and commit them to the criminal courts which still remained with the native agency under the authority of the Naib-Nazim. But Cornwallis thought it most unwise to 'leave the future control of so important a branch to the sole discretion of any Native'.[93]

It was, therefore, resolved by the Governor-General in Council to accept the Superintendence of criminal justice throughout the provinces.[94] As such, significant changes were effected in the administration of criminal justice.[95]

Muhammad Reza Khan was divested of his office of Naib Nazim and Sadar Nizamat Adalat was removed from

Murshidabad to Calcutta, and was placed under this Governor-General in Council who were to be assisted by Indian experts like qazi-ul-Qazat (Chief Qazi), and two Muftis. The Zillah Faujdari Adalats under the native Darogas were abolished, and in their place, four courts of circuits, one each at Calcutta, Murshidabad, Dacca and Patna, to be presided over by the two convenanted officers of the Company, styled as the Judges of the Courts of Circuits, and assisted by a Qazi and a Mufti, were established.[96] However, the decisions of the courts were to be regulated by the Muhammadan Law.

The policy of combining in Collectors the functions of revenue collection, Judge and Magistrate had failed to achieve the expected results. 'Such powers', observed Cornwallis, 'vested in an individual, and at a great distance from the seat of supreme control excites terror in the minds of the people, instead of inspiring confidence in its protection'.[97] To remedy this anomalous situation a great change was brought forth in the administration of justice in May, 1793. In the wake of the permanent Settlement a series of regulations which effected a complete separation of justice from the management of revenue, were issued.[98] By Regulation II of May, 1793 the Board of Revenue and the Collectors were deprived of their judicial and magisterial authority. Mal Adalats (revenue courts) of Collectors were abolished. Courts of judicature with civil and criminal jurisdiction under covenated (European) officers of the Company, higher in rank than the Collector and known as Judge-Magistrate, were established in every district. In all, 23 such district Courts of which seven, namely at Purnea, Bhagalpur, Ramgarh, Bihar (Gaya) proper, Shahabad, Saran and Tirhut, appertained to Bihar. Three city Courts, one each at Murshidabad, Dacca and Patna, were also provided.[99] The four courts of circuits established in 1793 for the Divisions of Calcutta, Dacca, Murshidabad and Patna were reorganised each with three European Judges.[100] Besides working as courts of circuits for the criminal justice, they were also to act as Courts of Appeal from District Courts: Sadar Diwani Adalat or Sadar Nizamat Adalat at Calcutta being the final court of appeal.[101]

Under Regulation II of 1793, Collectors and other officers of the government, and the Government itself in which it may be a party with its subjects, were made amenable to the courts of judicature for acts done in their official capacity.[102]

Though Warren Hastings had turned the merchants of the Company into Collectors and Cornwallis turned them into Judges, yet they were to be considered the first in importance in the civil service, and they were to be distinguished for their integrity, abilities, and knowledge of the manners, customs, and language of the natives, and their 'allowance were to be proportionate to the greatness of their trust'.[103]

Cornwallis sought to provide not only for better class of judges but also 'better class of Vakeels' by ensuring the possession of some measures of qualification for the office which they understood, and by subjecting them to due control.[104] Regulation VII of 1793 laid down that Vakeels (pleaders) were to be appointed from amongst the graduates of Calcutta Madarsa and Benaras Sanskrit College. If sufficient number of candidates were not supplied by these institutions, 'men of character and liberal education might be appointed by the Judges'.[105] Thus, pleading was made a distinct profession to be undertaken by persons so authorised by the Sadar Diwani Adalat. Nevertheless, the scheme of Cornwallis failed to bring about any major change in the personnel of pleaders immediately.[106]

Police Reforms

Police system of Warren Hastings did not work well. Zamindars and Farmers of Revenue who were entrusted with the police-work, proved to be means of tyranny instead of protection. Magistrates, too, were incapable under the system.[107] As such reforms of Cornwallis effected a radical change in the police administration. In December, 1792, the Government undertook the police-work directly into its own hands.[108] The Rules of 1792 further amended by Regulation XXII of 1793 placed the police of the country 'under the exclusive charges of the officers appointed to the superintendence of it on the part of the Government'.[109] Police establishments of Zamindars and Revenue farmers were disbanded. Districts were divided into police "Thanas", each under the charge of a 'Daroga' with adequate staff appointed by the 'Magistrate on a fixed salary. The Daroga was to apprehended the criminals and commit them to the Magistrate under 24 hours of arrest. Chaukidars, Pasbans, and Dusadhs of the rural police were all to work under the Daroga.[110] In fact, the Daroga system of Cornwallis represented the might of the Government in rural areas and removed the danger of rebellion by the Zamindars who were deprived of their right of sovereignty.

The Code of Cornwallis, though based on racial discrimination, laid down the foundation in this country of government by written laws and regulations in place of personal rule of the monarch'.[111] However, underlying principle of the Cornwallis Code to exclude the natives from the higher posts of trust, responsibility, and dignity which were reserved for the Englishmen of the covenanted service, led to the degeneration and debasement of the people of the provinces. 'And as the character of the Englishmen', rightly observed J.W. Kaye, 'as administrators continued to improve, the debasement of the natives became more complete'.[112]

The Revenue Reforms

The Permanent Settlement

The most important as well as the most controversial of all these reforms associated with the name of Cornwallis, is the Permanent Settlement of Land Revenue in the provinces of Bengal and Bihar, a measures of far-reaching consequences, highly acclaimed and equally denounced from its very inception to this day.

The mode of revenue collection of Warren Hastings had "proved fallacious to the Company and ruinous of the country.[113] Commenting on the revenue system of Hastings, Kaye has rightly observed that "while the Government had been great losers under the system, it has benefited no class of community."[114] As a matter of fact, ever increasing demand in revenue and frequent changes in settlement had ruined the Zamindars and raiyats alike, and it has been equally bad for the new sovereigns, for it had made the flow of revenue uncertain and the Zamindars rebellious. Though the English had overcome the challenge posed by the revolt of Raja Chait Singh of Benaras, yet it had assumed wider dimensions after the disaffected Zamindars of Bihar grieved by the revenue policy of Hastings had espoused the cause of Raja Chait Singh. The episode must be fresh in the minds of the alien administrators while deciding the course of future policy, particularly the revenue policy. In fact, the revolt of Raja Chait Singh and its wide repercussions caused by the large scale participation of the landed aristocracy in Bihar,[115] were in no small measure responsible for hastening the Permanent Settlement of lands with the Zamindars in the provinces of Bengal and Bihar, which was later on extended to Benaras. It was not without reasons that Pitt's India Act (Section 39) ordered an 'enquiry into the complaints of the dispossessed Zamindars', and directed the Company to establish permanent rules by which 'Tributes Rents and Services should be in future' rendered and paid to the United Company by the Rajas, Zamindars, Polygars, Talookdars and other land holders'.[116] Accordingly, the Court of Directors in their dispatch of 12th April, 1786, wrote to their Governor-General in Council at Fort William in Bengal that 'a moderate jummeh (assessment) if regularly and punctually collected unites the consideration of our interest with the happiness of the natives and security of the land-holders more rationally than only imperfect collection of an exaggerated jummah to be enforced with severity and vexation'. As such they authorised the Bengal Government for fixing a permanent 'jummah' to be considered as the permanent and unalterable.[117] The Directors also instructed 'the settlement to be made in every practicable instance with Zamindars' wherein they conceived to be the true spirit of the 39th section of the Act 24th of George III.[118] The Directors further directed the Government of Bengal to make forthwith the settlement for a period of ten years and to make it permanent on their approval, if the arrangement proved satisfactory.[119]

Cornwallis, however, deferred the decennial settlement, continuing the annual one till 1789, with a view to obtain sufficient information about all aspects of the land revenue system in Bengal and Bihar.[120] The Decennial settlement with Zamindars and other landholders, with a promise to make it perpetual on approbation of the Home Government, was announced by a proclamation on 10th February, 1790. The Court of Directors adopted the measure after a great deal of deliberation and sent their authorisation in their Dispatch of 19th Sept., 1792.[121] Accordingly, the ten years 'Settlement was declared' to be permanent by a proclamation of 22nd March, 1993.

The Permanent Settlement was thus made with the Zamindars who became independent proprietors of land and their revenue was fixed in perpetuity.[122] In Bihar there were only four principal Zamindars, those of Sannout, Tirhoot, Shahabad and Champaran. Remaining Zamindars were in number some thousand.[123] They included Zamindars, Talukdars, Choudharies, Mukarraridars and Mils.[124] Rules and Regulations were framed to effect the Decennial and Permanent Settlement. They were all incorporated in the famous 1793 Code of Cornwallis.

Regulations I of 1793 effected the Permanent Settlement which laid down "Jumma assessed on lands of actual proprietors with whom a settlement has been concluded, is accordingly declared fixed in perpetuity".[125] Regulation II of 1793 provided: 'Zamindars are privileged to transfer to whomsoever they may think proper, by sale, gift or otherwise their proprietary rights in the whole or any part of their respective estates without applying to Government for its sanction to the transfer; and that all such transfers will be held valid, provided that they be conformable to the Muhammadan or Hindu Law'.[126] However, the Zamindars and other landholders could be imprisoned and their property attached if they fell in arrears.[127] Regulation III of 1794 laid down more clearly that on failure to pay the revenue instalment, a part or whole of the estate of the defaulting Zamindar could be sold[128] to secure the arrears. At the same time, powers, functions and jurisdictions of the revenue authorities like the Collectors and the Board of Revenue[129]were defined.

The settlement rules of 1789-93 laid down separate principles of assessment for Bengal, for Bihar, and for Orissa, In Bihar, the standard was to be the average produce of land in any ordinary year. Regulation VIII of 1793 (Sections 49-51) provided that if any land had paid the same revenue for twelve years past, that was to be accepted as the settlement rate and was not to be increased. In other cases average produce of the land and prevailing rates of jumma were to form the basis of assessment.[130] Further, to afford security to the tenants and raiyats, the system of granting 'Pattas' (written declaratory leases) to them by the Zamindars, was devised and the Zamindar were enjoined not to take more rent from the tenants and raiyats what was agreed upon in the 'Patta'.[131]

Zamindars were also enjoined to effect improvement in agriculture by 'increasing the number of reservoirs, embankments and other artificial works', so that adequate supplies of grain might be available 'in seasons of scarcity' and famines.[132]

The Results

The Permanent Settlement secured immense financial gains and invaluable political advantages to the Company. The land revenue was settled at the highest point ever reached in which the share of the government was fixed at 89 per cent of the estimated 'jumma' leaving only 11 per cent to the Zamindars.[132] It ensured the Company sufficient, fixed and uninterrupted flow of revenue for its 'investments, wars and other expenses of the Government'.[133] If economic gains of the Permanent Settlement for the Company were great, the political advantages were greater. It turned, as was intended by Cornwallis, into solid supporters to the British interests and power in this part of the world',[134] atleast that class of powerful Zaminedars who wielded a sort of political power and sovereignty in their Zamindari, and who had always been refractory' and rebellious providing leadership to the people during disturbances. 'Looking at it solely from political point of view', rightly remarked Seton Karr, 'it was the means of allaying apprehensions and removing doubts, while it proved strong incentive to good behaviour, and something beyond passive loyalty in seditious and troubleous times'.[135] Dr. Tara Chand found in the Permanent Settlement a bargain with Zamindars by which the political power was taken away from them (Zamindars), and in return, they were endowed with unlimited powers of ownership of land. Explaining the point further he says: 'Henceforth two parties to the bargain settled down to a period of peaceful cooperation, one exercising the political authority, the other economic powers, and both preying upon and oppressing the tiller of the soil'.[136] It was all in this background that during the great revolt of 1857, many of the rajas in Bihar, like the Rajas of Deo Estate in Gaya, Hathuwa, Bettiah, Doomraon and Darbhanga, and Zamindars of Sursand, Pandaul and a host of others, sided with the Government.[137]

However, exorbitantly increased assessment and the sale-law sometimes adversely affected the two bargaining parties, marring the peaceful cooperation between them. The sale-law not only reduced the size of hundreds of Zamindaries in Bengal and Bihar in course of twenty two years time, but also unsettled and ruined one third of the defaulting Zamindars while realising arrears of revenue from them.[138] Pointing out to this aspect of the evil effects of the sale law, Earl of Moira had observed: 'The sales of land which violate the rights of whole communities, are much more productive of the ruin of the landed interest and contribute much more to drive the class of proprietors to act of desperation'.[139]

As a matter of fact, the effects of the Permanent Settlement were far-reaching. It changed the structure of society by destroying the village-community, creating new social classes and establishing new property relations. It was hoped by Cornwallis that the fixed state-demand would 'restore this country to a state of prosperity' and render our subjects the happiest possible in India'.[140] But its results and facts pointed to the contrary. According to the Fifth Report of the Finance Committee of Bengal the Permanent Settlement had produced more distress and beggary, and a greater change in the landed property of Bengal than had happened in the same space of time in any other age or country by the mere effect of internal regulation.[141]

Though the Permanent Settlement affected all classes of community, the cultivators were the worst sufferers. Its immediate effect on them were lamentable, for they were left at the mercy of the Zamindars. Sir John Shore, the chief exponent of the Settlement, had made it clear that the regulation of the rents of the raiyats was properly a transaction between the Zamindars and landlord and his tenant and not of Government.[142] It was because of this that led the Finance Committee of 1830 to remark in its report of 12th July, 1830, that in the permanently settled districts of Bengal nothing was settled and little was known except the Government assessment.[143] The result was obvious. The Zamindars, except in a few special cases, exacted from the raiyats as much as they could be made to pay, and there was no doubt that what was left to the actual cultivators after all these extractions, was little more than sufficed to keep souls and bodies together.[144] Though the systerm of granting 'Pattas' (declaratory leases) to the cultivators was planned to safeguard their interest, but in actual operation it proved to be a 'pious wish' and 'futile'.[145] On the issue of granting 'Pattas', the Zamindars in the various districts of Bihar acted and reacted differently, in most cases their attitude being unfavourable to the raiyats.[146] In fact, 'it was decreed', rightly observed Kaye, 'indeed, that the ryots had no rights, and he was left to fight it out with the Zamindars'.[147] But he was too weak against the Zamindar, and the courts of law were beyond the reach and means of the raiyats. Armed with Regulation IV of 1794 the Zamindars were able to 'claim any rates they pleased'.[148] Consequently, illegal exactions of Zamindars went on unabated. The fact led the Finance Committee of 1880 to report that the rent of the raiyats in Bihar had during the last fifty years been illegally and arbitrarily enhanced out of all proportions. The whole condition of the agricultural industry were such as to render it precarious.[149]

The Permanent Settlement opened the flood-gate of fraud, money making, corruption and litigations[150] which brought distress, beggared the people and viciated the age-old cordial and harmonious atmosphere in the society. The settlement had left ample scope for conflicting rights and claims of Zamindars and tenants. Civil suits relating to the rent payment were brought before the Court in such an alarming number that they remained pending for years. By the year 1798 such five thousand cases were pending in the Provincial Court of Appeal for the division of Patna alone.[151]

Administrative Changes After Cornwallis

The 1793 Code of Cornwallis, covering all branches of administration, was all comprehensive but not all perfect. Working of the Cornwallis code revealed its weaknesses, "yet even this greatest reverence could not hide the defects of the code, nor the utmost piety avoid some attempt to correct them.[152] To remedy the defects several changes were made in almost all branches of administration during the periods of subsequent Governors General who were, too a great extent, influenced by the political ideas and thought current in their country. In some branches of administration changes were so considerable that they almost modified the Cronwallis code, though basic structure remained there. Even in other areas of administration, principles of Cornwallis system were challenged and repudiated. As early as 1799 Wellesly wrote to the Directors: It is a radical imperfection in the constitution of our establishment in India, that no system appears to have been adopted with a view either to conciliate the goodwill or to control the disaffection of this description of our subjects, whom we found in possession of the Government, and whom we have excluded from all shares of emoluments, honour and authority, without providing any adequate corrective of those passions incident to the loss of dignity, wealth and power.[153] Such able officers like Munro[154], Elphinston,[155] and Malcolm[156] were no less critical of Cornwalis system.

Changes in Land-Revenue Administration

It would be advisable, from the point of importance, to start with changes in land revenue administration, for reforms, in other branches of administration followed as a natural corollary.

The working of the Permanent Settlement had brought to the face glaring evils of the Settlement. It had resulted in great increase in litigation and crime.

The powers of the Zamindars under the Permanent Settlement, augmented by the Regulation IV of the 1794, and the "monstrous provisions of Regulation VII of 1799,[157] had increased so much that it was deemed necessary to control them by bringing organisational changes in revenue administration through decentralization, and by removing defects in the existing regulations.

The Regulation X of 1807 and Regulation I of 1809 provided for a Board of Commissioners with general power of supervision and control for upper provinces. The Regulation XIII of 1811 authorised that individual members of Board of Revenue with all the powers of Board vested in them, be deputed in outlying districts to supervise revenue settlement and works of the revenue officials. By the Regulation V of 1812 the abuses in the system of granting 'pattas' (declaratory leases) were removed. The Regulation gave greater protection to the raiyats in matters of destraint on account of arrears of rent, and against enhancement of rent increases where land passed into the hands of new purchaser.[158] But the radical changes in revenue administration had to wait till the passing of the Charter Act of 1813 when " the unhesitating acquiescence in the Cornwallis system ended".[159]

Changes in Administration of Justice and Police after Cornwallis

Cornwallis system of justice and police equally needed reforms. The Permanent Settlement and the Sale-Law had resulted in phenomenal increase in litigations and huge files of pending cases.[160] To prevent increase in litigations fees were reimposed on registering suits[161] and to reduce the number of pending cases the number of Judges and the powers of Courts were increased.[162]

Under Regulations of 1794-95 and 1797 the number of the judges of the Provincial Courts of Appeal was increased from three to four and provision was made that appeals could be heard by the Provincial Courts of Appeals even when some of their judges were on circuit.[163] The powers of the Provincial Courts of Appeal were also increased. Now they could hear appeals to the extent of Rs. 5000[164]. Their power was further enhanced in 1808 under Regulation XIII. It was provided that all cases ultimately appealable to the Sadar Diwani Adalat (Suits above 5,000 rupees) could be instituted in the Provincial Court of Appeal.[165] The powers of the Single Judge of Provincial Courts and Sadar Court were further augmented by Regulation 13 of 1810.[166]

By Regulation II of 1801 the Sadar Diwani Adalat and Sadar Nizamat Adalat were reconstituted. As suggested by Wellesley, the Governor-General and his council discontinued to work as their judges, for it was "essentially necessary to the impartial, prompt and efficient administration of justice, and to the permanent security of the persons and properties of the native inhabitants of these provinces that the Governor-General in Council, exercising the supreme legislative and executive authority of the state should administer the judicial functions of the Government by the means of the Courts of justice distinct from the legislative and executive authority of the state".[167] The Sadar Adalats were now to be presided over by a

Chief Judge (still a member of the Council) and two puisne judges appointed from the covenanted servants of the Company. The reorganisation was effected in 1805, and the number of judges was raised to four including the Chief Judge.[168]

Under Regulation 49 of 1803 the Sadar Diwani Adalat was empowered to appoint Sadar Amins in every District and City with 0powers to try property cases up to the value of Rs. 100.

Criminal Justice and Police

Reforms were also effected in the administration of criminal justice.[169] The powers of the Magistrates were enhanced with a view to suppress crime and to give relief to the prisones. By 1807, Magistrate were empowered to punish crimes by imprisonment for a maximum period of one year.[170] In 1810, they were given powers of release the prisoners on bail pending his trial.[171] Provisions were also made for the appointment of Joint and Assistant Magistrates for the quick disposal of criminal cases.[172]

The Police system of Cornwallis proved to be an extensive failure.[173] It failed to give protection to the person and property of the people. Reports from Tirhut and Bhagalpur indicated that robberies had increased greatly.[174] Darogas under the Cornwallis system were as corrupt as their predecessors.[175] Moreover, Darogas were quite incapable to manage the powerful Zamindars and extensive territorial jurisdiction.[176] To remove these defects reforms were effected in police administration. In 1807 Police Amins were appointed to assist the Daroga and to conduct investigation against them.[177] But the office of the Police Amin was abolished in 1810 by Regulation VI of that year. In the meantime the Police Superintendent was appointed for the divisions of Calcutta, Dacca and Murshidabad to coordinate and supervise the works of Magistrates.[178] His authority was extended to the division of Patna in 1810.[179] At the same time powers of the police were enhanced by Regulation IX of 1808. Under the provisions of the Regulation Zamindars and other landholders could be imprisoned on mere suspicion of being negligent of their duty or being in connivance with robbers. Any resistance to the warrant by police was declared to be a crime.

Reorganisation of the Chaukidari System

Under the changed circumstances need was felt to reorganise the Chaukidari or the subsidiary rural police system as an official police organ beyond the control of the Zamindars. William Blunt, the Superintendent of Police of the Lower Provinces, formulated an experiment in Murshidabad on the lines of one successfully operating in the city of Benaras. He submitted to the Government in October, 1812, his draft of a regulation as a general plan of the new chaukidari system.[180] Under the scheme Chaukidars were to be appointed on a monthly salary of Rs. 3/- from a fund raised through contributions by the community for its own benefit and protection[181] under the supervision of the Magistrate. No regulation was passed immediately but the system allowed to be introduced in Patna (Bihar) after Murshidabad and Dacca.[182] Subsequently, the new Chaukidari system was formally effected by Regulation XIII of 1813, just before the arrival of Lord Moira.

Sweeping Reforms and Indianisation of Lower Service: Administrative Changes from Moira to Bentinck

The arrival in India of Lord Hastings (Moira) as the Governor-General of Bengal coincided with the passing of the Charter Act of 1813. Though this Act did not make any substantial change in the constitution either of the Home-Govt. or of the Company's Govt. in India, it was significant in many respects. Discussions, investigations and reports preceding the passing of the Charter Act of 1813, and its passage and provisions, were indicative not only of definite liberal trend in British political thinking towards the polity and people in India, but it also ushered in an era of Utilitarian liberalism and reforms in England as well as in India.[183] By abolishing the monopoly of the Indian trade of the East India Company, the Charter Act of 1813, diminished its commercial interests and compelled the Company to give more and more attention to the administration and well-being of the people of India. One of the select committees of the House of Commons appointed to look into the affairs of the East India Company did its work so well that its Fifth report in 1812 is the standard authority on the judicial and police arrangements then in force and on land tenures.[184] Consequently, the Court of Director sent its famous Dispatch on the 9th Nov., 1814.[185] Accordingly, revolutionary measures were adopted. Considerable and significant changes making a distinct break from the established tradition in politics and administration[186] were affected in the administrative system of British India during the period (from Lord Hastings to Lord William Bentinck) under review. However, till the assumption of office in 1827, by Lord William Bentinck, the attitude of the Govt. of India in several respects was more conservative than that of the authorities at home.[187]

Reforms in the Field of Judicial Administration (Civil Justice): Indianisation of Judicial Service begins under Moira

The Cornwallis system of land revenue administration and virtual exclusion of Indians from any respectable share in the administration of justice head resulted in the heavy load on the superior courts manned by the European judges. Hence, this policy of Cornwallis was modified under the instructions from the Court of Director[188] during the period of Lord Hastings. With a view to improve the efficiency of the judicial machinery and to remove the congestion in the business of the Court, and delay in justice and to add to the respectability of Indians, more and more native officers with additional powers were associated with the administration of civil justice.[189] In 1814, every Thana was provided with a Munsiff with definite judicial functions.[190] They were to be appointed or removed by the Provincial Court of Appeal on the recommendation of Zillah and City Judges. Selection was to be made normally by considerations of fitness, with a preference for Pargannah Qazis who were all Muslims. The Munsiff could try cases upto the value of Rs. 64/- instead of previous amount of Rs. 50. In some cases of local civil suits, they were empowered with original jurisdiction. In addition to judicial duties, they could be employed by Zillah and City Judges for investigating the question of local rights and usages. Thus Munsiff's powers and functions were further extended.[191] Likewise, under the same Regulation, Sadar Amins with enhanced powers and status, were to be appointed for every district of big cities, their number depending on the requirement of the area. They could try original suits for money and personal property to the value of Rs. 150.[192] On reference Sadar Amins could hear appeal from the Court of Munsiffs. Appeals from their

Courts could be made in the courts of superior European Judges. However, Munsiffs and Sadar Amins enjoyed no power to try cases of European or Americans.[193] Powers and status of Sadar Amins and Munsiffs were further raised in 1821. Their numerical strength could also be increased. Sadar Amin's power of cognizance was now extended to the value of Rs. 500 and that of Munsiff's to Rs. 150.[194]

A Temporary Set Back

Increasing use of Native Officers in the administration of justice received a temporary set back on the departure of Lord Hastings. John Adams who assumed the charge of Supreme Government in January, 1823 revived the policy of Europeanisation of judicial service in the name of efficiency. But the inadequacy of the Company's Civil Service stood in the way. This resulted in the pending of civil suits in large number which stood in Purnea at 1,667 and in Tirhut 3,168.[195] As a measure of relief the separation of the office of Magistrate and Judge was suggested so that the Judge could devote his time and energy exclusively to the disposal of civil suits. In fact, Lord Hastings had given serious consideration to the idea as early as 1815. However, it was in 1823, that the office of Judge and Magistrate was separated in the districts of Jungle Mahals, Purnea and Tirhut in Bihar, alongwith Hughli, Jessors and Nadia in Bengal.

Augmentation Again

With the assumption of office by Lord Amherst as the Governor-General of Bengal, the policy of Adams was reconsired and the use of native agency in the judicial service was again augmented with increased powers and perks. By a Regulation of 22nd July 1824, Sadar Amins were empowered to execute their own decrees as well as those of Munsiff's. Besides Sadar Amins could now try suits upto the value of Rs. 500. At the same time, instead of fees or stamp duties in suits, he began to receive a fixed allowance and establishment cost.[196] However, no provision was made for the increase in powers or number of Munsiffs. With the result that their number was quite inadequate, for example in the districts of Saran and Champaran there were only 8 Munsiffs for 15 thanas.[197] Nevertheless, the Directors were decidedly in favour not only of increasing the number and powers of 'these functionaries', but also granting 'them adequate allowances'[198] The Zillah and City Judges also in their reports on the state of administration under Munsiffs held similar views. A judge from Patna Division even observed that Munsiffs generally looked "more to the respectability of the office than to emoluments derived from them".[199] Judges of the Sadar Diwani Adalat including the Chief Judge stood for the extension of powers and status of native judicial officers.[200] However, further effective measures in this regard had to wait for Lord William Bentinck.

Sweeping Reforms Under Bentinck

Lord William Cavendish Bentinck, a typical representative of a new spirit of the liberal era in England, assumed in July, 1828, the charge of Company's Government in India in the wake of a great financial crisis[201] due to wars during the period of Lord Hastings and Lord Amherst. Ironically enough, there was the expediency of economy on the one hand, and on the other, the Directors wanted to present a good picture of liberal reforms in India to win the renewal of their Charter in 1833. The new spirit in the internal administration of India showed itself in two ways which often came into conflict. On the one hand, there was a far more respectful study and appreciation of Indian laws and customs as had been shown since the time of Warren Hastings, alongside ...... was an equally strong conviction that it was the duty of the British Government to introduce into India the best result of the Western activities.[202] It was in this background that sweeping reforms in society, administration, and education were introduced during the period of Lord William Bentinck.

Progressive Indianisation of Judicial Service Under Bentinck

It was but natural that the progressive Indianisation of Judicial service 'to secure a prompt administration of justice to the natives of India in civil cases as was instructed by the Court of Directors in their Dispatch of 23rd July, 1824, began with Bentinck. It also confirmed the policy of economy as well as sound principles of administration. The Civil Finance Committee appointed by the Governor General in November 1828 to suggest ways and means for economy in administration, in their Report of 12th July, 1830, also recommended the increased use of Indian Officers in judicial service under the superintendence of European Judges.[203] However, the Committee was not in favour of Indianisation of Executive and Magistracy.[204] Final reforms, as proposed by Butterworth Bayley in his Minute of 5th Nove., 1829, took shape in Regulation V of 1831 under which the office of the Registrar was abolished and that of Principal, Sadar Ameen was established. Indian judicial officers, viz., Munsiffs, Sadar Amins and Principal Sadar Amins, were now privileged with enlarged powers and higher salaries.[205] However, European Judges were authorised to regulate their proceedings, as also to report on their conduct and ability to the native agency and propriety of declaring 'all natives of India eligible to the judicial office received the approval and appreciation of the Court of Directors.[206] Thus, the opening of the judicial service to all Indians irrespective of their religious persuasion signified in practice the end of virtual monopoly which the Muslims enjoyed in the legal profession of the country under the Mughals and under the early administration of the East India Company.

Restoration of Certain Judicial Powers to Collectors

The period under review also saw some of the Judicial powers being transferred to Collectors with a view to relieve pressure of business in civil courts. The Collector was empowered in 1817 to use summary process with powers to arrest in realising the arrears of rent, though cognizance of such suits still remained vested in the Zillah (Distt.) and City Judges.[207] The successful implementation of Regulation VII of 1822 in the Western provinces investing the Collectors with powers to determine suits relating to irrigation, boundaries, crops and other local rights prompted the Government in 1825 to extend the provisions of this Regulation to the Collectors of Khas Mahals, Sundarbans and other areas such as the Hill lands of Bhagalpur.[208] The need was felt even before this to empower the Collectors with authority to hear, investigate and determine by summary process and subject to a regular suit in the civil court, all suits, claims, demands of rent, arrears or exaction of rent, between landholders or farmers of land, and their under-tenants, or between any other persons concerned in the receipts and payment of the land rents.[209] Regulation XIV of 1824 largely fulfilled these objectives. However, the revenue suits were still required to be instituted in the civil courts and the power to execute decree also remained vested in the Judge. Regulation VII of 1831, and Regulation VII of 1832 removed these anomalies on the lines suggested by Bayley in his Minute of 5 Nove. 1829.[210]

Separation of Judiciary and Magistracy

The office of Magistrate and Judge united in 1781, continued to be so during the period of Cornwallis and that of subsequent Governors-General. But large number of pending civil suits in the courts after the Permanent Settlement in the three provinces compelled the Government to reconsider the scheme. The separation of office of Magistrate and Judge had become necessary to spare the Judge to devote his time and energy exclusively to the disposal of civil suits. Though Lord Hastings had given serious consideration to the idea as early as 1815, yet it was in 1823 that the office of Magistrate was separated from Judge, and transferred to Collector in the districts of Jungle Mahals, Ramgarh, Purnea and Tirhut in Bihar, alongwith Hughly, Jessore and Nadia in Bengal.[211] Nevertheless, this separation could not be extended to other districts immediately due to inadequacy of covenanted servants. But 'on Bentinck's accession to Government this principle found general support' and by July, 1832, the arrangement was extended to the districts of Bhagalpur and Shahabad in Bihar alongwith Rajshahi, Sylhat, Cuttack, Benaras, Gorakhpur, Allahabad and Fatehpur.[212] As a matter of fact, circumstances and factors were also working in the same direction. In 1831, Sessions work of Divisional Commissioners of Revenue and Circuit, created under Regulation 1 of 1829, had to be transferred to the District Civil Judges, who, in turn, were divested of their Magisterial duties[213] which were made over to Collectors of Revenue. Thus, District Judges became Civil as well as Sessions Judges, and Collector became Magistrate as well'.

District and City Courts

Increasing Indianisation of judicial service necessited the change in the constitution and powers of District and City Courts presided by European Judges. With gradual increase in the powers of Indian Judicial Officers, there was proportionate rise in the powers of Indian Judicial Officers, there was proportionate rise in the powers of European Officers. A Regulation of 1814 increased the cognizance of District and City Courts to Rs. 5000[214] which was extended to Rs. 10,000 in 1817. With the abolition of the Provincial Courts of Appeal from 1831 to 1833, the jurisdiction of the District and City Courts became unlimited.[215] However, appeal could be made to the Sadar Diwani Adalat which also witnessed changes in its constitution and powers.[216]

The Beginning of Jury-system

With a view to exempt the non-Muslims from the operation of Muhammad Law, the District and City Judges were permitted to deliver their judgements, both in civil and criminal suits, independent of Indian law officers under them, obtaining the assistance of respectable Indians as 'Panchs', assessors and jurors.[217] Thus, a beginning was made in India of the Jury-system.

Criminal Justice and Police

Lord Moira initiated sweeping reforms in the domain of administration which anticipated the works of Bentinck. Steps had been taken, just before his arrival, to reorganise the rural police (Chaukidari) system. But Hastings was against the proposed extension of the regular stipendiary police beyond the establishment of Darogas. He was of the opinion that the chaukidari-system should arise out of the society and be subservient to it, and if the chaukidars were made stipendiary servants of Government they would behave as masters of the people and that an authority would be established pregnant with the most odious tyranny'.[218] As such he allowed to extend the provisions of Regulations XIII of 1813 only to the district headquarters of all the magistrate. In the division of Patna alongwith the divisions of Murshidabad and Dacca, it was affected in February, 1814.[219] Incorporating all these ideas and modifications, the reorganisation of chaukidari system was completed by Regulation XXII of 1816. While one of the modifications extended the chaukidari establishment to the headquarters of the Joint-Magistratte, the other abolished the power of the community to elect its own Panchayat.[220]

Police Darogas

Steps were also taken to reorganise the official police. Regulation XX of 1817, regarded as the first police manual, defined the powers and duties of the Police 'Darogas' incorporating all their previous rules regulations and enactments concerning them. Districts were divided into several thanas or police stations. Each thana was provided with one 'Daroga', one 'Munshi' or writer, one 'Jamadar', one Sergeant and nearly twelve armed constables. The Daroga was to keep an eye on all the villages and village watchmen of his thana, and had to send a monthly report to the Magistrate. Power of Daroga regarding simple thefts and burglaries underwent certain modifications after Regulation XI of 1832.[221]

Increase in the Power of Magistrate

The period witnessed an increase in the authority of the Magistrate over Police Darogas, Kotwals, Jailors and subordinate staff of criminal jails. The magistrate now had wide powers of appointment, transfer, suspension or dismissal of these officers.[222]

Considerations of economy and efficiency demands decentralisation in the constitution of courts, hence, increase in the powers of the Magistrate's court. Under Regulation XII of 1818, the consonance of his court was extended to burglary and theft, to buying and receiving stolen property, and escaping from jails and other places of cofinement. In 1831, the Magistrates discretionary authority increased considerably even in the commitment of heinous crimes.[223]

Native Agency and the Criminal Justice

Though the Directors had recommended 'liberal' admixer of native with European authority in the magistrial department of police as in the other departments of civil administration,[224] their representatives in India were unwilling to associate natives in the administration of criminal justice. As a matter of fact, the principles of Cornwallis here died hard.[225] And as such, Indian judicial Officers were allowed limited powers in 1821 to the effect that the (European) Magistrates and Joint-Magistrates were authorised to refer the trial of petty offences and simple thefts to the Law Officers as well as Sadar Amins appointed under Regulation II of 1821.[226] And, in 1832, their power of sentence was extended from one month and 30 rattans to hard labour.[227]

Divisional Commissioners of Revenue and Circuit as (Criminal) Judges of Circuit and Superintendent of Police

Provincial Courts of Appeal and Circuit erected by Cornwalis and Barlow for the six divisions of Calcutta, Murshidabad, Dacca, Patna, Benaras and Barailli had sunk very low and become 'woefully inefficient'[228] with the passage of time. Bentinck found them "as resting places for those members of the service who were deemed unfit for higher responsibilities."[229] At the same time "as the courts of Circuits, they were especially defective". The period between confinement and trial was infinitely too long. The prisoner was kept, unjustly perhaps, for months in confinement. Any measure to increase the 'goal deliveries could not fail to be blessing to the people'.[230] Hence, Bentinck abolished these Provincial Courts of Appeal, and uniting efficiency with economy,[231] transferred their circuit duties to 20 Divisional Commissioners of Revenue and Circuit established under Regulation I of 1829.[232] Commissioners of Revenue and Circuit were to hold Sessions of jail-delivery twice in a year in each district and general delivery for any of the cities and districts under his jurisdiction, whenever required or instructed by the Sadar Nizamat Adalat.[233] All the functions and powers of the Superintendent of Police[234] were also vested in him, rescinding the Regulation XX of 1808 and Regulation VIII of 1810.[235] The office of the two Superintendents were abolished. Thus, Magistracy, Police, Collectors and other executive officers were all brought under his control and Superintence for which he was to visit frequently all parts of his jurisdiction.[236]

'It was', rightly remarked J.W. Kaye, 'a great thing to increase the number of goal-deliveries, but it was not necessary to this end that the functions of the judge and tax gatherer should again be combined in the same person'. Revenue Commissioners were turned into Judges of Circuit who were to superintend both the finance and the criminal justice of their different divisions. 'They were to look after the Company's coin and they were to sit in judgement upon gang-robberies a blending of Somersat House and the old Bailey'.[237]

Distt. Civil-Judges also as Sessions-Judges

Multiple Union of offices in the Divisional Commissioners

of Revenue and Circuit, naturally, affected adversely the efficiency in all the branches of administration over which the Commissioner presided. The fact was realised soon. And, as a remedy, the sessions duties with provision of monthly jail-delivery began to be transferred from 1831 to the District Civil-Judges[238] who, thus, also became Sessions-Judges. The process was completed in 1835, when the Government was empowered to transfer any part or the whole of the duties connected with the criminal justice from any Commissioners of Circuit to any Session-judges and to define the powers-which shall be exercised by each respectively.[239] However, powers were not defined till 1871 and the Commissioners continued to exercise judicial powers occasionally.[240]

Collector as the Chief Executive Officer in the Distt.

The 'Permanent Settlement' gave permanency to the office of the Collector but it left him only as revenue officer. 1793 Code of Cornwallis divested the Collector of all his judicial authority and magisterial duties which were made over to the Judges of Civil Courts. However, the expediency demanded the reversal of this system of Cornwallis. Many experienced and able officers believed : 'We should form a very erroneous judgement of this important influence of the office of Collector, if we supposed that it was limited merely to revenue matters instead of extending to every thing affecting the welfare of the people. In India whoever regulates the assessment of the land, really holds in his hand the mainspring of the country'.[241] Inconformity with this principle, a permissive regulation of 1821[242] provided for the exercise of magisterial powers by the Collector. Further, a regulation of 1822 not only invested the Collector with judicial authority in the Settlement of land revenue but also in the preservation of law and order.[243]

Regulation I of 1829 created the all comprehensive and powerful office of Divisional Commissioners of Revenue and Circuit; and the Collectors were placed under their immediate authority. Under Regulation VII of 1831 the Sessions works of Division Commissioners of Revenue and Circuit had to be transferred to the Civil judges who were also the Magistrates. 'It was necessary, therefore, to divest them of their magisterial duties. So another class of functionaries had to be found to take up these dropped responsibilities; and, accordingly, they were flung to the Collectors. The warmest admirer of Lord William Bentinck and his system admitted that this was a mistake.[244] Nevertheless, Collectors of revenue, thus, became Magistrates as well. Consequently, the Collector were, once again, the Chief Executive Officer in the District with functions of magistracy and police and powers to adjudicate in rent and revenue cases.[245] Thus, the double institution of Divisional Commissioner and District Officer permanently modified the Cornwallis' structure and supplied the orthodox model for future British Colonial administration'.[246] By 1831, several districts of Bihar like Jungle Mahals, Ramgarh, Purnea, Tirhut, Bhagalpur and Shahabad, were placed under these powerful District officers. The year 1833 witnessed further upward revision in the duties and powers of the Collector. Regulation IX of the year provided for the more speedy and satisfactory decision of judicial questions cognizable by them.[247] Provisions were also made in 1833 for the appointment by the Governor-General in Council, of uncovenanted Deputy Collectors to assist the Collector.[248] The office of Dy. Magistrate was also created in 1843. These posts were open to Indians irrespective of their caste, creed or religion. But the people of Bihar could not take advantage of these provisions as they lagged behind in English Education.

New Revenue Policy

The Cornwallis system of revenue administration had provided for the Collector as the Chief Revenue Officer in the district under a Collective Board of Revenue at the Presidency. Extensive and ever increasing territorial jurisdiction, duties and powers of the Board of Revenue as constituted under Regulation II of 1793 and added by subsequent regulations obtaining upto the period under review, had become unmanageable and demanded decentralisation. The appointment of the Board of Commissioners for the Upper Provinces under Regulation X of 1807 and Regulation I (Section 2) of 1809, were the steps in the same direction. Even more important measure for the decentralisation of the Board of Revenue was adopted in the year 1811. Regulation XIII of the year authorised the Board of Revenue to depute one of its members with full powers of the Board to any part of the country to control and superintend the settlement and collection, and the conduct of the officials. It was under this permissive regulation that the Board of Commissioners for Bihar and Benaras was constituted in 1817. The jurisdiction of this Board extended to the districts of Ramgarh, Bhagalpur and Purnea in Bihar. All the provisions of Regulation XIII of 1811 with regard to constitution, powers and duties of the Board were made applicable to this Board also.[249] Still the respective jurisdiction of the Boards of Commissioners so established were too extensive to be easily controlled and efficiently managed'.[250] As a measure of remedy a Special Commission was appointed for the 'ceded and conquered provinces' in 1821;[251] and the Board of Revenue was reconstituted in 1822.[252] Under this new arrangement the Board of Revenue at Calcutta became the Board of Revenue for the Lower Provinces or the Sadar Board, to which were transferred the districts of Bhagalpur and Purnea. The Board of Commissioners for Bihar and Benaras came to be known as the Board of Revenue for Central Provinces or the Central Board. Rest of the territories were placed under the Board of Revenue for Western Provinces or the Western Board. Yet the respective jurisdictions of the three reconstituted Boards proved to be too vast to secure efficient and effective management. In the absence of personal communication, as was reported by Holt Mackenzie, Secretary to the Government in Territorial Deptt. of the Board with the Collectors, the business went slow and public records were loaded with voluminous correspondence. And, at the same time there were frequent cases of embezzlement and defalcation of public money.[253]

The Office of Divisional Commissioners of Revenue and Circuit: Revenue Treads down Other Branches of the Service

The collective Boards supervising the Collectors entirely by correspondence had failed to answer the purpose.[254] The answer was found, as was proposed by Mackenzie, in the appointment, under a Sadar Board of Revenue, of several Divisional Commissioners of Revenue to superintend the affairs of a moderate extent of the country. The proposal also conform to Bentham's advocacy of the individual officer as against the Collective Board, his principle of inspectability, and of 'reducing the field of Service' to the limits in which personal control could be effectively exercised.[255] The proposed office of the

Commissioner of Revenue, to which was to be annexed the duties and powers of the Courts of Circuit and Superintendents of Police, was considered equally advantageous to the administration of justice and police as it combined efficiency with economy.[256] Accordingly, Bentinck's Government passed Regulation I of 1829, and created the office of Divisional Commissioner of Revenue and Circuit for 20 Divisions, excluding the division of Delhi, of centrally administered territories of the Company. Of these 20 Divisions, 3 Divisions, namely, 1. Saran—comprising districts of Saran, Shahabad and Tirhut, 2. Patna—comprising the districts of Patna, Bihar and Ramgarh, and 3. Bhagalpur—comprising the districts of Bhagalpur, Monghyr, Malda and Purnea, appertained to Bihar. The Regulation was to take effect from Ist March, 1829.[257]

The Divisional Commissioners of Revenue and Circuit were to exercise powers and authority vested in the Boards of Revenue and Courts of Wards. They were placed under the control and direction of the Sadar Board of Revenue at the Presidency. In their proceedings both were to be guided by orders issued by the Government from time to time.[258] As we have noted earlier,[259] Provincial Courts of Appeal and Circuits, and the office of the Superintendents of Police were abolished and their duties and powers were made over to the Divisional Commissioners of Revenue and Circuit.[260] Thus, not only Collectors but also the magistracy and police were all placed under his superintendence and control.[261]

The Vicissitude of Kanoongos

One significant aspect of the revenue administration of the period had been the changing fortunes of Kanoongos, who were supposed to be repository of vital information concerning revenue administration, and whom Warren Hastings had discontinued for sometime, and again restored in 1774. The office of Kanoongos found no place in the administrative arrangement affected in the wake of Permanent Settlement.[262] But the exigencies of the situation demanded the revival of the Kanoongo's office. In fact, in the Upper Provinces, it had continued to work, and Regulation IV of 1808 specifically provided for the appointment of Kanoongos for Benaras and for the 'ceded and conquered provinces'. Lord Moira's Government revived the office of Kanoongos in the Lower Provinces, particularly in Bihar in 1816.[263] The Collectors of Bihar, Shahabad, Saran and Tirhut were authorised to appoint two Kanoongos for each of the pargana under their jurisdiction. The arrangement was extended to the districts of Ramgarh, Bhagalpur and Purnea alongwith several districts of Bengal in 1817.[264] Provisions were also made for the appointment of Patwaris in every village.[265] It was then widely hoped that the measure in progress for re-establishing the office of Kanungos in Bengal and Bihar would afford the means of redeeming to a great extent atleast that knowledge of landed tenure, and of the interests of all classes connected with land, the want of which had so long and seriously been felt.[266] However, of less than a decade-working of the office of Kanungo proved contrary to this general belief in superior revenue circles. In 1827, it was found that Kanungos had done nothing.[267] Even in Bihar where they were selected from old body of Kanungos of their immediate descendants, Kanungos were generally inefficient and corrupt. Hence, the office of Kanungo was finally abolished in 1827.[268]

The Final form of the Administration : Administrative Changes from 1835-1858

Alarmed by the sweeping reforms during the period from Lord Moira to Lord Bentinck the Court of Directors instructed the Government of India not to take any measure or pass any new laws affecting in any material degree the civil and military administration inconsistent in principle with their instructions or recorded opinions,[269] yet the period undr review (1835-1858) witnessed far reaching changes which centred round the following themes :

(1) Separation and re-union of the offices of Collector and Magistrate,

(2) Changes in police administration : Divisional Commissioner vis-a-vis Superintendent of Police.

(3) Judicial reforms : Augmentation in the powers and salary of the native Judicial Officers, and attempt for bringing the naturalborn-British subjects under the jurisdiction of Company courts.

(4) Reorganisation of administrative Units.

(5) Separation of the Government of Bengal from the Government of India.

(1) Separation and Re-union of the Offices of Collector and Magistrate

The Government of Bentinck had combined the offices of Collector and Magistrate.[270] But this union of offices could not deliver the goods. It was generally believed that too great a burden had been placed upon the Collector. His engrosing revenue duties resulted in the neglect of general administration, and that of lower criminal justice and police.[271] Hence, Lord Auckland, with the sanction of the Court of Directors, decided in 1837, to bifurcate the offices of Collector and Magistrate. The process of the separation of the two offices continued till 1845 when it was completed in all the districts of Bihar, except the independent joint magistracies of Patna, Maldah and Champaran.[272]

The bifurcation of the offices of Magistrate and Collector proved to be short lived. Within years there was a clamour in the highest official circle to re-unite the two offices. Cecil Beadon, Secretary to the Government of Bengal, observed at the end of 1853: 'we have suffered a grievous loss of power, maintaining a separate class of Collectors charged with special duties insufficient to occupy their time and yet inhibited from rendering assistance to the other branch of executive government'.[273] Right from Sir Cecil Beadon and Sir F.J. Halliday to Lord Dalhousie and Lord Canning, all were in favour of the revival of the joint office of Magistrate Collector.[274] Dalhousie believed that the separation was injurious both to the administration and interests of the people. In his last dispatch as Governor of Bengal to the Government of India on the 28th April, 1854, he held that the separation of the offices of Magistrate and Collector had been an error and that the true theory of government in India was the entire subjection of every civil officer in a division to the Commissioner at the head of it. Lord Canning in his Minute of the 18th Feb., 1857, expressed his opinion that reason, no less than experience pointed to the necessity of concentrating the whole executive power of the Government in each district of Bengal in the hands of one experienced men. He thought that the division of authority was to be avoided rather than sought.

As regards the people, he fully believed that the patriarchal form of Government was, in their present condition, ' most congenial to them and as regards the governing power, the concentration of all responsibility upon one officer can not fail to keep his attention alive, and to stimulate his energy in every department to the utmost, while it will preclude the growth of those obstructions to good Government which are apt to spring up where the two co-ordinate offices divide the authority"! It was under these considerations that the offices of Collector and Magistrate were finally re-united in 1859.[275] At the same time independent-Joint-Magistracies were converted into full Magistracy-Collectorships.

(2) Changes in Police Administration : Divisional Commissioner vis-a-vis Superintendent of Police

The period of Lord Auckland witnessed not only the separation of the offices of Magistrate and Collector, but also the separation of the duties and powers of the Superintendent of Police from the Commissioner of Revenue & Circuit. It was generally admitted that the transfer of the Supervision of Police to the Divisional Commissioners of Circuit had resulted in a want of uniformity and co-ordination in the direction and management of Police administration.[276] As such the office of the Provincial Superintendent of Police was revived in 1837 under Act XXV of that year. The Act transferred the power of the supervision and control over the police to the Superintendent of Police, and left the Divisional Commissioner only as the Commissioner of Revenue.[277] However, this arrangement, too, was found unsatisfactory. It could not bring about any improvement in the situation with regard to the problem of peace and security. Hence, the office of the Superintendent of Police was abolished in 1854, and his duties and powers were once again made over to the Divisional Commissioner.[278] It was only after the enactment of the Indian Police Act in 1861 that this tug of war for control over the police between the Divisional Commissioners of Revenue and Superintendent of Police came to an end. The Act, which reorganised the Police on modern lines, divested the Divisional Commissioner of his police powers, and provided for Inspector-General, Deputy-Inspector-General, and District Superintendent of Police.[279]

The above discussion touched only one aspect of the police administration, viz., the superior control and supervision of the police. But the exigencies of the situation demanded complete re-organisation of the police-system to which Kaye refers to as a mighty Engine of injustice. Committee, appointed to look into the affairs of the East India Company, in its report in 1832 revealed glaring defects in the Police administration of the Company's govt. in India. As such the Court of Directors in 1836, instructed the Govt. of India to re-organise its police system on the lines of 1829 Robert Peel Reform of London Police. Accordingly, Lord Auckland appointed a Police Committee headed by W.W. Bird, to investigate into and to report on the whole affair of the Police and criminal administration. The committee in its report pointed out several defects in the police administration, and recommend suitable measures including the separation of judicial and police powers of Magistrate, to improve the same.[290] It deplored the neglect of the ancient rural police, the village-chaukidars, with regard to their meagre pittance, and their deployment only at the headquarters of the Magistrates and Joint-Magistrates. F.J. Halliday, later the Lieutenant-Governor of Bengal, and then a member of the Police Committee, opined that though corrupt, the village-chaukidars were not wholly ineffective. He also recommended a regular and large police force (Civil constabulary) with adequate salaries, under a General Superintendent of Police, District and Assistant Superintendent of Police. He wanted the designation of Darogah to be changed to Inspector of Police, and next in rank, sub-Inspector of Police, with enhanced salary.[291] Concurring in with the views of Frederick Halliday, an anonymous writer in the Calcutta Review observed. "It is incumbent upon the Government to change the name of Darogah, because it is one with which the most odious associations are connected, - one, which is almost synonymous with 'dakoit' - which carried terror in its very sound, which reminds the poor cultivators of him over whom there is no control, of him who lives upon cruelty and extortion, and whose very vocation is corruption. No real native gentleman, however distressed his circumstances, will consent to take a Darogahship as long as it bears its present designation.[292] At the same time, the writer advocated for the employment of educated and respectable persons with adequate salary as police officers to the charge of a thana, instead of employing uneducated persons on salary with "impossibility of living decently".[293] However, no immediate measure was adopted for the improvement of the Bengal Police writing about whom in his Modern India in 1852, Sir George Campbell remarked that it (the Bengal Police) had "attained an unfortunate notoriety as being more active for the evil than good".[294]

Nearly a year after assuming the charge of the Government of Bengal, Bihar and Orissa as the first Lieutenant-Governor, Sir F.J. Halliday, moved with definite proposals for police and criminal reforms to the supreme Government.[295] But nothing was done even after the lapse of complete one year. The Lieutenant-Governor, therefore, pressed the question again in June, 1856, with his elaborate Minute of 30th April, 1856, in which he admitted the badness of mufassil police, and the inefficiency of the measures previously taken to improve them. At the same time he considered it vain to improve the agency for the detection and apprehension of criminals unless the agency for trying them was also improved as the badness of the Police and the inefficiency of the tribunals act and reach on each other, and both are concerned in bringing about the deplorable existing circumstances'..... 'Whether right or wrong the general native opinion is that the administration of criminal justice is little than a lottery, in which however the best chances are with the criminals .... the corruption and extortion of the police, which causes it to be popularly said that dacoity is bad enough, but the subsequent police enquiry very much worse." To relieve this situation Frederick Halliday suggested 'indispensably necessary' five following measures - (1) the Improvement of the character and position of the village chaukidars, (2) adequate salaries and fair prospects of advancement to the stipendiary police, (3) the appointment of more experienced officers as Covenanted Zilla Magistrate, (4) a considerable increase in the number of uncovenanted Deputy Magistrates, (5) improvement in the criminal courts of justice. He asked for one hundred more Deputy Magistrates, and for the junction of judicial and executive power in all Magistrates. In addition to these indispensable measures, he also dwelt upon the importance of (1) extended use of Honorary Magistrates, (2) good roads and (3) systems of vernacular education.[296]

The proposals of the Lieutenant-Governor did not bear general fruit until after 1858. However, he succeeded, in 1856, in procuring the passing of a Chaukidari (or village police) Act which provided for the watch and ward of those larger towns and villages to which it was applied. Chaukidars were to be appointed by the District-Magistrate on such salaries as they though fit. The cost was to be recovered from the inhabitants assessed by Panchayats. Any surplus to be available from tax funds was to be spent on sanitary and other improvements.[297]

Though a military police was raised in the wake of the Santhal Insurrection[298] the establishment of a Civil Constabulary had to wait till the reforms of 1860, and the complete reorganisation of the Police administration on modern lines till the passing of the Indian Police Act (V) in 1861.

(3) Judicial Reforms (i) Augmentation in Powers and Salary of the Native Judicial Officers

Lord Auckland continued the policy of the augmentation of the native agency with increased salary, in the judicial service of the Company as initiated by his immediate predecessors. Changes in the administration of justice, viz., the abolition of the Provincial Courts of Appeal and Circuit and consequent increase in the duties of the European District-Judge during the period of Bentinck had made the policy more expedient. To lessen the burden of work of District Judges additional District and City Judges were appointed. They were authorised to refer certain case of appeal to the principal Sader Amins, and at the same time, proposals were made by the Sadar-Diwani Adalat to refer summary appeals from Sadar Amins and Munsiffs to the principal Sadar Amins, whose decisions were appealable in the Courts of the District Judges.[299] Incorporating these proposals an Act was passed in 1837. This Act invested the Principal Sadar Amins to adjudicate the suits of any value referred to them by the Zillah or city Judges, including those suits in which the Government or its officers were involved. Appeals could be made against their decisions to the Zillah Judges in cases of the value of Rs. 5,000 and to the Sadar Diwani Adalat in cases valued above that amount.[300] With the increase in their powers, there was corresponding increase in their salary and establishment allowance. It was the considered view of Lord Auckland that as from year to year we must give them power, it becomes absolutely necessary to reside them in dignity and character.[301]

Attempts to bring European - British Subjects under The Jurisdiction of the Company's Courts

During the period under review serious attempts were made to bring the European-British Subjects under the jurisdiction of the same laws and courts of the Company to which Indians were also subjected. Infact, the way for this was paved by the Charter Act 1833.

The Charter Act of 1833[302] was significant in many respects. First of all, it proclaimed, setting aside the racial discrimination, the equality of all British Subjects - whether European or Indian.[303] For giving practical shape, so far law and justice was concerned, to this principles of equality the Act not only provided for the consolidation and codification of varieties of law prevalent in the Company's territory in India, but also adding fourth member-the law member, to the Governor-General's Council, gave them extensive powers of legislation, with certain limitations, even to repeal, amend or alter any laws or regulation then inforce or to be in force thereafter. Their Acts possessed the same force and effect' as any act of British Parliament and were to be taken notice of by all courts of justice whatsoever within the territory of the Company.[304] This Supreme Court of Judicature at Calcutta was also brought under the direct perview of the laws enacted by the Governor-General-in-Council. Earlier statutes requiring registration in the Supreme Court, of regulations passed by the Company's Government in India were automatically rescinded.

The Charter Act of 1833 expressly provided that it was 'expedient that subject to such special arrangements as local circumstances may require, a general system of Judicial establishment and police, to which all persons whatsoever, as well as Europeans as natives, may be subject, should be established in the territories subject to the Company at an early period; and that such laws as might be applicable in common to all classes of inhabitants .... due regard being paid to the rights, feelings and peculiar usages of the people, should be enacted, and that all laws and customs having the force of law within the same territories should be ascertained and consolidated, and, as occasion may requires, amended.[305] To execute this provision of consolidation and codification of laws, the Act directed the Company's Supreme Government in India to appoint a law commission—the Indian Law Commission. (Sections 53-55 of the Act). Accordingly, the Ist Indian Law Commission was constituted with Macaulay, the law member, as its President.[306] The Law Commission was to take its own course which was definitely arduous and long.[307] Under the new circumstances it had become expedient to remove immediately the legal anomalies caused by conflicting series of laws-English and Indian, enforceable by two different and hostile judicatures - King's Courts and Company's Courts. Apart from territorial jurisdiction over the Presidency towns, the Kings' Courts possessed a personal jurisdiction over British-born subjects, in some cases involving India born subjects. The peculiar aspect of the matter had assumed greater dimension as the doors of India were "unsealed for the first time to British subject of European birth."[308] And they were permitted to settle in, and to acquire landed property in the Company's territory in India. With this the chances of natives to be wronged by European British subjects had increased tremendously as the latter were under the control of the Supreme Court at the Presidency town alone both in civil and criminal cases, a fact, which kept the former at a great disadvantage.

Natives in the interior wronged by British born subjects were deterred from going before the Supreme Court as the procedure there was very slow and the litigation ruinously expensive. Making a comparison of this aspect with that of England, Macaulay observed : "The expenses of litigation in England are so heavy that people sit down quietly under wrongs and submit to losses rather than go to Law Court, and yet the English are the richest people in the world. The people of India are poor, and the expenses of litigation in the Supreme Court are five times as great as the expenses of litigation at Westminister". In fact, the mission of the Supreme Court, he remarked, had been to beggar every rich native within its jurisdiction.[309]

Macaulay's efforts bore fruits and the Act XI, generally known as Macaulay's 'Black Act'. (so called by its opponents), was passed in 1836. This Act rescinding the clause 107th of the Charter Act of 1833, and declaring that no one residing in the Company's territories in India "shall by reason of place of birth or by reason of discent" be exempted from the jurisdiction of the Courts excepting the Munsiff's Courts of Civil Justice of the Company brought the European British subjects under the jurisdiction on of the Company's Courts in Civil suits.[310] Act VI of 1843, placed them generally under the Munsiff's Courts also.[311] However, in criminal matters, they continued to enjoy the right to be tried in the Supreme Court to the great detriment of the natives. Describing the state of things a contemporary English writer wrote in the Calcutta Review: "Innumberable instances are on record which show, how lamantably this indulgence has been abused, and how frequently British Europeans after the commission of outrages, which at Calcutta or at home would have been visited with the most codign punishment, have baffled the most strenuous efforts of justice. The only remedy at present is a prosecution in the Supreme Court to which as it is not in the power of poor people living at the distance of several leagues to resort, there is no real redress for wrongs: that salutary influence which the presence of neighbouring and competent authority can not fail to exert over a community is unfelt by British European subjects. Unrestrained in their actions, with large sums at their command, they had been known to equal the worst zamindars in cruelty and oppression. False charges, connivance of at perjury, even subornation of perjury, affrays, unnecessary disputes-have been as things of every day occurrence with them.[312] Some of the indigo-factors themselves had acknowledged in their evidence before the Police Committee appointed by Lord Auckland in 1838 that law did not provide that protection to the natives against the oppressive conduct of the British-born subjects which they had every right to demand from their rulers.[313]

Attempts of Macaulay and that of his Law Commission through its draft Penal Code (1837) to establish the principle of legal equality had been confined to the civil matters only due to the violent opposition of the European Community. For the same reason recommendations of the Law Commission of 1843, regarding the trial of British-born subjects charged with heinous crimes.[314] During the Governor-Generalship of Lord Dalhousie fresh attempts were made to bring the British-born-subjects under the full jurisdiction of the Company's Courts in India. Four Bill to this effect[302] introduced by Bethune, the Law-Member of the Governor Gentral's Council, met with stiff resistance by the European Community. A counter agitation by the natives were of no avail and Bills were withdrawn.[315]

In the meantime, Act XVII of 1837, Act XXXI of 1838, Act V of 1844, Act XIX of 1850, only provided for fines and punishments by the District Courts and Magistrates for particular offences committed by the British-born subjects under special circumstances. Act V of 1844 authorised the Magistrates in Bengal and Bihar to take Muchelkes (penal-recognisances) from European British subjects.[316] Act VII of 1853 empowered the Magistrates to punish only petty crimes by fines upto Rs. 500. None of these Acts however, applied to theft, perjury and other serious offences committed by the Europeans in the interior. Only the Supreme Court at Calcutta still had the power to award capital punishment[317] and the British-born subjects continued to enjoy the special privileges in criminal matters.

(I) Augmentation in the Powers and Salary of the Native Judicial Officers

Lord Auckland continued the policy of the augmentation of the native agency with increased salary, in the judicial service of the Company as initiated by his immediate predecessors. Changes in the administration of justice, viz., the abolition of the Provincial Courts of Appeal and Circuit and consequent increase in the duties of the European District Judges during the period of Bentinck had made the policy more expedient. To lessen the burden of work of District Judges additional District and city Judges were appointed. They were authorised to refer certain case of appeal to the Principal-Sadar Amins: and at the same time proposals were made by the Sadar-Diwani Adalat to refer summary appeals from Sadar Amins and Munsiffs to the Principal Sadar Amins, whose decisions were appealable in the Courts of the District Judges.[317] Incorporating these proposals an Act was passed in 1837. This Act invested the Principal Sadar Amins to adjudicate the suits of any value referred to them by the Zillah or City Judges, including those suits in which the Government or its officers were involved. Appeals could be made against their decisions to the Zillah Judges in cases of the value of Rs. 5,000, and to the Sadar Diwani Adalat in cases valued above that amount.[318] With the increase in their powers, there was corresponding increase in their salary and establishment allowance. It was the considered view of Lord Auckland that as "from year to year we must give them power, it becomes absolutely necessary to reside them in dignity and character.[319]

(4) Reorganisation of Administrative Units

Organisation of administrative units, as we have noted in various chapters, underwent changes from time to time, sometimes in the wake of political events (risings and rebellions) of magnitude, and at others for the sake of administrative convenience. A clear picture emerged in 1829, when by Regulation I of that year the office of the Divisional Commissioner of Revenue and Circuit was created. Out of the 20 Divisions created for Bengal, Bihar, Orissa and 'Ceded and conquered territories', 3 Divisions appertained to Modern Bihar. They were (1) Patna Division, comprising the districts of Patna, Bihar (Gaya) and Ramgarh, (2) Saran Division, consisting of the districts of Saran, Champaran, Shahabad and Tirhut, (3) Bhagalpur Division which included the districts of Bhagalpur (with parts of Monghyr), Purnea and Maldah. A change took place in this arrangement in 1834, when the Division of Saran was abolished and its constituent districts, excluding the district of Tirhut, were amalgamated in Patna Division, Tirhut being included in the Division of Bhagalpur. This arrangement was further affected by the Santhal Insurrection of 1855 as a result of which a new non-regulation district of Santhal Parganas was created under Act XXXVII of 1855, and placed under Bhagalpur Divsion.[320] It was at this time that the district of Tirhut was added to the Division of Patna.

Likewise, South Bihar witnessed momentous changes during the period. Under Act XIII of 1833 a special administrative unit of South West Frontier Agency was created for the tribal people of Chotanagpur region in the wake of Kol and Bhumij Risings. By 1837 this Agency incorporated in it the districts of Singhbhum, Manbhum, Lohardaga and Hazaribagh, abolishing the old districts of Jungle Mahals and Ramgarh. Subsequently, in 1854, by Act XX, South-West Frontier Agency was transformed into the Division of Chotanagpur with Commissioner as its head under the Leintenant-Governor[321] instead of Agent to the Governor-General.

(5) Separation of the Government of Bengal from the Government of India

It was unfortunate that instead of palliating the evil consequences resulting from the union of the three provinces of Bengal, Bihar and Orissa under the latter Mughals mercantile Government of the East India Company added through its conquests a vast tracts of the country to the Presidency of Bengal. Whereas each of the three provinces required a separate Governor, one Governor-General in Council was 'responsible for the general administration and policy of all British India as well as for the particular administration of Bengal. This burden was infact more than he could bear. The details of Bengal administration tended, therefore, to be relegated to subordinate authorities ... The reform of the Govt. of Bengal was long overdue.'[322]

The idea of relieving the Governor-General was first mooted, though from a different angle of view, by Sir John Malcolm in 1826.[323] Again, the Civil Finance Committee, instituted under the direction of the Court of Directors by Lord William Bentinck, in its letter of 2nd August, 1830, recommended the separation of the supreme Government from the local charge of the Presidency of Fort William, and the separation of the lower Provinces of Bengal from the upper Provinces,[324] if the administration of Bengal were not to fall into confusion.

The Charter Act of 1833 provided for the division of the overgrown Presidency of Bengal a separate charge under a Governor for the Upper Provinces of Bengal.[325] But economic considerations ruled supreme. With the termination of its commerce under the Act[326], the Company became concerned more and more with the recovery of its assets and dividends.[327] Taking advantage of sections 56 and 57 of the Act of 1833, a Lieutenant-Governor (without a Council) for the North West Upper Provinces was appointed in 1836 under an Act of 1835.[328] This reduced the area under the Government of Bengal but that was not right remedy for the real problem, for though the Charter Act of 1833 made the Governor-General of Bengal the

Governor-General of India.[329] He continued to be the Governor of the Presidency of Fort William in Bengal as well. 'The absurdity of the legal position' connected with this dual role of the Governor-General was mitigated by authorising him to appoint a senior member of his Council as Deputy Governor of Bengal, but the Act did nothing to improve the administration of the three Provinces of Bihar, Bengal and Orissa "which remained under a minimum supervision for another twenty years".[330] In fact, the provisions of the Act were far from adequate to the needs of the country.

Writing about the lamentable state of things in his Modern India in 1852, George Campbell observed: The Government of Bengal proper must be heaviest of all. The Governor has the administration of the great provinces of Bengal, Bihar and Orissa with subsequent additions - Assam, North East Frontier Agency, South Western Agency, Arracan, and Tenasserim.... and he has the charges of a number of petty independent states : .... and many other miscellaneous charges.

"Of late years, the Governor-General having been so much absent, there has generally been a Deputy Governor of Bengal; and latterly the duties of Governor-General and Governor of Bengal have been found to be, too much for one man, and the Governor-General has even when present nominated a Deputy Governor .... Although the Governor General may select the Deputy Governor from the Members of Council, in practice it has become the custom to consider the appointment the right of the Senior Member, and he has invariably been appointed. The consequence is a constant change in the holder of the office. In 12 years upto 1850 the reigns had been held by 9 successive Governors or Deputy-Governors. The present Deputy-Governor has served in the army with credit for 52 years, but has never had any experience of any kind in civil affairs".....'It is no wonder that such a Government is inefficient, that nothing has generally been done beyond mere routine, and that Bengal has suffered in consequence.[331] As a matter of fact, 'Bengal was under-administered, and demanded continuous and thoughtful care, if abuses were not to grow, and multiply '. But what of this, when the responsible Govt. was preoccupied with the French intrigues in the peninsula or a Maratha war or trouble with Sikhs and Afghans, and when

Directors were insisting on strict economy.[323] The separation of the administration of Bengal from the general administration of India had become the crying need of the time.

Credit, as W.S. Seton-Karr wrote in 1854, must go to Lord Dalhousie for persuading, on the eve of the renewal of the Charter of the Company in 1853, the Home authorities to make the Bengal proper a separate governmental charge.[333] The Charter Act of 1853 provided that the Governor-General of India should cease to be the Governor of Bengal, and that a separate Governor should be appointed for the Presidency of Fort William in Bengal, and that until a separate Governor of such Presidency should be constituted, to authorise and to direct the Governor-General of India-in-Council to appoint a Lt. Governor from amongst the servants of the Company of ten years service in India.[334] Here again, economy proved a stronger factor than efficiency, and the Court of Directors authorised the Supreme Government in India to appoint a Lt. Governor (without a Council) for the Lower-Provinces of Bengal. Accordingly, Frederick James Halliday was appointed, who took over his charge on 28th April, 1854, as the first Lt. Governor of Bengal, Bihar, Orissa and Assam.[335]

Nevertheless, if this was the fate of Bengal where the 'agitators could shout aloud,[336] what can be said of Bihar where the people could not shout? And as a result, even at this late stage separate status and special position of Bihar as a province was not taken into account, and Bihar remained altogether neglected and fully appended to Bengal as an inferior partner which naturally undermined Bihar's proper growth. We have the example of North-Western Provinces which was created in 1836, and which with a shorter period of its separate Lt. Governorship, and despite setbacks of famines, saw more development of agriculture-irrigation, education, and other public works.[337] Bihar's progress in these fields had been insignificant. On the contrary, with the start of the English rule, the seat of the government of Bihar alongwith the centre of activities was shifted to Calcutta. Consequently, Patna and its neighbourhood which even at the beginning of our study had been a flourishing centre of international trade and industry,[338] and oriental learning, was deprived of everything. Sir John Strachey quoting extensively Sir Ashley Eden, Lord Lawrence, and the Report of the Famine Commission of 1880, had dwelt at length upon the lamentable condition of peasantly, agriculture and industry in Bihar under the Company-rule.[339] Racial discrimination even in the matters of civil and criminal justice encouraged the planters and others of ruling race to abuse their privileges and commit outrages on native peasants. In fact, the European planters had surpassed the worst zamindars in their tyrannies and oppressions.[340] In Bengal the outrages of the Indigo factors began to decrease after the Nil-Darpan drama highlighted the problems of peasants and raiyyats. There were indigo disturbances followed by the appointment of an Indigo Commission and its reports. The Lt. Governor of Bengal undertook vigorous measures in the light of the Report of the Indigo-Commission.[341] However, the problems of the Bihar peasants groaning under the cruelties and oppressions of the European Indigo factors[342] were not undertaken with the same vigour and intensity either by the Govt. or by the leaders of Bengal. The reason of this step-motherly treatment meted out to Bihar-peasants was that due to distance of th seat of government from Bihar neither the Government nor leaders of Bengal were fully alive to the problems of Bihar. There were no Dinbandhu Mitra, the author of Nil-Darpan, to depict the pitiable plight of the peasants, no Rev. J. Long, the publishers, and no Seton-Karr, the Secretary to the Government of Bengal, in Bihar, to create a great sensation through the official publication of the translation of the drama-Nil-Darpan.[343] The peasants and raiyyat in Bihar who could not go to their fields and grow crops of their choice, had to undergo the intimidation, coersion, open violence, frauds and harassments in the Courts by the European Indigo planters till the arrival of M.K. Gandhi in 1917.[344]

The unnatural union of Bihar with Bengal affected adversely the people of Bihar in various ways. Cornwallis had started the policy of exclusion of Indians from the services. Moira and Bentinck attempted to palliate the evil results of that policy and provided for the appointment of the natives to the Junior revenue, judicial and executive posts. However, the people of Bihar remained a loser in this field also as they did in to take to the English education early[345] as compared to the people of Bengal. Consequently, the English educated Bengalees flooded the services in Bihar. Descendants of those prosperous Bengali officers, now on decline, can still be found in good number in many of the cities of Bihar. It was in the last quarter of the 19th century that the Government, with a view to check the flow of Benglies to Bihar, undertook some effective measures to encourage English education in Bihar, and also passed orders to reserve some jobs exclusively for Biharies.[346] Nevertheless, the issue later on proved to be the main plank of the movement for the separation of Bihar from Bengal and Bihar for Biharies.[347]

References

1. For details Supra Bihar under Warren Hastings.
2. Tarachand, Freedom Movement in India, Vol. I. p. 242.
3. Gleig, Memoirs of Warren Hastings, Vol. I, p. 317.
4. Forrest's Selections from the State Papers, Warren Hastings, Vol. III, Appendix, A. p. 277.
5. Committee of Circuit's Proceedings, 28 July, 1772, pp. 162-68.
6. Mill and Wilson, The History of British India, Vol. III, p. 364.
7. Firminger, Fifth Report, Vol. I, Introduction, p. XII.
8. *Ibid.*
9. R. Dutta, The Economic History of India under Early British Rule, p. 79.
10. Cambridge History of India, Vol. V. pp. 414-415.
11. W. W. Hunter, Bengal M.S. Records, 1894, Vol. I, p. 18.
12. B. B. Misra, The Central Administration of the East India Company 1774-1834, Oxford Univ. Press, London, 1959, p. 114. ft.
13. Committee of Revenue proceedings, 23, Nov. 1773, pp. 3453-77.
14. Cambridge History, Vol. V. p. 149.
15. Vide R. Datta, Economic History, p. 59.
16. Proc. of the Governor-General in Council, 17 & 31 May, 1776.
17. Firminger, Fifth Report, II, pp. 410-417.
18. Sixth Report of the Select Committee of Secrecy 1782, p. 23.
19. Proc. of the Governor-General in Council (revenue), Vol. 47.
20. Revenue Consultations, July 16, 1777.
21. Gleig, II, pp. 329-30.
22. R.B. Ramsbotham, Studies, in the Land Revenue History of Bengal, 1769-87, pp. 96-131.

23. Proc. of the Governor-General in Council, Revenue, 20 Jan., 1781.
24. Vide Cambridge History of Indian V p. 427.
25. F. D. Ascoli, Early Revenue History of Bengal, 1917, pp. 35-36, also J. C. Sinha, Economic Annals of Bengal, p. 194.
26. J.R. Hand, Early Eng. Ad. of Bihar, p. 25.
27. J.R. Hand, Eng. Ad. of Bihar, 1781-85, pp. 25-26.
28. Harrington, Analysis of the Bengal Regul., 1807, II, pp. 41-43.
29. *Ibid.*
30. Cambridge History, V, p. 428.
31. James, Selections from the Revenue Chief of Bihar at Patna, p. 20.
32. Hand, pp. 20-42.
33. James, Selections from the Correspondence of the Revenue Chief of Bihar, p. 35.
34. *Ibid.,* pp. 35-36.
35. *Ibid.* p. 38.
36. Cambirdge History, V. p. 309.
37. General Regulations for the Admn. of Justice, Augs. 15, 1772. Colebrook's Digest, Suppl. volume.
38. Niranjan Dhar, The Administrative System of the East India Company in Bengal, 1774-86, Vol. II, pp. 58-59.
39. N. Mazumdar, Justice and Police in Bengal, 1765-93, p. 96.
40. John William Kaye, The Admn. of East India Co. Kitab Mahal, Allahabad, 1966, p. 327.
41. Forrest, Selections from the State Papers of the Governor-General of India, II, Warren Hastings, p. 290.
42. H. Cowell, the Hist. and Consult. of the Courts and Legis. Autho. in India, p. 31.
43. N. Mazumdar, Justice and Police in Bengal, p. 98.
44. J. W. Kaye, The Admn. of the East India Co., Judicial System, p. 328.
45. N. Mazumdar, Justice and Police in Bengal, p. 98.
46. Bihar through the Ages, p. 618.
47. W. H. Morley, Digest of Indian Cases, Vol. II, pp. 549-587; also Kaye, Administration of the East India Co. Supreme Court, pp. 328-331.

48. 21 of the George III, Chapt., for details J.W. Kaye, *op.cit.*, pp. 329-332.
49. Selections from the Judicial Records of the Bhagalpur Distt. Office, Ed. K.K. Datta, State Central Record Office, Patna, Introduction, p. ii.
50. Bengal Administrative Report, 1911-12, p. 40.
51. Asim K. Datta, Proc. of the Ind. Hist. Cong. Calicut session.1976, p. 34
52. J. W. Kaye, The Admn. of the East India Co., p. 333.
53. J. E. Colebroke, Suppl. to the Digest of the Regulations and Laws enacted prior to 1793, Vol. III. p. 125.
54. Bengal Revenue Consult, dt. 24 Jan. 1776.
55. B.B. Mishra, Judicial Admn. of East Ind. Co., Patna, 1961, pp. 300-304.
56. Siyar, Vol. III, p. 193.
57. A. Spinal, Cornwallis in Bengal, pp. 43-44.
58. Bengal Rev. Consult. 5th July, 1782.
59. Original Consult., Bengal Rev. Deptt. 6th Apr.
60. B. B. Misra, The Central Admn. of the East Ind. Co., pp. 319-320.
61. Penderel Moon, Warren Hastings and British India, Hodder and Stoughton, 1947, pp. 107-108
62. Cambridge History, V, pp. 208-209.
63. J. Reginald Hand, Early English Admn. of Bihar, 1781-85, p. 59.
64. *Ibid.*
65. For details J. C. Sinha, Economic Annals, pp. 110-146.
66. Cambridge Histroy, Vol. p. 212.
67. J. Malcolm, Sketch of the Political Hist. of India, Ed. 1811-15, p. 40.
68. Romesh Dutta, The Econ. Hist. of India, Ed. 1811-15, p. 40.
69. *Ibid.*
70. Adam Smith, The Wealth of Nations, Modern Library edition, p. 71.
71. Special mention may be made of Section 39.
72. Fort William India House Correspondence, Vol. IX, pp. 204-226.
73. F. D. Ascoli, Early Revenue History of Bengal, pp. 38-40.
74. Bd. Rev. Progr. Ist June, 1786, pp. 7-11 para 30-36.

75. Letter to the Court, 3rd July, 1786, Fort William India House Correspondence, Vol. IX, pp. 254-274.
76. Cambridge History, Vol. V. pp.431-32.
77. Charles Ross, Correspondence of Ist. Marquess Cornwallis, Vol. I, p. 238.
78. Lord Tiegnmunth, Memoris of the Life and Correspondence of John Lord Teignmunth, Vol. I, pp. 128-129.
79. J. W. Kaye, Admn. of the East India Co., Indian Reprint, p. 88.
80. P. E. Roberts, Hist. of British India under the Company and the Crown, Clarendon Press, 1938, p. 222.
81. Act 26th of George III, Chap. 16.
82. Ross, Correspondence of Cornwallis, I, pp. 208-215.
83. Fort William India House Correspondence, Vol. X, Ed. Reghubir Singh, p. Introduction 5.
84. Cambridge History, V, p. 434.
85. Tarachand, History of the freedom movement in India, Vol. I, p. 249.
86. J. W. Kaye, Administration, p. 88.
87. Fort William India House Corresp., Vol. X, Introd., p. 3.
88. Eric Stokes, The English Utilitarians and India, Oxford, 1955, p. 25.
89. Mill & Wilson, The Hist. of Brit. India, Vol. V. p. 341.
90. Seton-Karr, Cornwallis, Rulers of India Series, pp. 99-100, & 121.
91. John Shore, Notes on Indian Affairs, Vol. II, p. 57.
92. Vide L.S. S. O'Malley, History of Bengal, Bihar and Orissa under the British Rule, p. 282-283.
93. For details, Letter to the Court 18th Aug., 1787 Fort William India House Corresp. X,. p. 512.
94. Letter from the Court, 28 Mar., 1788, Fort William India House Corresp. X. p. 338.
95. Cambridge Hist. of India, V. p. 442.
96. *Ibid.*
97. For details see H.R. Ghoshal, Economic Transition in the Bengal Presidency, 1793-1833, Patna Univ. 1950-pp. 22-26.
98. Colerbrook, Suppl., III, p. 130, 27th June, 1787.

99. Minute of Cornwallis, 30 Dec., 1790, para 10-27, Bengal Consult., 3rd Dec., 1790 also Ross, Corresp. of Cornwallis, I, pp. 523-24.
100. Bengal Revenue Consult., 3rd Dec., 1790.
101. For details A. Spinal, Cornwallis in Bengal, pp. 70-74.
102. Regulation II, of December, 1790.
103. Vide J.W. Kaye, Admn. of the East India Co., p. 336., ft.
104. A Spinal, Cornwallis in Bengal, p. 87.
105. Regulation III of May, 1793.
106. Regulation V of 1793.
107. *Ibid.*
108. Section I of Regulation II of 1793, for details O'Malley, History of Bengal, Bihar and Orissa, pp. 280-82; also Ross Correspondence, p. 558.
109. J.W. Kaye, Admn. of the East India Company, p. 338.
110. Thornton, History of British Empire in India, II, p. 542.
111. Bengal Revenue (Judicial Consult., 26th April 1793, Ni. 1.
112. For details see Chitranjan Sinha, The Vakeels in the Early Days of British Rule in Bengal, Indian History Congress, Varanasi Session, 1969 '; also Dr. K.K. Basu, Native pleaders in an Early District Court in Bengal, History Records Commission, 1945.
113. B.B. Misra, Central Admn. p. 234.
114. Revenue (Judicial) Consult. 7th, Dec., 1792.
115. Harrington, *op.cit.,* Vol. I, p. 510.
116. B.B. Misra, Central Admn. pp. 231-33.
117. Tarachand, Freedom Movement, Vol. I, p. 251.
118. J. K. Kaye, Admn. of the East India Co., p. 419.
119. Letter from the Court, 12 April 1786, Fort William India House Correspondence, Vol. X. p.132.
120. J. W. Kaye's Admn. of the Company, p. 176.
121. See Supra Chap. The Revolt of Raja Chait Singh.
122. Letter from the Court, 12 April 1786, For William, India House Correspondence, Vol. X. p. 134.
123. *Ibid.,* pp. 131-32.
124. *Ibid.,* p. 128.
125. *Ibid.,* p. 132.

126. Letter to the Court, 6 Nov., 1788, *Ibid.,* pp. 662-663.
127. Forest, Selection from the State Papers, Cornwallis, Vol. I. pp. 204-206.
128. For details, Badenpowell, The Land Systems, I, pp. 411-16.
129. Letter to the Court, 6th Nov., 1788, Fort William, India Home Correspondence, X, p. 663.
130. Nand Kishore Singh, Working of the Permanent Settlement in Bihar, Indian History Cong. Varanasi Session, 1969.
131. Section 4, Regulation I of 1793.
132. Preamble to Regulation II of 1793, also Article 8 of the Proclamation, See Baden-Powell, The Land System, I. p. 410.
133. Regulation XIV of 1793.
134. Section I.
135. Sections 3-15 of Regulation II of 1793.
136. Sections 31-33, 36-42, 44-46 of Regulation II of 1793.
137. For details Baden-Powell, The Land systems I, pp. 414-416, 427-428.
138. Firminger, 5th Report, Vol. II, Introduction, pp. XVI-XVII.
139. Section 1, Regulation II of 1793.
140. R. Rickards, India of Facts, 1829, ed. Vol. I, p. 360.
141. J. C. Sinha, Preface to Economic Annals of Bengal, 1927, ed., also Tarachand, Freedom Movement, Vol. I. p. 254.
142. Minute of Lord Cornwallis, 3rd Feb. 1790, *op.cit.*
143. W.S. Seton-Karr, Marquis Cornwallis, Rulers of Indian series, p. 72.
144. Tara Chand, Freedom Movement, Vol. I, p. 254.
145. See S.N. Sen, 1857, also Patna Comm. Reports, Mutiny Bundles, State Archieves, Patna.
146. W.W. Hunter, Bengal MS Records, Vol. II, p. 109 also Report on the Land Revenue System, Bengal & Orissa, 1882-83. submitted to the Govt. of Bengal, 31st Oct., 1883. p. 4.
147. Lord Moira's Revenue Minute of 21st Sept., 1815, vide Firminger's Fifth Report, II, p. 60.
148. Minute of Cornwallis, 3rd Feb. 1790, *op.cit.*
149. Vide John Capper, The Three Presidencies of India, London, 1853, p. 281.

150. Minute of Sir John Shore, 18th June, 1789, vide Baden-Powell, The Land System, Vol. I, p. 619, note I).
151. Report of the Select Committee, 1831-32. Vol. XI, p. 4.
152. J.W. Kaye, Admn. of the East India Co. p. 198.
153. For details, J.C. Sinha, Econ. Annals, p. 273; and Baden-Powell, The Land System, I. pp. 632-33 also W.W. Hunter, Bengal 175 Records, Vol. I, pp. 123-133.
154. For details R.N. Sinha, Bihar Tenantry, Bombay, 1968, pp. 70-73.
155. Kaye's Administration, p. 198.
156. C.D. Field, Land holding—The Relation of Landlord and Tenants in various countries, pp. 565-566.
157. Vide Sir John Strachey, India, its Admn. and Progress, pp. 425-27 also Calender of Persian Corresp., X, pp. 312-13; & Bengal Zamindar's Settlement Report, Vol. I, pp. 61-76.
158. For details W.W. Hunter, Bengal MS Records, I, pp. 88-116.
159. Bengal Judicial Civil Proceedings, 18th December, 1800.
160. Cambridge, V. 455.
161. Wellesley to the Court of Directors April 22, 1799, vide Thomson & Garrat, The Rise and Fulfilment of British Rule in India, 1958, ed. p. 207.
162. Edward Thomson, Making of the Indian Princes, pp. 272-73 and Romesh Dutt, the Econ, Hist. of India, Under Early Brit. Rule Sixth ed. pp. 163-165.
163. G.W. Forrest, Select, from the Min. and other official writings of Elphinston, p. 102.
164. Edward Thomson, Making of the Ind. Price, p. 272.
165. Baden-Powell, I, p. 636.
166. 2, 3, Sections of Regul., V. of 1812.
167. Cambridge History of India, Vol. V. p. 457.
168. B.B. Misra, The Central Admn. p. 260, also A.B. Kieth, Constitutional Hist. of India, 1600-1935, p. 143.
169. Regul. XXXVIII of 1795 & Regul. VI of 1797.
170. For details B.B. Misra, Central Admn. pp. 261-67.
171. Cambridge Hist. V. p. 457.
172. Section 2 of Regul. 12 of 1797, and Regul V of 1798.
173. B.B. Misra, Central Admn., p. 265.

174. *Ibid.,* p. 266.

175. Preamable to Regulation II of 1801.

176. Regul X of 1805 & also Regul. XV of 1807.

177. For details see B.B. Misra, Cent. Admn. *op.cit.* 344-361.

178. Sect. 19 of Regul. IV of 1807.

179. Regul. XIV of 1810.

180. Regul. XVI of 1810.

181. Imper. Gaz of India, Vol. IV, p. 386.

182. Sel. from the Judicial Rec. of Bhag. Distt, office, 1792-1805. Ed. K. K. Datta, p. 249.

183. Fifth Report, Vol. V. p. 130.

184. B.B. Misra, *op. cit.*, pp. 347-348.

185. Regulation XII of 1807.

186. Regulation X of 1808.

187. Regulation VIII of 1810.

188. William Blunt to Dowdeswell, Judicial Secretary to the Govt. of Bengal, 31 Oct. 1812, Bengal Criminal (Judicial) Consult. 14 Nov. 1812, No. 6.

189. *Ibid.,* No. 8.

190. *Ibid.,* No. 9.

191. T. Eric Stokes, The English Utilitarians and India, Oxford Univ. Press, London 1959.

192. A.B. Kieth, Constitutional Hist. of India, p. 127.

193. Bengal Dispatches, Vol. LXVII, Judicial Dispatch of Nov. 9, 1814.

194. B.B. Misra, The Central Admn. of the East India Co., 1773-1834, p. 361.

195. Cambridge Hist., Vol. V, p. 459.

196. Judicial Letters from the Court, dt. 9 Nov. 1814, Bengal Distratches, Vol. LXVIII, I.O. Records, Vide Cambridge Hist., Vol. V, p. 458.

197. *Ibid.,* also G. Campbell, Modern India, p. 181.

198. Sections 3-4 of Regul, XXIII of 1814.

199. For details B.B. Misra, Cent. Adm., pp. 274-277.

200. Sections 68-75 of Regul. XXXIII of 1814.

201. Sections 13 & 68 of the Regul. XXIII of 1814.

202. Regulation II of 1821, Sections 1-4.
203. B.B. Misra, Central Administration, p. 277.
204. *Ibid.,* p. 278.
205. Bengal Civil (Judicial) Consul. 12, Oct., 1830, No. 42.
206. Judicial Dispatch to Bengal, 23rd July, 1824, para 9, Home Misc. 530, p. 794.
207. Bengal Civil (Judicial) Consul., 12 Oct., 1830, No. 67.
208. *Ibid.,* Nos. 72-73.
209. The Asiatic Jrl., Jan.-Apr. 1833.
210. Ramsay Muir, Making of British India, pp. 277-78.
211. Bengal Civil (Judicial) Consultations, 12th Oct., 1830, No. 69.
212. *Ibid.,* No. 1, paras 52-55.
213. For details J. W. Kaye, The Administration of the East India Company, pp. 50-51.
214. Judicial Dispatch to Bengal, 11 Sept., 1833, para 19.
215. Misra, Central Administration, p. 284.
216. Section 15, Regulation XIX of 1817.
217. Regulation IX of 1825.
218. Preamble to Regulation XIV of 1824.
219. For details Misra, Cent. Admn., pp. 285-86.
220. Home Misc. No. 530, f. 769, 12 June, 1823.
221. B.B. Misra, *op. cit.,* p. 289.
222. Act VII of 1831.
223. Section 6, Regulation XXIV of 1814.
224. Regulation 5, 1831, and Regulation 2, 1833.
225. For details B. Misra, *op. cit.,* p. 294.
226. Sections 2-5, of Regulation 6 of 1832.
227. Lord Moira's Minute, 2nd Oct., 1815, paras 41-43.
228. Regulation III of 1814.
229. For details B.B. Misra, Central Administration, pp. 365-66.
230. For details F. J. Shore, Notes on Indian Affairs, Vol. II, pp. 378-80.
231. Regulation XVII of 1816 with particular reference to Section 7.
232. For details B.B. Misra, Cent. Admn. pp. 368-369; also N.C. Roy. The Civil Sev. in India, Firma K.L.M., Cal. 1958, pp. 19-20.

233. Judicial Dispatch to Bengal, 9 Nov., 1814, para 16.

234. Cambridge History, Vol. V, p. 460.

235. Sections 3-4 of Regulation III of 1821.

236. Section 3, Regulation II of 1832.

237. J.W. Kaye, p. 346.

238. L.S.S. OMalley Hist. of Bengal, Bihar & Orissa, p. 351.

239. Kaye, p. 347.

240. Revenue Consultations, 30 Dec., 1828, Nos. 19-21.

241. Of the 20 Div., 3-Saran, Patna and Bhagalpur were in Bihar, Bengal Rev. Consult. 30 Dec. 1829, No. 22.

242. Section 5, Regulation I of 1829.

243. The Ind. Police Commission Report, 1902,-3, Bengal Sec. press, Calcutta 1909, para 14.

244. Preamble to the Regulation I, 1829.

245. J. W. Kaye, Admn. of the East India Co., p. 347.

246. Regulation VII of 1831.

247. Act III of 1835.

248. Report on the Admn. of Bihar & Orissa. During 1911-12, Bihar & Orissa Govt. Press, Patna, 1913, para 115.

249. Minute of Thomas Munro, 22 Jan., 1821, Selections from Revenue Records, North-west Provinces, Vol. III. p. 63.

250. Regulation IV of 1821.

251. Sect. 14-18, Regulation VII of 1822.

252. J. W. Kaye, the Admn. of the East India Co,. p. 348.

253. N. C. Roy, The Civil Service in India, p. 21.

254. Eric Stoke, The English Utilitarians and India, p. 164.

255. Sect. 8 of Regul, IX of 1833, for details B.B. Misra, Central Admn. p. 160.

256. Sections 16-25, Regulation IX of 1833.

257. Regulation I of 1817.

258. Sects. 4-5, Regul. XXIV of 1817.

259. Misra, Central Administration, p. 145.

260. Regulation I of 1821.

261. Regulatin III of 1822.

262. Bengal Revenue Consult., 10 Dec. 1828, No. 53, paras 3-4.

263. Eric Stoke, The English Utilitarians & India, p. 151.

264. *Ibid.,* p. 152.

265. Bengal Revenue Consult, 30 Dec., 8128, Nos. 19-21.

266. *Ibid.,* No. 22.

267. Sect. 2 Regul. I of 1829.

268. See Supra Criminal Justice & Police of this chapter.

269. Sects. 5-7, Regul. I of 1829.

270. Preamble to the Regulation I of 1829.

271. For details R. B. Ramsbotham, Studies in the Land Revenue History of Bengal, pp. 137-160.

272. Regulation II of 1816.

273. B. B. Misra, Central Admn. pp. 167-68.

274. Regulation XII of 1817.

275. Bengal Revenue Consult. 17, Mar. 1820, No. 1.

276. B.H. Badenpowell, The Land System of British India. p. 679.

277. B. K. Sinha, Office of the Kanungo in Bihar, Bengal Past & present, January-June, 1967, pp. 15-16.

278. D.P. Sinha, Aspects of Brit. Soc. & Admn. Policy during the Administration of Lord Auckland, pp. 4-5.

279. Regulations I of 1829, VII of 1831, IX of 1833.

280. Minute of the Police Committee, 18 Aug., 1838, Cal. Review. Vol. V. Jan-June, 1846.

281. Report on the Admn. of Bihar & Orissa. During 1911-12, Bihar & Orissa Govt. Press, Patna, 1913. p. 33.

282. Quoted N. C. Roy, The Civil Service. in India. pp. 23-24.

283. Cambridge History of India, Vol. VI, Indian edition, S. Chand & Co. 1964, p. 28.

284. C.E. Buckland, Bengal under the Lieutenant-Governors, Cal., 1901, Vol. . I. pp. 24-55.

285. L.S.S. O'Malley, Hist. of Bengal, Bihar & Orissa, p. 383.

286. Report of the Bihar Police Commission, 1961, Bihar Govt., Secretariat Press, Patna, 1961 p. 6.

287. Report of the Salaries Com., 1885-86, Bengal Secret. Press, Calcutta, 1886, para 9.

288. *Ibid.*

289. Section 4, Act V of 1861, see J.C. Curry, The Indian Police, Faber & Faber, London, 1932, pp. 4-18.

290. Minute of the Police Committee, 18 August, 1838, Calcutta Review, Vol. VI, 1846, pp. 145-46.

291. *Ibid.*

292. Calcutta Review, Vol. VI, 1846, p. 154.

293. *Ibid.*

294. Quoted Buckland Bengal under Lieutenant-Governors, I. p.3.

295. For details *Ibid.,* pp. 25-26.

296. *Ibid.,* pp. 26-27.

297. Cambridge History of India, Vol. VI, pp. 27-28.

298. For details Buckland, II, pp. 27-28.

299. D.P. Sinha, Aspects British Social and Administrative policy in India—During the Administration of Lord Auckland, pp. 280-81.

300. Act XXV of 1837.

301. D.P. Sinha, Administration of Lord Auckland, pp. 291-92.

302. 3rd & 4th of William IV, Chapt. 85.

303. Sections 53 & 87 of the Charter Act of 1833.

304. Section 43 and 45, 46 of the Charter Act of 1833, see Cambridge History of India, Vol. V.I. pp. 6-7)

305. Preamble to Section 53 of the Chapter Act of 1833.

306. J. W. Kaye, the Administration of the East India Company, p. 102.

307. Cambridge History, VI, p. 8.

308. *Ibid.*

309. Quoted John Strachey, India, Its Administration and Progress, 2nd Ed. Macmillan, London, 1903, p. 116-117.

310. *Ibid.,* also D.P. Sinha, *op. cit.,* p. 249.

311. B.B. Mitra, Administrative History of India, p. 513.

312. Calcutta Review Vol. VI, 1846, pp. 145-146.

313. Minute by the Police Committee, 18 Aug. 1838. vide *Ibid.*

314. For details, Report of the Law Commissioners, 4th Ncv., 1843, paras 7-8, 48.

315. For details Calcutta Review, Jan-June, 1850, Vol. VIII pp. 377-85.

316. British Paramountcy and Indian Renaissance, ed. R.C. Majumdar, Part-I, p. 346.

317. For details B.B. Misra, The Administrative History of India, pp. 513-525.

318. *Ibid.,* pp. 525-527.

319. D.P. Sinha, Aspects of British Social and Administrative Police in India. During the Administration of Lord Auckland, pp. 280-81.

320. Act XXV of 1837.

321. D.P. Sinha.... Administration of Lord Auckland, pp. 291-92.

322. Supra Chapter-Santhal Insurrection.

323. Supra Chapter Kol and Bhumij Rising.

324. Combridge-History of India, Vol. IV p. 8.

325. Sir John Malcolm. The Political History of India, 1754-1823, Chapter X, also Buckland, Bengal under Lieutenant Governor, I.P. Introduction XV.

326. For details see B.B. Mishra, Central Administration of the East India Company pp. 55-56.

327. 3 & 4 of William IV, Chapter 85, Section 38.

328. *Ibid.,* 55, 4 & 5.

329. *Ibid.,* SS. 11-17.

330. 5 & 6 of William IV, C 52.

331. 3 & 4, William IV, C 85, 39-65.

332. Cambridge Hist., Vol. VI, p.9.

333. Sir George Campbell, Modern India p. 228, also quoted Buckland, Bengal, Under Lt. Governors, I, PP. Introduction, XIII-XIV.

334. Cambirdge Hist. VI. p. 21.

335. For details Calcutta Review, Vol. XXII, 1854.

336. 16 and 17 of Victoria, Chapter 95, Section 16.

337. For details of his appointment to the office, rank, salary and etc. see Buckland, Bengal under Lt. Governors, Part I, pp. Introduction XVII-XIX.

338. W.S. Setorn-Karr, Calcutta Review, Vol. XXII, Jan. 1854.

339. J.W. Kaye, Administration of the East India Company, pp. 277-309, also Michael Edwards, British India, 1772-1947, Sidgewick and Jackson, London, 1967, p. 120.

340. For details of Buchanan Reprots on Patna, Gaya & Shahabad.

341. John Strachey, India, its Administration and Progress, 425-27, 458.

342. Calcutta Review, Vol. VI, 1846, pp. 145-146.

343. Buckland, Bengal under the Lt. Governors, Part I, pp. 183-208, and Minute of the Lt. Governor, Sir. J.P. Grant on the Report of the Indigo Commission vide *Ibid.,* pp. 238-271.

344. For details K.K. Datta, Freedom Movement, I. pp. 167-92.

345. For details Buckland, Bengal under Lt-Governors, I, pp. 196-208.

346. For details K.K. Datta Freedom Movement in Bihar, Vol. II, pp. 167-92. & B.B. Misra 'Mahatma Gandhi's Movement in Champaran, Govt. of Bihar, 1963.

347. Michael Edwards, British India, pp. 118-119; also letter dated the 22nd August, 1871, alongwith a report on the state of education in Bihar, from the Commissioner of Patna to the Govt. of Bengal.

348. Letter dated 3rd Oct. , 1872, from R.H. Wilson, Officiating under Secretary to the Govt. of Bengal to the Commissioner of Patna, and letter dated the 18th April, 1879, from the Govt. of India to the local Govts.

349. For details V.C.P. Choudhary, The Creation of Modern Bihar, Yugeswhwar Prakashan, Patna, 1964.

CHAPTER 6

The Revolt of 1857-1858 and Bihar: The Climax

The great Revolt of 1857-58, shaking to its roots the very foundation of the British Empire in India, was an all India Movement. Hence causes of its outbreak in Bihar also were more or less, similar to those elsewhere in India. A century of the British rule, beginning with Plassey and followed by political, administrative, fiscal, social, and religious changes, left 'behind a blazing trail of discontent and disaffection'[1] among all classes of the people which growing in volume and intensity culminated in the Revolt of 1857-58.

'Every conquest and rule of a foreign power, whether Imperial or colonial, has in it a stain of evil, it wounds the spirit of the conquered country. A strange element foreign to the soil, to the manners, to the blood of the country and encroaching on its customs and institutions, and also the very means of subsistence of the people, builds up stresses and strains (which no Bentinck or Ripon can palliate). The case of India under British rule furnishes the singular instance of the natural reaction of a highly seasoned and mature people under a sense of subjection.[2]

India had been ruled by alien conquerors many a times in the past, but there had been a marked difference between the English conquerors and their predecessors. The Imperial Britons always remained aliens in true sense of the term. With the growth of their territory and power, grew the sense of English racial superiority and arrogance;[3] and with that widened the gulf between the ruled and the ruler. Like many keen observing. English officers, William Tayler, Officiating Commissioner of

Patna, while reporting his superiors at Calcutta in 1855, clearly emphasized this point:" Separate as we necessarily are from the millions around us by our habits and ideas, we are still further and without the same necessity isolated from their hearts by an utter absence of all individual feeling or sympathy'.[4]

During the preceding years of the Revolt a widespread feeling of discontent and disaffection was prevalent in Bihar. Referring to the state of mind of the people, Tayler wrote to the Government: "Minds of the people in these districts are at present in a very restless and disaffected state, and they have generally conceived the idea that there is an intention on the part of the Government to commence and carry through a systematic interference with their religion, caste and their social customs".[5]

Mention may be made in this regard of an anonymous petition[6] supposed to be from the principal inhabitants of the province of Bihar and Zillah Azimabad (Patna) to the Lieutenant Governor of Bengal. The petitioners claimed that the grievances of the people of Hindustan would run to a volume, but three things had chiefly attracted the attention of the people, (1) the establishment of (English) Schools in every village, (2) the destruction of Musjeeds and the Temples of Hindoos for formation of road, (3) the passing of rule whereby in making appointments in the public service preference (is) given to persons possessing a knowledge of the English language. Thus when our religion are destroyed, and we are deprived of the means of earning our bread, life will be burden to us.

It was further claimed in the representation that the zamindars and Rajahs of Muzaffarpore, Arrah, Chapra, Azimabad, Sahebganj and Bhaugulpore, and Sepoys attached to the jails and collectorates of these districts' had ' formed themselves into a party', and had 'made preparations, for a battle to defend their religion and honour'. The petitioners also threatened that disturbances would occur in several places , if (1) English schools were not abolished, (2) destruction of Masjeeds and Hindoo Temples were not prohibited, (3) measures for prevention of baptism of Natives were not adopted, (4) Act for attendance of females at the court were not annulled, (5) and if situation on Omedwars conversant with Persian and Arabic languages without giving any preference to those acquainted with English language were not conferred.[7]

As a matter of fact, as late Dr. Rajendra Prasad, 1st President of India, had rightly remarked, ' the people of India had never accepted the rule of the East India Company with alacrity'.[8] From the very beginning of the establishment of the Company's political sway the people had reacted actively against the alien-rule, and had resisted its growth in different parts of the country, including Bihar. In Bihar alone we find a series of battles, resistance movements, insurrections, plots and conspiracies against the growing English supremacy. Battle of Siraj-uddaula, activities of Raja Ram Narain, battles of Mir Qasim, disturbances by Bihar Zamindars during the revolt of Raja Chait Singh of Benaras, and Wazir Ali, the Sannyasi raids, various tribal risings of South Bihar leading to the Kol and Santhal Insurrections, and the Wahabi Movement, are burning examples of active resistance against the alien-rule. The great Revolt of 1857-58 came as a climax.

Bihar, true to its tradition, played a glorious role in the great Movement of 1857-58. The first shots for the Revolt were fired on the 10th May, 1857 at Meeruth, and its echoes were heard nearly a month later in Bihar at an insignificant village named Rohini near Deoghar in Santhal Parganas where a Company of the 32nd Nattive Infantry and the 5th Irregular Cavalry wereaflamed.

The Sepoys' Revolt at Rohini

In the evening of the 12th June, 1857, the Sawars of the 5th Irregular Cavalry at Rohini rose in rebellion and murdered Sir Norman Leslie, the Adjutant, and injured Major Macdonald and Dr. Grant.[9] However, Major Macdonald suppressed the outbreak firmly & cruelly,[10] courtmartialling and hanging the three leaders on the 16th June. The Headquarters of the Regiment was transferred to Bhagalpur.

After the failure of this mutiny at Rohini not only the 5th Irregular Cavalry & Rohini became quiet, but the whole of Bihar seemed to be so. However, this peace proved illusory.In fact, it was the lull before the storm. Bihar rose again with renewed vigour from July, 1857. This time lead was provided not by the sepoys but by the people , " an event unique in the annals of the mutiny, a popular outbreak without a military rising'.

Anxiety at Patna and Danapur

Since the Mutiny at Meerut Company's authorities-civil & military, of important stations in provinces were on alert to preserve the peace in their respective stations and regions. So were William Tayler, Commissioner of Patna Division, and Major General Lloyd, commanding Danapur Division. The province of Bihar with Patna as its capital was of paramount importance. During the critical period of the 'Mutiny', it had become all the more important, for Patna not only commanded the land route and water line between Calcutta and Allahabad, but also had in its proximity Danapur, the Divisional headquarters of the Army with three Native Regiments— the 7th, 8th & 40th N.I, one company of European, and one of the native Artillery and Her Majesty's 10th Foot.[11] Naturally, both the places were the source of constant anxiety to the British authorities. Danapur, like all other regimental centers, was sitting on volcano. Moreover, Danapur Sepoys came mostly from the neighbouring districts of Shahabad, where subsequently, even according to English standards, the movement 'assumed all the dignity of a national revolt'.[12]

Patna, according to Colonel Malleson, was the most Inflammable city in India, the headquarters of the intriguing Wahabis[13] and to William Tayler, the Commissioner, 'every Wahabi was a potential rebel.'[14]

Wahabi leaders Arrested

Tayler knew that Patna was 'a very sink of disaffection and intrigue',[15] and troubles were apprehended any moment after revolt at Meeruth. Hence, he took every precautionary measure to preserve the peace of the city and to provided protection to the European community in case of danger. He, through his letter of the 19th June, also directed District Officers of Chapra, Arrah, Gaya, Muzaffarpur, and Motihari, to deal with the anti-British outbreaks sternly and to raise extra police force for the purpose: and himself 'adopted some highly repressive measures'[16]. Since Tayler expected troubles from the Wahabi leaders of Bihar, he resorted to' 'treachery',[17] and arrested Shah Muhammad Hussain, Ahmad-Ullah, and Wazir-ul-Haque, prominent Wahabi leaders of Patna on the 19th June.[18]

Rising of July 3rd at Patna

After the arrest of the Wahabi leaders Tayler tried to disarm the people of Patna, and accordingly issued orders to surrender all their arms and not to leave their homes after 9 P.M. But all the 'unnecessary harshness and illegal proceedings'[19] could not dampen the spirit of the people of Patna. And they rose in rebellion on the 3rd July, 1857.

The hero of the 3rd July Patna rising was Peer Ali, a book-seller who was noted for his anti-British feelings.[20] Arms and men were collected at the house of Peer Ali, and on the fateful evening of 3rd July a strong party of rebels with flags and drums, parading the streets of Patna city attacked the local Catholic Mission with a view to finish the inmates.[21] As soon as the information reached the local opium Godown, Dr. R. Lyell, Principal Assistant to the opium Agent proceeded to quell the disturbances at the head of fifty Nazeeb guards and some Sikh sepoys. But before Dr. Lyell and his party could do anything, he was shot dead and them beheaded by the insurgents. At the death of their leader Nazeeb guards resorted to firing causing the death of a rebel. Even then the rebels did not disperse[22]. In the mean time, J.M. Lowis, Magistrate of Patna and Mr. Mangles, Assistant Magistrate, rushed to the spot alongwith 100 men of Sikh Battalion headed by Captain Rattray himself. The insurgents, though gave a fight, could not withstand the onslaught of the disciplined Sikh sepoys and dispersed with heavy losses[23]. However, prominent rebel leaders like Ali Kareem[24] and Peer Ali escaped unhurt.[25] But the following two days were the days of thorough search for rebel leaders and repression let loose on them.[26] Peer Ali and Ghashita, and employee of Lutf Ali, the famous banker of Patna who was suspected of financing the organization of Peer Ali, were hanged on the 8th and 9th July respectively.[27]

The Mutiny at Danapur

Though the rising of the 3rd July, 1857 was suppressed, yet there was danger from Danapur Regimental Centre. To avert that danger, William Tayler, Commissioner of Patna suggested the disarming of the Danapur Sepoys. The Govt. of India left the decision of disarming the sepoys of Danapur on the wisdom of General Lloyd, who was reluctant to take that drastic measure,[28] and vacillated long to take any definite action. Finally, he resorted to a half measure and resolved not to disarm the sepoys but to deprive them of the percussion caps. 'This was to render their fire arms harmless without subjecting them to any degradation or humiliation.[29] Nevertheless, while officers endeavoured to persuade the sepoys to surrender the caps in their actual possession, the sepoys of the 7th and 8th Native Infantry broke into open mutiny. The soldiers of Her Majesty's 10th Foot who were patrolling nearby European Hospital, fired upon the mutineers causing the death of a number of rebels. Consequently, men of the 40th Native Infantry who were till then orderly and peaceful, also joined the insurgents. Then all the mutineers went off towards the river Sone in the direction of Arrah.[30]

The Mutineers at Arrah

On their arrival at Arrah in the morning of the 27th July, the mutineers from Danapur were welcomed and joined by the local Nazeeb Guards. William Tayler suspected previous understanding between the two.[31] At Arrah the rebels burnt the two indigo factories and raided government buildings.[32] Next, attacking the jail building they released the prisoners and then looted the treasury containing Rs. 85,000.[33] Now they began their hunt for the Europeans. But the Europeans were not taken by surprise.[34] In view of the apprehended trouble they had already taken certain measures for their safety. The women and children, and most of the non official Europeans found it safe to march to Danapur.[35] It was also decided to fortify the two-storey detached house of Vocars Boyle, Railway Engineer to the Company, where the Europeans could take shelter in case of emergency.[36]

As soon as the English authorities at Arrah received the intelligence that the mutineers had crossed the river Sone, and were marching towards Arrah, they took shelter in Boyle's fortified house defended by fifty of the captain Rattray's Sikhs, sent by Tayler from Patna.[37]

The Mutineers after plundering the Treasury and European bungalows on 27th July rushed to Boyle's bungalow in the evening and laid seize to it. Though the Sikh soldiers offered stern resistance, rebels were successful in occupying its outhouse where from and from behind the trees in the compound, they continued their musket and gun shots throughout 27th, 28th, 29th July.

Mutineers under the leadership of Kunwar Singh

In the meantime, the Mutineers found themselves greatly strenghtened in terms of men and morale, resources and leadership, by the joining, with his men, of Babu Kunwar Singh who, according to Tayler, was "driven into rebellion by the shor-sightedness of the Bengal Govt."[38] The Revolted sepoys now 'placed themselves under Kunwar Singh's order.[39]

It might be debatable whether Babu Kunwar Singh, one of the foremost leader of the Great Revolt, in joining the revolt was motivated by his personal grievances against the Company's Govt. due to its failure to relieve him from bankruptcy or by the higher ideal to end the alien rule on a premeditated plan, as was believed by some contemporaneous British officials, i.e., E.A. Samuells, Commissioner of Patna division, H.C. Wake, Magistrate at Arrah, A. Money Magistrate of Gaya and Colonel Maleson,[40] but once the Octogenarian hero took the cause of the revolt, he, did not pause for a moment and sacrificed everything to the cause he was fighting for. Undaunted by heavy odds, he displayed unbounded energy and resolution, skills quality of leadership. Moreover, he "obtained more success against the English in the battlefield and carried on a more vigorous and prolonged campaign.[41]

Nearly two years long fight of Kunwar Singh against the English began from Arrah, his district headquarters, when he took the leadership of the Mutineers from Danapur, and attacked the English Garrison there. The Garrison, as we have noted earlier, put a resolute resistance. However, 500 strong European and Sikh troops [42] sent from Danapur under Captain Dunbar of Her Majesty's 10th Regiment to relieve the besieged, was severely defeated with heavy losses. The loss included Dunabar and several of the English officers. Vanquished and reduced Govt. forces made a disorderly retreat, and retreat became a route. Describing the event Mc Donell recounted, "of the four hundred men who had gone out on the day before, full of health and hope,one half had been left behind to gorge the vulture and jackals, and of those who returned only about fifty were wounded."[43] Not only the result of the expedition to Arrah had been very, as was reported by General Lloyd to the Commander in Chief,[44] but also the situation was critical, for the people 'of the country had turned against' the English.[45]

Babu Kunwar Singh's Raj

After the defeat of the English forces under Captain Dunbar, Babu Kunwar Singh "proclaimed himself ruler of the country " and assumed the title of Maharaja or Raja.[46] He now established his own machinery of administration on the English model and appointed his own officers. Reporting the matter to his authorities at Calcutta, Samuells, the Commissioner of Patna, observed that all acts of Kunwar Singh during the short time he considered his Raj to be firmly established and that he was desirous of modelling his government one that of the Govt. which he had superceded.[47]

In fact, Arrah passed for the time being under Kunwar Singh's control.[48] Major General Lloyd, commanding Danapur Division, had himself admitted that the (English) troops were "inadequate to cope with Koer Singh and Mutineers in Arrah"[49] However, Kunwar Singh's Raj proved to be short-lived. Major Eyre who was on his way to Allahabad, hearing the presence of Mutineers at Arrah, broke at Buxar. Reinforced by 25 High-landers form Ghazipur and 154 men of 5th Fusileers under captain L'Estrange, he marched to Arrah and gained decisive victories. After severe fighting against the rebel forces under Kunwar Singh at Bibiganj near Arrah on 31st July, Eyre regained Arrah on 2nd and 3rd August 1857.[50] Major Eyre not only made the rebels disperse but also disarmed that hostile people of Arrah.[51] Native officers acknowledging the authority of Kunwar Singh were hanged as an example after trial by drum head court-martial.[52] However, all the condemned " met death with dignity".[53]

Babu Kunwar Singh, with his men and the Mutineers, left Arrah to take a better position at Jagdishpur, his ancestral home-town and stronghold. But Eyre also attacked Jagdishpur on the 11th August after adequate preparations and reinforcement. Though, resolute resistance was offered by Babu Kunwar Singh and his men, " but muskets had no chance against howitzers",[54] Jagdishpur was captured by Eyre on 12th August. The town, the palace and principal buildings around it were blown up.[55] From Jagdishpur Kunwar Singh retired to the jungles of Jitaura, south of Jagdishpur. But he was hotly pursued by Eyer's party.[56] Consequently, Kunwar Singh had to leave the jungles of Jitaura (Jagdishpur) on 14th. Captain L 'Estrange destroyed, Kunwar

Singh's new place there and Captain Jackson, with the volunteers, on their way back to the camp, set fire to the residences of Omar (Amar) Singh and Dayal Singh, the two brothers of Kunwar Singh".[57] Thus, Kunwar Singh's army was defeated, his strong-hold destroyed; but the old lion was not tamed'.[58] Dislodged from the jungles of Jagdishpur, he turned to the hills of Rohtas.[59]

From Juthora (Jagdishpur) Kunwar Singh first went to Nokha near Sasaram, where he halted for sometime and was "furnished with supplies by the Zamindars holding villages in the neighbourhood, but the most conspicuous among them were the maliks of Burgon, who went so far as to come to Sasaram and openly proclaimed that the Company's raj had ceased".[60] However, Kunwar Singh could not hold long in Sasaram because of the opposition offered on behalf of the Govt. by Shah Kabiruddin, Honarary Deputy Magistrate of Sasaram,[61] and he proceeded towards Rohtas, hovering in this area for most of the days of August, waiting for a junction with the 5th Irregular of Bhagalpur and Ramgarh Mutineers who had already marched from Hazaribagh to join Kunwar Singh.[62]

Kunwar Singh's Campaigns outside Bihar

The presence of Kunwar Singh and his brother Amar Singh along with the Mutineers in the vicinity of Rohtas "threatened the Grand Trunk road, the land artery of the British communications. But Kunwar Singh had "wider views and bolder plans. He rightly perceived that the war would be won or lost not in the lower provinces but in northern India".[63] Accordingly, he moved out of Bihar. Throughout the month of September he was reported to be hovering in the Mirzapur-Rewa region, threatening both.[64]

In Rewa itself, with the entry of Kunwar Singh, the Raja of the place fled from his Capital, and a "large body of armed People" surrounded the house of lieutenant Willoughby Osborne.[65] The old warrior had plans to join Tantia Tope and Nana Sahib and as such from Rewa he move to Banda by the end of September.[66] On 20th October he proceeded from Banda to Kalpi[67] at the invitation of Nana or the Gwalior Contingent or both, to participate in the projected assault on Kanpur.[68] As a matter of fact, Kunwar Singh at the head of 40th NI alongwith Gwalior Contingent led by Nana Saheb and Tantia Tope took part in the battle of Kanpur.[69] After the defeat of rebel forces at the battle of Kanpur, Kunwar Singh with his forces moved to Lucknow, "the most important seat of war", where he was warmly welcomed by the Shah of Oudh and was presented with a robe of honour along with a 'Farman' for the District of Azamgarh.[70] Kunwar Singh now marched towards Azamgarh. In February, 1858, Koer Singh was somewhere between Lucknow and Dariabad, headquarters of the district of Bara Banki.[71] British troops under Colonel Milman opposing the march of Kunwar Singh was defeated on 22nd March at Atraulia and even chased to Azamgarh, which itself was subsequently occupied by Kunwar Singh on 26th of March.[72] An attempt by Colonel Davies on 27th March to recapture Azamgarh was frustrated. And, thus 'Azamgarh remained virtually under Kunwar Singh's control'.[73] But it was too much for the mighty British Empire to bear such defeats and occupations of a district by the rebels. Probably, Kunwar Singh understood it well and, as such he was planning to return to Bihar before it was too late. Even before this the Commissioner of Patna, through the Secretary to the Govt. of Bengal had informed the Governor-General of the intended return of Kunwar Singh and of consequent anxiety and alarm among the officials in Bihar.[74] Realising the gravity of the situation, the Governor-General immediately sent Lord Mark Kerr and Sir Edward Lugard to deal with Kunwar Singh and to vindicate the honour of the British arms. The old chieftain and his forces 'fought well, and with more determination than usual and it was not without a severe struggle that they were defeated and expelled from the city".[75] However, the rebels "retired in good order", Kunwar Singh could not be captured, though reward for his apprehension had been raised to Rs. 25,00.[76]

Under the circumstances, Kunwar Singh finally decided to return to Shahabad to renew the struggle in his home province, Bihar; and from Azamgarh he proceeded towards Ghazipur.[77] But he was hotly pursued by Brigadier Douglas and Colonel Cumberlege. Nevertheless, the old warrior covered his retreat, with "regularity and devoted courage" as has been testified by Sir E. Lugard in his letter of 16th April, 1858:; and at the same time "fought a series of brilliant rear-guard action".[78] Despite Govt.'s

"Utmost endeavours to capture" Kunwar Singh and to prevent his party from crossing the river Gogra, the veteran chieftain forced his passage to Maniar in Ghazipur District by the night of 20th April , 1858,[79] where he found himself amongst friends. The wants of his troops were voluntarily supplied by the villagers who were almost universally in his favour.[80] Now, Kunwar Singh decided to reach Bihar by crossing over the Ganges near Balia. Contrary to the orders of the Govt. The zamindars of Sheopur welcomed Kunwar Singh cordially and furnished him with 20 boats for crossing the Ganges.[81]

Kunwar Singh Reenters Bihar

Naturally, Govt. Officials on both sides of the river were alarmed and they took all possible precautionary measures to prevent Kunwar Singh's entry into Bihar.[82] Orders were given to the Magistrate of Arrah and Chaprah to be most careful in removing all boats from the left bank of the Ganges and the right bank of Gogra. Parwahnahs on the same subject were issued to the zamindars and the bodies of the police and zamindar's men were placed on each Ghat particularly at the Sheopur and other nearby Ghats. The Magistrate of Ghazipur gave the most stringent orders on his side to have the boats removed. The villagers in Shahabad were warned that in the event of any of the inhabitants giving "assistance to Koer Singh entire village will be severely punished.[83] In spite of such preventive measures taken by the Govt. Kunwar Singh with his men crossed the Ganges safely on the 21st April , 1858 "by baffling the efforts of Douglas and outwitting Colonel Cumberlege.[84] It was a wonderful feat, : Even his opponents spoke high of his masterly retreat across the Ganges".[85] Thus, against heavy odds, the old hero force-marched bravely and unmolested to Jagdishpur by the 22nd of April, 1858.[86] However, while crossing the Ganges he was hit by a cannon ball resulting in the loss of one arm and wound in his thigh.[87] But he remained undeterred in his resolve to renew the contest, and on reaching Jagdishpur he was greatly strengthened by the joining of Amar Singh with his men and materials.[88] The troops of Kunwar Singh and Amar Singh took their position in the jungles of Jagdishpur. On the other hand, the Govt. forces were not sitting idle. A strong detachment under Capt. Le Grand of 35th Foot marched from Arrah to Jagdishpur. Le Grand wanted to repeat Eyre's exploits in the self- same jungle[89], but the dying lion could still strike, and strike with effect.

The End of Mortal Life of Immortal Hero

On the 23rd April, the British troops had to retreat with heavy losses, Le Grand himself being killed. As a matter of fact, retreat soon became a complete rout.[90] But the old lion was not destined to repeat his exploits. It proved to be his last victory. He died in his liberated Jagdishpur on 26th April, 1858,[91] both of physical injuries sustained at Sheopur Ghat while crossing the Ganges, and fatigue of a prolonged warfare.

Thus came to an end the mortal life of the greatest immortal hero of Bihar, one of the foremost leaders of the Great Revolt of 1857, who opposed the alien rule in a wider theatre of war. Even against heavy odds, he fought with a rare resolve and achieved brilliant successes. And not the least, he inspired a band of fighters against the growing strength of the British power, possessed of various means of modern warfare'.[92]

Amar Singh Leads the Bihar Fighters

Amar Singh, the younger brother of Kunwar Singh, though reluctant in the beginning to join the movement,[93] proved to be the great leader of the Revolt in Bihar. Like his brother, he valiantly fought the English against heavy odds. While Kunwar Singh had been out of Bihar to fight at various fronts, Amar Singh took command[94] of the home front providing the most needed and able leadership to the rebels. In fact, it was he who in the absence of Kunwar Singh kept alive the flames of the great movement in Bihar. He had well understood the futility of open fight against the English and from the very beginning adopted the plan of guerilla warfare. After the first fall of Jagdishpur in mid August 1857 he made the Kaimur Hills his home—where from, he carried on his incessant fight against the English.[95] He suddenly used to appear on the Grand Trunk Road and disrupt the English supplies and communications.[96] Despite handsome rewards announced by the Govt. on the heads of Amar Singh and his compatriots, namely, Nishan Singh, Harkrishna Singh,[97] they could not be arrested as they were protected with fidelity by the people.[98] Colonel Fisher moving along the Grand Trunk Road was directed to halt at Dehri with his column. He rushed there on 3rd , Sept. Captain Rattray was also ordered to send as many of his Sikhs as he could spare from Gaya. On the 28th Sept., 1857 Lieutenant Baker, 2nd in command of the Rattray's Sikhs, surprised Amar Singh's village of Sirohi. But Amar Singh was not there. A Jamadar, a havaldar and two sepoys were captured there and hanged two days afterwards. In the beginning of October, Amar Singh and the 5th Irregulars were in the neighbourhood of Rohtas.[99] In December Captain Rattray came to Arrah with his headquarters. Early in February, 1858, he arrived at Sassaram and Colonel Mitchell organised an advance on Rohtas. He could easily occupy the Fort as Amar Singh's men had retired, "but it was evident from the preparations that had been made in Rohtas and its neighbourhood', that Amar Singh had contemplated holding the place in force at some future time, it was probably intended to be a rallying point for the rebels driven out of Oudh and Gorakhpur.[100]

All the exertions of the civil and military officers of the Govt. to contain the menace of Amar Singh and his men proved futile. With the re-entry of Kunwar Singh into Bihar and subsequent defeat of English forces under Le Grand at the end of the April 1858, the situation became all the worst for the Govt. Valiant fights of Amar Singh and his men at various places against the English forces under Capt. Rattray, Brigradier Corfield, General Lugard, Brigadier Douglas, during May and June, 1858,[101] "and his swift movements created an alarm amongst the British officials from Gaya to Ghazipur, and from Arrah to Azamgarh.[102] All the attempts of the Govt. to arrest Amar Singh and to subdue the rebels were frustrated. On the contrary, the English troops had to be, 'confined to the stations; and the interiors of the district of Shahabad, Patna and Bihar (Gaya) had been abandoned to the rebels', who were "offering a reward all over the country for the heads of Government officers.[103] As a matter of fact for the month of July. Shahabad remained under the virtual control of Amar Singh,[104] who with the help of Harkishan Singh[105] ran a parallel govt. on the English model, appointing his own civil, military and judicial officers, and punishing the zamindars and people friendly to the English Govt.[106] In the mean time, Nishan Singh, a brave General of Kunwar Singh and Amar Singh was captured, tried, and blown away from a gun on 7th June, 1858 at Sasaram.[107] Saran Singh was also captured and blown from a gun on the 19th July, whole of the male members of his family were also destroyed.[108] Nevertheless, Amar Singh's men, like Joodhar Singh and Meghur Singh[109] and many others continued to be active in groups, fighting relentlessly and harassing the enemy at different places in a wider area.[110] Under the circumstances a vigorous campaign had to be undertaken by the Govt. Brigadier Douglas on 13th October, 1858 ordered seven columns of his troops to besiege the Jagdishpur jungles from several directions to overpower the insurgents.[111] But the plan did not succeed as the insurgents evacuated the place safely before the arrival of the British troops.[112] However, in October – November, fresh offensive by Brigadier Douglas in concert with Major Henry Havelock using the mounted columns and long range Enfilled rifles were at last successful in annihilating Amar Singh's troops.[113] But the English forces could not lay their hands on Amar Singh and other leaders. In fact, Shahabad fighters did not surrender expecting reinforcement from Oudh and Gorakhpur.[114]

Amar Singh, with a view to continue the struggle with the help of Nana Saheb's forces entered the Nepal Tarai in October, 1859,[115] where he was defeated and apprehended by the Gorkha troops and was handed over to the English authorities in December, 1859. He was kept in Gorakhpur Jail. But he died of dysentery in the jail Hospital on the 5th February, 1860, before his trial.[116] With the death of Amar Singh, the movement in Bihar came to an end. Amar Singh, though not a great general like his brother, yet like his brother, fought with grim determination, vigorous efforts, rare tacts of guerilla warfare, exemplary courage and bravery, securing an exalted place amongst the leaders of the great revolt.

As in Rohilkhand and Awadh,[117] movement under the leadership of Kunwar Singh and Amar Singh in Shahabad and adjoining districts where the people protected the rebels by fidelity[118] and were bent up destroying everything European,[119] had assumed the dimension of a national war. Even according to the English standards "the movement in Shahabad had all the dignity of a national revolt and was supported by many of the minor zamindars and more or less openly by all the Rajput population of the district".[120] Mr. W.C. Wake, the Magistrate of Shahabad complained to the commissioner of Patna, that not one zamindar great or small in the whole of Shahabad rendered the slightest assistance before or after the disturbance and with exception of Raja of Doomrao, had offered any since. Neither at any time had a single deserter been apprehended through their means.[121]

Kunwar Singh inspired a band of fighters against the mighty British Empire. As was, though in another context, well observed by the then Lieutenant-Governor of Bengal and Bihar, "his name had always been a tower of strength to the rebels in this part of the country."[122]

Kunwar Singh's aim (and also that of Amar Singh) was not only to destroy alien authority but also substitute in its place own system of government, calculated to serve the best interests of his people.[123] And at the same time, like Mir Qasim, he had also established a gun manufactory at Jagdishpur with a view to provide himself with adequate war implements.[124] After the fall of Jagdishpur Amar Singh shifted this workshop to the hills where he had to retire. According to the statement of a sepoy who served under Amar Singh till his arrest, the guns and cannon balls were manufactured by a mechanic brought from Calcutta. A regular training was given to the new recruits.[125] Regular training and drills are also corroborated by Ramtahal Gwala's deposition.

Disturbances in Gaya

The district of Bihar (Gaya) was also disturbed during the Revolt. Ever since the Mutiny at Meerath there was excitement among all sections of the people in Gaya[126] and anxiety among the officials, more so because of the proximity of Grand Trunk Road. Nevertheless, nothing significant happened immediately after the mutiny at Danapur. However, a carpenter, spreading rumours and disaffection, was tried and executed.[127] After the receipt of intelligence of the mutiny at Danapur and disaster of Dunbar in Shahabad, there was a great deal of panicy among the officials and other Europeans at Gaya and they all left the town.[128]

By the evening of 3rd August, 1857, Mr Money, though managed to dispatch to Calcutta the treasure consisting of Rs. 7 lakhs, himself had to join the escorting party of H.M.S 64th when pursued by an attacking mob of revolted Nazeib quards and freed prisoners of local jail. The rebels overtaking the British party attacked them twice in the rockies near the Dobhi Road. However, the attack was repulsed and the party thereafter reached Raniganj unmolested by 12th August.[129] In the meantime in Gaya, there was no government and there was lawlessness for 13 days. Unfortunately, no leader or a man from landed aristrocracy rose to occupy the city.[130] and it was easily re-occupied by the Govt. forces on 16th August, 1857. But the interiors of the district were still disturbed.[131] In Nawada sub-division Hyder Ali Khan with the help of a large follower and a gun taken from Hisua fort had taken possession of the Rajgir pargunnah declaring that the British Raj was over. However, Capt. Rattray who was sent against him was successful in defeating and capturing Hyder Ali Khan.[132] In the north and west of the district Jeodhar Singh had brought the English rule to an end and had been making land grants to his men as an independent ruler.[133] He remained active for a long time.

The Mutineers of the 5th Irregular cavalary from Bhagalpur also created troubles in the District. In the last week of August, 1857, marching through Madanganj, Hasua and Nawada, they destroyed public buildings and levied contributions from zamindars and other rich sections.[134] In early September, they approached Gaya. Captain Rattary encountered them on the 8th September near Bodh Gaya, but the rebels 'inflicted considerable loss' on the English forces and reached Gaya before Rattray.[135] Here the insurgents attacked the house of European judge and released 400 prisoners from the jail and proceeded towards Tikari early on the 9th September.[136] On reaching Tikari they are said to have levied a contribution of rupees one lakh from the Raja and Rani.[137] The Mutineers now marched towards the river Sone via Daudnagar and crossing the river on 17th, they joined the forces of Amar Singh on the other side.[138]

Fresh alarm was caused in the district of Bihar (Gaya) by the movements of the 32nd N.I. which had mutinied in the Bhagalpur Division. The Mutineers however, continued their march without visiting Gaya.[139] In early January of 1858 Kushal Singh, a Thikadar of several villages, and Jamuna Singh of Khowra with 2000 men raised the standard of revolt under the Wazirganj Thana and declared themselves as Rajas.[140] More formidable than all these was the revolt of Jeodhar Singh and his brother Hetam Singh. A party of 42 Naziebs sent out to effect the capture of Jeodhar Singh failed miserably as he had taken position in his strongly fortified house and the attack was for the present abandoned.[141] Thus he had established himself between Arwal and Daudnagar, collecting revenue and punishing people and villages friendly to the govt. Jahanabad thana was attacked and burnt on 24th June 1858 . The Daroga was cut to pieces and his mangled body afterwards hung up by the heels on a tree opposite the side of the thana. The Nimandawa dak bungalow was also destroyed on the following day, and Judhar Singh is said to have boasted that he would destroy every public building between the Sone and Monghyr. This was enough for the Govt. A vigorous campaign was undertaken to clear the district of rebels. Hetam Singh, brother of Jeodhar Singh was surprised and defeated on the 29th June. Jeodhar Singh himself was completely defeated with a loss of about 100 men, in an encounter near Kasma on the morning of the 4th July 1858.[143] This was the end of trouble in the district.

Commotion in North Bihar

Since the mutinies in the Upper Provinces, the Europeans in the Lower Provinces of the Presidency of Bengal were alarmed. So were they in the North Bihar. Writing to the Secretary to the Govt. of Bengal on the 17th June, 1857, H. Richardson, Magistrate of Muzaffarpur, apprehended trouble any moment. And hence he had already adopted certain measures for the protection of the European community in the District.[144] Armed with the powers of arrest and summary trial of 'Mutineer or a Deserter' under Act XVII of 1857.[145] Mr. Tayler, the Commissioner of Patna, advised all the District officers, including that of Saran, Champaran and Tirhut, of his division,' to be stern in suppressing anti-British outbreak".[146] Accordingly, arrests were made in the interiors and 'among the Mussalman's in Muzaffarpur, which included one fat Thanadar with a lot of mutineous correspond- dence.[147] Major E.S. Holmes , commanding the `12th Irregular Cavalary at Sugauli in Champaran, went a step further. Declaring Martial law throughout the District he was hanging right and left-mostly sepoys returned from the scene of action.[148] This high handed policy of Holmes instead of checking the insurgent spirit among the sepoys, added flames to the fire. Simultaneous with the rising of Danapur, Major Holmes own 12th Irregulars at Sugauli, not only rebvolted but also savagely murdered him and his wife, Dr.

Garner, the Surgeon, his wife and their little son.[149] The insurgents also killed Mr. Bennet, the Dy. Post-Master, and after loot and arson proceeded towards Siwan.[150] At Siwan the rebels made an attack on the houses of Mr. Lynch, the Dy. Magistrate and Mr. Macdonel, the sub-Dy. Opium Agent who made their escape with difficulty.[151]

With the receipt of the intelligence of the mutiny of the 12th Irregulars at Sugauli and their march towards Siwan the English officers and other Europeans of the town of Chapra abandoned the station on the 28th July in panicky and left for Danapur.[152] But the rebels from Sugauli marched towards Azamgarh without visiting Chaprah. The station was re-occupied, unopposed and undamaged, on the 12th August, 1857. In the meantime order had been preserved by a native gentlemen, Kazi Ramazn Ali, who received the thanks of Government with the highest praise and substantial reward.[153] However, Chapra did not remain peaceful for long. The rebels in small and scattered parties soon became active.[154] A small body of the insurgents, in December, crossing from Gorakhpur into the Saran District attacked the post of Guthani. All the 55 Sikhs of the detachment fled away without facing them.[155] And there was an attack on a somewhat larger scale on the night of the 21st June, 1858, on Captain Miles' post at Etwa. The attack was successfully repulsed.[156]

After the revolt at Danapur and the success of the insurgents in Arrah Martial Law was declared on the 30th July, 1857 , in all the districts of Patna Division; and on the following day operation of Act XVI of 1857, was extended to the whole of the lower provinces. It was on this date, July 31st, that Mr. Tayler, the Commissioner of Patna, issued orders directing the abandonment of all the outstations his Division.[157] And it was in the wake of this order that the English officials and residents at Muzzaffarpur abandoned the station. Taking advantage of this situation a detachment of the 12th Irregulars stationed there rose in revolt. They looted the Monghyr mail and made an attack on the Treasury and other Government offices. Being successfully opposed by the Nazeebs and Nazirs of the Foujdari Court, the insurgents plundered the residences of the Judge and the Collector and then proceeded towards Motihari, even taking with them, besides properties, horses, one thana Jamadar and four or five of the new Sawars.[158] The station was soon reoccupied and safety measures against future dangers were also adopted but a feeling of insecurity still prevailed.[159] There was always apprehension of an attack, at one time by the mutineers from Dacca,[160] and that other time from Azamgarh.[161]

The districts of Saran, Champaran and Tirhut remained disturbed for long due to hostile activities of revolutionaries from Gorakhpur under Muhammad Hussain Khan. Tirhut also was at one time further menaced by the mutinous Sawars from Jalapaiguri.[162] It was only after vigorous efforts and the joint operations of the British and the Gurkha Armies[163] that the districts of the north Bihar could be cleared of the revolutionaries.[164] Rajas like that of Bettia hand Maharaj Chattudhari Singh of Hathwa and zamindars like Bishun Prakash Singh of Tirhut, zamindars of Pandaul and Sursand displayed loyal spirit by helping the Govt. with money and men for which they received the highest praise.[165]

Commenting on the nature of the movement in north Bihar, Sir F.J. Halliday, the then Lt. Governor of Bengal, on the one hand observed: 'In these districts too, as in Shahabad, great uneasiness' had been caused by the late successes of the rebels": and on the other hand, he' dismissed with very brief notice, " the three districts north of the Ganges, as there had never been anything in the shape of a popular movement."[166]

Widespread Revolt in Chotanagpur Division

During the Great Revolt the British authority was seriously challenged[167] in the Division of Chotanagpur. The fact is corroborated by volumes of official documents. Writing about mutiny in Chotanagpur and Cuttak, Sir F.J. Halliday, the then Lt. Governor of Bengal, observed in his Minute: "During the whole period of the outbreaks, the Division of Chotanagpur has been a source of anxiety and uneasiness, and from time to time of embarrassment and difficulty, and even of actual danger. In fact, no division in the whole of Bengal has been subject to such continued disturbance as this province.[168]

Here, in this Division, the rising started first from Hazaribagh, on the 30th July, 1857, in the afternoon, two companies of the 8th Bengal Native infantry broke out in open mutiny, made an attack on the jails, liberating all the prisoners both from Penitentiary and District Jail, looted the treasury containing Government Papers and Bank Notes amounting to Rs. 74,000, and burnt three bungalows and part of the catchery papers. The jail workshops were plundered by the prisoners.[169] The rebels marched off to Ranchi and the English officers of the Station saved their lives by timely flight.[170]

Two companies of the Ramgarh Battalion, about 30 Sawars of Irregular cavalry, with two guns under Lt. Graham were sent from Doranda (Ranchi) to deal with the situation at Hazaribagh. But these detachments also revolted under the leadership of Jamadar Madho Singh on their way when they received the information of the actual rising of their comrades of the 8th Native Infantry at Hazaribagh. The insurgents soon seized the guns, ammunitions, and carriage including four elephants, and turned back to Ranchi with hostile designs.[171] They effected a junction with the mutineers of the 8th Native Infantry from Hazaribagh at Bermo, twenty-five miles north of Ranchi.[172] No doubt existing that the headquarters of the corps stationed at Doranda would join them. Commissioner Captain Dalton along with other Europeans reluctantly quitted the station (Ranchi) and retreated on Hazaribagh.[173]

Captain Dalton easily reoccupied Hazaribagh and restored law and order with the help of loyal Sawars and sepoys under Lt. Graham and forty to fifty armed men provided by the Raja of Ramgarh.[1749] A special feature of the rebellion in Hazaribagh was the participation of the Santhals who availed themselves of the Mutiny of the Sepoys at the station to rise against the oppressive money landers and incidently against the Govt. too.[175]

Ranchi Under Temporary Control of the Rebels

With the flight of the civil and military officers from Doranda and Ranchi, the British-rule in the area for the time came to an end, and the insurgents got an upper hand. In fact, nearly for a month or so the township remained under the virtual control of the rebel-forces,[176] who were greatly strengthened after the joining of their cause by the main body of the Ramgarh Battalion including Infantry and Artillery at Doranda under the leadership of Jaimangal Pandey (Singh ?). Soon Thakur Bishwanath Singh Shahi, an influential zamindar of Burkagarh (Lohardagga), who had earlier joined the insurgents, at their request, assumed the supreme leadership; and promised to give the sepoys Badshahi pay.[177] Pandey Ganpat Rai of Bhaunro, a former Dewan of the Maharaja of Chotanagpur, was elected commander-in-chief.[178] Thakur Bishwanath Shahi, the Supremo took his seat in Captain Nation's Bungalow at Doranda, held regular courts and passed orders.[179] He also caused the Ghats to be closed to prevent the return of the English officers, and several breeches to be cut in the road leading to Ramgarh hat to make it difficult for the troops advance against Doranda.[180]

During their "Raj" the rebels took possession of the treasury, plundered and burnt the officers bungalow, thatched cutcherry-buildings, and the lines; destroyed the papers and records; broke open the jail and liberated the prisoners: illtreated the Christian Missions, and tried to destroy the German Mission Church at Ranchi.[181] However, the leaders could not keep in check the sepoys who were involved in indiscriminate plunder, arson and bloodshed,[182] and thus could not evoke popular support.

After their month long stay in Ranchi and Doranda, the rebel-forces, with a view to join Kunwar Singh and Amar Singh in Rotas Garh, left the place on the 11th Sept., 1857, and proceeded towards Chatra via Kaja and Chandwa.[183]

At Chatra on the 2nd October, 1857, the insurgents had a serious encounter with the English forces under Major English and Captain Earle. This grim battle was won by the British at 'a considerable loss', 46 Europeans and 10 Sikhs, 56 men killed or severely wounded.[184] The loss of the rebel forces were even greater, seventy seven were buried in one pit and above one hundred were lying wounded in the jungle. Four guns and wagons complete, ten elephants and much ammunition were captured.[185] Leaders, like Thakur Bishwanath Shahi, Ganpat Rai and Jamadar Madho Singh and others escape but Subedar Jaimangal Pandey and Subedar Nadir Ali were captured, tried and hanged on the spot.[186] With this decisive victory of the English the movement was crushed both in Hazaribagh and Ranchi.

In the meantime, after the departure of the insurgents from Doranda, Ranchi was reoccupied unopposed by the British. With the return of Commissioner Dalton accompanied by Major English, on the 23rd Sept., 1857,[187] normaly and authority returned to Ranchi. Martial Law had already been proclaimed (on the 18th August) in all the districts of Chotanagpur Division by the Lt. Governor. A great hunt was made for the leaders of the movement, the mutineers and bad characters released from Jails.

Thakur Bishwanath Shahi and Pandey Ganpat Rai who had escaped from Chatra and subsequently burnt the Thana at Barwa, and collecting a force of 1,100 men planned an attack on Lohardagga, were captured tried and hanged for 'rebellion' in April, 1858. Their entire property including all the villages under them were confiscated.[188] Tikayat Omrao Singh, Brij Bhukhan Singh, Shukha Bhukhari, Chama Singh, Sibboo Singh and many others suffered the same lot early in January, 1858 . More than 200 sepoys were hanged. Koreban Ally, a Jamadar in the collectorate, Balgobind Shahu, Seetam Choudhary, Buhoran Singh and hundred others had to undergo various terms of imprisonment and fine.[189]

Troubles in Manbhum

There were troubles also in Manbhum. After the mutinies at Hazaribagh and Doranda, in view of the imminent outbreak, Principal Assistant Commissioner and other European officers at Purulia 'retired to Raniganj;[190] and the sepoys of the Ramgarh Battalion on detached duty there rose in revolt on the 5th Aug., 1857. They looted the treasury, and bungalow, liberate the prisoners from the jail; and left for Ranchi[191] Though the sepoys did not create further trouble, but the tribal people like Santhals and Chuars were restive.[192] Santhals made an attack on the Raja of Jaipur and levied contributions.[193] Chuars looted Mahajans and threatened the zamindars.[194]

Raja Nilmani Singh Deo of Panchet raised the standard of revolt and defied the orders of the Asstt. Commissioner of Manbhum who alleged that the Raja in league with the Mutineers of Ramgarh Battalion, was arming his retainers and making preparations for war.[195] After an enquiry the Raja was arrested in early Nov., 1857 and detained in Calcutta till March, 1898.[196] Four pieces of artillery, with other munitions of war were also captured from his fort.[197] Manbhum became peaceful after his capture.

Serious Challenge in Sambhalpur

Serious challenge was thrown to the British authority in the District of Sambhalpur under the leadership of two brother-Surender Sai & Udwant Sai—who were related to the late Raja of Sambhalpur and who had lately been released from Hazaribagh jail by the mutineers there. They had collected a rabble of some

1,400 to 1,600 men.[198] Under their leadership, many of the principal zamindars and rajas in the district were also collecting 'Paiks' for the 'purpose of resisting the Government'. Though, the ordinary police was increased, extra semi-military police was raised, detachments and reinforcements of 40th Madras Native Infantry were summoned from Cuttack, yet 'Indeed', observed the Lt. Governor in his Minute on the Mutinies, "The whole country in the neighbourhood of Sambhalpur was now temporarily in the hands of the insurgents".[199] The rebels began to attack the English parties here and there. At one time in the early part of October, they killed Dr. J. Moore of the Madras Army in such an attack.[200] So bold had the rebels now become that they even ventured to attack Captain Leigh, the senior Asstt. Commissioner, and succeeded in killing and wounding several men of his detachment of the Madras Corps & 'Sebundi'. In December, 1857 the 'dak' road to Bombay was obstructed; and two of the dak stations were burnt.[201] Till the end of 1858 long and several operations under Major Bates, Major Wyndham and Colonel Foster had to be undertaken to defeat the Sai (Surendra, Udwant, Ujjwal and Chail) brothers and to crush the rebellion.[202] In fact, from the close of 1857 to the commencement of 1862 they remained in a state of war, ran a parallel government of their own and kept the whole country in a dangerous state of excitement.[203]

Widespread Insurection in Singhbhum

In Singhbhum a formidable opposition was organized[204] by Raja Arjun Singh of Porahat, popularly known as the Raja of Singhbhum. Like Kunwar Singh, he was well qualified for the role he was to play, and he had a large adherents in excitable and brave Kols; and he had faithful lietenants like his brother Kunwar Baijnath Singh and his 'Diwan' Jaggoo Deo and other courtier Raghu Deo. He was lukewarm and indecisive in the beginning, but circumstances and 'bolder spirits around him,[205] made him a fire-brand revolutionary. After the 23rd Sep., 1857, he was a proclaimed 'rebel' with a reward of Rupees One thousand on his head.[206] What started as a mere mutiny with the outbreak of sepoys at Chaibasa on the 3rd Sept. 1857, after the flight from the station of Captain Sismore, the senior Asstt. Commissioner, was now transformed into a revolt of the people[207] next in dimension to that of Shahabad.[208] Even hundreds of labourers and Brahmans,[209] besides the aboriginals of the various tribes, joined the movement. Procalamation had already been made to the effect that " the people belonged to the Almighty, the country to the king, and the Ruler thereof is Maharaja Arjun Singh." The people were made to believe that the English had left the country and that it had become the property of the Raja.[210] Thus Raja Arjun Singh and his men long defied the authority of the Government.

New Senior Assistant Commissioner, Lt. Birch, after reoccupying Chaibasa determined on a vigorous expedition against the rebel-forces. He, on the 23rd October 1857, first surprised Jaggu Diwan who had earlier expelled the police chauki at Charkradharpur. Jaggu Diwan was captured, summarily tried, sentenced and hanged. Lt. Birch, then, made well managed attack on the Raja's stronghold.[211] After some-resistance the Raja escaped with his men but the palace and the adjoining villages were plundered and burnt by the British troops.[212] But this did not deter the Raja and his brother from the path of revolution. Instead of being subdued, they now exerted themselves to the utmost to raise the whlole Kohlan in insurrection.[213]

A party of the English forces led by Commissioner Dalton himself, along with the senior assistant commissioner Birch, together with 50 or 60 Sikhs under Captain Hale & E. Lushington, in the pursuit of rebels, were themselves ambushed by not less than 3000 or 4000 Kols near Bar Pir by the side of the River Mogra on the 14th January 1858.[214] It was a severe fight. 'Not an officer escaped unhurt ..... The enemy is said to have left 150 dead on the field'.... The insurgent Kols even pursued the party for a distance of 7 miles.[215] Encouraged by this success the rebel-forces drove out the Raja of Saraikella with three hundred matchockment from Chakradharpur who was occupying the place on behalf of the English. The insurgents further defeated severely the British troops sent against them and thus terminated the British Raj from the area for the second time.[216] Under the circumstances Colonel Foster with his Shekhawati Battalion was summoned from Raniganj in mid-January, 1858. Vigorous exertions of Colonel Foster's Battalion and 100 Europeans compelled the insurgents to disperse and the rayatts to submit.[217] The resistance movement was now turned into a guerilla war. Raja Arjun Singh and his lieutenats, like his brother Baijnath Singh and Raghoodeo, in different parties remained active attacking the English camps, posts and the 'loyal' zamindars throughout the year, 1858.[218] However, with the improvement in the situation for the Government in other areas and surrender of some of the Porahat insurgents followed by the capture of Kunwar. Baijnath Singh in early February, 1859, Raja Arjun Singh's position was weakened. Yet the Raja was not inclined to surrender under the Queens' Proclamation. At last, Dalton adopted a clever device to capture the Raja. Arjun Singh's father-in-law, the Raja of Mayurbhanj, was prevailed upon by the Commissioner to exert his influence on Arjun Singh. On the 15th Fevruary, 1859, Raja Arjun Singh submitted himself to his father-in-law who surrendered him to the Commissioner.[219] Though Raghoo Deo and Shankeran still remained active for a year or two,[220] the movement on a wider dimension died down in Singhbhum with the surrender of Raja Arjun Singh. The Raja spent rest of his life as a state-prisoner in Benaras.[221] Letters recovered from the palaces of Raja's retreat indicate that he was in regular communication with other leaders of the movement in Chotangpur and the supreme leader Babu Kunwar Singh and Amar Singh. He had 'succeeded in causing a very universal belief amongst the people of his country that large force was to enter Singhbhum to place him on the 'Gaddi'.[222]

Civil Upsurge in Palamau

The movement in Palamau is unique in as much as there was a widespread rebellion without any mutiny. This was also perhaps the reason that here the movement, although started a little late, proved very serious for the Company.[223] However, it remains a fact that the leaders were certainly inspired by mutiny. Unfortunately, for the English, one of the two Bhogta leaders, 'Pitambar was at Ranchi when the outbreak took place and thinking that here was the end of British rule, and still confirmed in this opinion by the behaviour of the two companies of the 8th N.I., who passed through Palamau on their way to join Amar Singh, the two brothers (Nilambar and Pitambar Shahi) determined on declaring their independence.[224] After so determining, they plunged headlong into the movement and soon organized various classes of the Khairwars to which they belonged, and the Cheros into a fighting force. Many of the Chero Jagirdars were also induced to join them. Their first attack was directed against the 'loyal' Rajput Jagirdar, Thakurai. Raghubar Dial (Dayal) Singh of Chainpur.[225] But the attack on the 21st October, 1857 was repulsed with loss. The insurgents next attacked Shahpur and took possession of four old guns belonging to the Ranee. They broke into the Thannah, destroyed all the records and seized Burkundaz whom they later sacrificed to the Guns. Next day, 500 of them proceeded to Lesliegunj. The 'Tuhseel' Police and Abkaree establishments' fled on the approach of the rebels who plunered and burnt the Thannah, 'Abkaree Cutaries' and 'Tahseel' cutcherry. The disturbances now began to assume a more political aspect & expanded into an incipient insurrection.[226]

Notwithstanding the arrival of Lt. Graham's party with 60 men of the Ramgarh Infantry on the 7th Nov. at Chainpur, there assembled a great force estimated at several thousands.[227] As a matter of fact, as has been observed by the Lt. Governor in his Minute on the Mutiny: "By the end of November the whole country appeared to be up in arms, and Lt. Graham, with his small party, was shut up and besieged in the house of Raghubar Dial,[228] whilst the rebels were plundering in all directions." The factory of Rajhara Coal Company was plundered & destroyed. The Govt. Thannahs of Manka and Chattarpur were burnt. Ranka Fort of Kishun Dayal Singh was attacked.[229] Though with the arrival of relief from several quarters[230] the situation began to take a favourable turn for the English by the beginning of the year 1858, yet their difficulty was that in such a country of impractable hills and jungles, 'the whole of the side of the rebels', who received every information of their (English parties) movements, whilst it was with the utomost difficulty they were enabled to trace them (the rebels).[231] However, with the help of their military might and organisation, the British were able to create a dent in the movement.

While Lt. Graham defeated Premanand (Parmanand), the 'ilakadar' of Kundu and 'the influential leader of the Khairwar tribe',[232] Commissioner Dalton, by his diplomacy, won to his side many Chero jagirdars who were earlier coperating with the rebel leaders, and thus pretty well completed the secession of the Cheros from the Bhogata's alliance.[233] In the meantime several encounters had taken place and the rebels had lost some of their daring leaders. Most severe was the loss of the insurgents when Commissioner Dalton himself, after entering Palamau with a detachnt of the Madras Native Infantary under Major Mac Donel, a small party of Ramgarh cavalry, and a body of match- lockmen under Parganait Jagat Pal Singh, and joined by Lt. Graham, made an attack on the historic Palamau Fort occupied by the rebel forces. After a brave resistance revolutionaries had to leave the fort, leaving behind them guns, ammunitions, supplies and baggage, besides several killed and wounded. Letters to Nilambar and Pitambar Shahi, and Naklant Manjhi were found with the baggage, and amongst them communications from Amar Singh, promising immediate assistance from Kunwar Singh.[234] The Commissioner remained in the 'Bhogta country' for a month but he could not capture the two Bhogta brothers, who, though now reduced in strength , had waged a guerilla war against the British Govt. "A full retaliation was, however, exacted for all the 'mischief' done by them.[235] Their villages were destroyed their goods and cattles seized and their estates confiscated to the State.[236] Undaunted by these retaliatory measures, Nilambar and Pitambar Shahi and their compatriots continued the resistance movement for a long time, still expecting assistance from the revolutionaries in Shahabad which the authorities tried to stop. But despite their best efforts 1,100 rebels had actually entered Palamau under Sidhu Singh and Ram Bahadur Singh to join the Bhogtas.[237] However, Nilambar and Pitambar Shahi were eventually captured, tried and hanged. And, with their capture the district was tranquillized. Thakurai Raghubar Dayal Singh of Chainpur, Thakurai Kishun Dayal Singh of Rauka & Bhikhari Singh of Meenka were granted 'jagirs' in recognition of the local services they had rendered.[238] The leaders and rank who took part in the movement, were punished.

It is a good tribute to the people of Palamau, though written in another context by an English officer, that "Palamau is a country rich enough to support them (the rebels from Shahabad) and strong enough to offer them a revolt against a large force (of the Govt.)[239] Undoubtedly it was a popular movement, 'active upsurge'[240] in Palamau where the whole countryside was in flame. Barring a few Rajput Jagirdars, the landed proprietors and the people 'made common cause'.[241]

1857 Movement in Chotanagpur was a 'wide-spread revolt,[242] a revolt of the people. Even Dr. R.C. Mazumdar concedes that 'the mutiny was merged into a general rising of the civil population in Singbhum and

Palamau.'[243] The Company-government had a hard time. The suppression proved to be a difficult task. In fact, no Division in the whole of Bengal had been subject to much continued disturbance as this province.[244] Though, there was no concerted move under one leadership in the area and there was no leader of the stature of Kunwar Singh, there is a long list of daring leaders. With the exception of Raja Arjun Singh of Porahat big Rajas and Zamindars, like Maharaja of Chotanagpur, Rajas of Ramgarh and Saraikella and Jhalda.[245] Thakur of Kharsanwa, Thakurais Raghubar Dayal Singh and Kishum Dayal Singh of Palamau actively helped the Govt. for which they were suitably rewarded. But there were hundreds of Jagirdars, Ilakadars and Paraganaits who with all their resources faught against the Govt.

One special feature of the movement in Chotanagpur is the largest participation by the tribal masses. The Santhals in Hazaribagh, the Kols in Singhbhum, various classes of Kharwars and the Cheros in Plamau provided real base to the popular movement and they suffered a lot. This is the reason that the writers even see this movement as a continuation of the earlier disturbances of the tribal people of this area against all outside encroachment—the rebellion of the sepoys only providing an opportunity for the smouldering discontent of the triabal people manifesting itself in open outbreaks.[246]

"There is no doubt that all who had revolted in Bihar wanted to work under the common leadership of Kunwar Singh and after his death under Amar Singh; and that those who were conducting the movement in Shahabad remained in constant communication with their fellow workers[247] in different parts of Bihar. The ultimate aim of all, whether civilian or sepoys who had revolted at different times and at different places, had been to join the main body of rebels under Kunwar Singh and Amar Singh. In fact, as has been observed, though in another context, by the then Lt. Governor, Kunwar Singh's 'name' had always been a tower of strength to the rebels in this part of the country.[248] However, it would not be quite correct to say that "the leaders in different parts of Bihar planned to stand and fight together.[249] A close perusal of the facts clearly shows that there was no concerted moves with a 'definite policy and plan of action.[250]

Incidently, this being also the most important cause of the failure of the movement.

Suppression of the Movement

With their superior military might, better organisation, plan, skill, and strategy, diplomacy and vast resources, backed by a powerful nation; and with the active help of friendly Indian princes (including Nepal Darbar), local loyal rajas and loyal battalions and Regiments (including the Sikhs), the British with a sense of higher ideal to save their national glory and empire, could suppress in Bihar, too, the Movement of 1857, which they took as one of the greatest national calamities.[251] As in other theatres of war so in Bihar, suppression of the great Revolt was marked by terrible ruthlessness and vengeance somewhat mitigated after the Queen's Proclamation.[252] Gradually, the whole of the province was brought under Martial law. Through para I of the Circular, dated 31st July, 1857, the Governor-General in Council observed with approbation the zealous exertions of the local civil authorities for the apprehension and condign punishment of the mutineers and deserters concerned in the present revolt, to show that the just fate of the Mutineers was 'death, and that the British Government was powerful to inflict the penalty. Several special Acts[253] in 1857-58, with harsher provisions for the apprehension, trial and punishment of different category of rebels were enacted and enforced.

Repression and reprisals knew no limits. Execution of rebel leaders, long term imprisonment, transportation, confiscation of properties more than damages caused,[254] burning or destruction of houses or villages of prominent leaders, imposition and forcible realisation of collective fines from villagers who joined Kunwar Singh enmasse, and disarming and even flogging of such people, were the general features.[255]

Tayler, the 'pro-consul' of the Division of Patna, even before he was duly empowered, let loose repression on the people of Patna, after the July 3rd rising. Without observing the 'niceties of cross-examination', and punctilios of judicial ceremonies',[256] sixteen were sentenced to death, fourteen being hanged within three hours of sentence, two transported for life, seventeen were imprisoned for various terms by Tayler. The House of Peer Ali, 'principal in the riot', was razed to the ground, and a post was placed on the site telling the crime and fate of the owner and his accomplices.[257] Peer Ali was hanged on the 8th July. Even the Governor-General believed 'that in the course of Mr Tayler's proceedings men were condemned, and executed upon insufficient evidence.[258] Tayler had also issued directives to all his District Officers to suppress the outbreak sternly.

When Major Eyre regained Arrah, he disarmed the people, and after a drum-head court martial hanged as an example to all the native officers who acknowledged the authority of Kunwar Singh.[259] After the fall of Jagdishpur on the 12th August 1857, 'Principal buildings within Kunwar Singh's premises were soon heaps of blackened ruins'.[260] 'The whole town including newly built Hindu Temple, for Eyre believed that the Brahmans had instigated the rebellion, was blown up. Kunwar Singh's new palace at Jataura, and houses of his brothers, Amar Singh and Dayal Singh, were all destroyed or set on fire.[261] All the properties including Kothies' at Arrah, and estates of Kunwar Singh and Amar Singh were confiscated.[262]

Not only Sarnam Singh, a great rebel leader, was captured and blown from a gun but also the 'whole of the male members of his family' were destroyed.[263] Lt. Stanton while searching for the escaped prisoners (from Gaya), and plunders discovered in the village of Etwa some property belonging to Mr. Solano. The house in which the properly was found was set on fire, and subsequently the whole village was destroyed.[264] Unfortunate Major Holmes, before he was killed by the rebels at Sugauli, had been, 'hanging right and left-mostly sepoys returned from the scene of action."[265]

Likewise in the Division of Chotanagpur, not only the houses but also the villages, for they had been the nests of the rebels, connected with the leaders and their lieutenants, were destroyed or burnt. All the palaces of retreats, places and forts of Raja Arjun Singh of Singhbhum, at Porahat, Chakradharpur and elsewhere were destroyed. The Lt. Governor mentioned in his Minute on the Mutinies (30 th Sept., 1858) that after destroying Chakradharpur Colonel Foster proceeded to Porahat, burning villages and seizing large quantity of grain and cattle.'[266] In Sambhalpur, Kolabira of Udwant Shahi[267] and in Palamau the villages of Sunya and Chemu, the Bhogta leaders,[268] met the same fate.

Babu Kunwar Singh, the supreme leader to the movement in Bihar, died a natural death after a prolonged fighting. Amar Singh died of dysentery in Gorakhpur jail Hospital before his trial. But hundreds of followers and leaders met death heroically in battle fields. A good number were captured, tried and hanged or blown from guns. Equal number had to undergo sentences of transportation or long term imprisonment. In Shahabad Amnesty under the Queen's Proclamation of November, 1858, was granted to all except the fourteen leaders mentioned below:

Amar Singh, Harkishan Singh, Joodhar Singh, Seedha Singh, Needha Singh, Ram Bahadur Singh, Meghun Singh, Ibrahim Khan, Debi Ojha, and the four brothers of Harkishan Singh,Lachuni Singh, Kashi Singh, Anand Singh and Radhe Singh.[269]

Properties of all these rebel leaders were confiscated. Even after vigorous attempts to apprehend these leaders, several of them remained active till May, 1859. Many went underground and several took to the Nepal Terai. Harekishan Singh was arrested on the 29th August, 1859 in Benaras. His trial took place in November-December at Arrah. He was sentenced to be hanged by the neck until he be dead at the chowk of Jagdishpur, by R.J. Richardson, officiating Judge of Shahabad, and Special Commissioner under the Act XIV of 1857.[270] Mr. Wake, the Magistrate of Shahabad thought of indiscriminate burning of villages. But it was not approved by the Commissioner. However, the whole population in the district were disarmed by A. Money, the new Magistrate. He resorted to flogging and other humiliating measures to make them surrender their arms.[271]

In Chotanagpur Division, lives of a few prominent leaders were spared. Raja Arjun Singh of Porahat and his brother Kunwar, Brijanath Singh were tried for waging war against the Government . As a special consideration.[272] their lives were spared but thier ostate and propertios were confiscated, they were exiled to live as a state prisoner in Banaras.[273] Raja Arjun Singh died at Banaras in 1890, Leader to be aparted was Nilmani Deo of Banchet who after his capture, was detained in Calcutta for about a year and half.[275] Rest of the leaders were tried and hanged. Jai Mangal Pandey and Mandir Ali, Subedar of the Ramgarh Battalion, were tried on 3rd October 1857 under the provisions of Act. AVII of 1857, were sentenced to death and executed on the very ground where they had made such an obstinate resistance to the British troops two days previously.[276] In the Division of Chotanagpur follwing leaders were tried and sentenced under Act AIV of 1857-58.

Koreban Alli, a Jamadar of the Principal Assistant in the Collectorate Deptt., and Balgobind Shahi were transported for life for 'rebellion and causing the proclamation of the Padshahi Raj' on or about the 4th August.

Tikayat Omrao Singh and Shaikh Bhikharee were given capital sentence and forfeited the property of every description and were executed on 8th Jan., 1858. Thakur Bishwanath Shahi and Diwan Pande Ganpat Rai forfeiting all their properties, were hanged on the same day sentences were passed (16th & 21st April, 1858 respectively). Buhoran Singh was capitally punished and hanged on 5th Jan. , 1858. Seetam Choudhary convicted to 10 years' hard labour and a fine of Rs. 250/-. Chama Singh and Siboo Singh were sentenced to 7 years labour. [277] Nilambhar Shahi and Pitambar Shahi also forfeited their properties and were executed.[278]

A court Martial held under the provisions of Act XIV of 1857 at Ranchi on 1st November, 1857 by Major Mac Donell transported for a period of 7 to 14 years more than two hundred sepoys of the Ramgarh light Infantry Battalion. Another General Court Martial by the same Major passed orders for forfeiture of property and various terms of imprisonment on a long list of sepoys.[279]

References

1. For a detailed study of the causes see R.C. Majumdar, ed. BritishParamountcy & Indian Renaissance, Part I; The Sepoy Mutiny and the Revolt of 1857; Freedom Movement In India, Vol.I; also S.N. Sen., Eighteen Fifty Seven; and Tarachand, History of the Freedom Movement in India, Vol. II.

2. S.B. Choudhury, Civil Disturbances, P.XIX.

3. Charles Ball, History of the Indian Mutiny, 2 Vols, London, 1858-59 , Vol. II, p. 36, also S.N. Sen. Eighteen Fifty Seven, Delhi,

1957, 2nd Reprint, 1977, P. 29.

4. William Tayler, Officiating Commissioner of Patna to W.Grey,Secretary to the Govt. Of Bengal, Dated 27th June, 1855, No. 623, Patna Divisional Commissioner's Records, Central Record Room, Patna Secretariat, (State Archives).

5. Ibid.

6. Enclosure to Letter No. 611, dated 8th Oct., 1855, from Govt. of Bengal, to Commissioners of Patna & Bhagalpur Divisions, Vide Bhgalpur Commissioner's Correspondence, Vol.No. 403, (1832-56).

7. Ibid.

8. *President's Foreword, K.K. Datta's History of the FreedomMovement in Bihar, 3 Vols. , Published by the Govt. of Bihar, Patna 1957, Vol. I, -II.

9. Military consultations, 10th July, 1857, No. 412.

10. For details Charles Ball, History of thc Indian Mutiny, Vol, .I, P416.

11. Colonel G.B. Malleson, History of the Indian Mutiny, 2 Vols,London, 1878-80, Vol. I, p. 40.

12. E.A . Samuells, Commissioner of Patna, to A.R. Young, Secretary to the Govt. of Bengal, No. 1515 dated 25th Sept., 1858, Patna Archives.

13. Malleson, History of the Indian Mutiny, Vol. I, pp. 52-53, 547,550.

14. Quoted G.W. Forrest A, History of the Indian Mutiny, 3 Vols, Edinburg & London, 1904-19132, Vol. III, pp. 400-401.

15. William Tayler, 'Our Crisis', Calcutta, 1858, p. 5.

16. K.K. Datta, Freedom Movement in Bihar, Vol. I, pp,. 17-19.

17. J.W. kaye, A History of the Sepoy War in India, 32 Vols., London, 1864-78, Vol. III, pp. 83-84.

18. For detail see Ibid, also Forrest, History of the Indian Mutiny, pp.400-402; and Tawyler 'Our Crisis', pp. 30-33.

19. G.W. Forrest, History of the Indian Mutiny, vol. III, p. 405

20. Parliamentary Papers, Vol. 44, Part II of 1857-58, Paper No. 2316, p. 14, Enclosure 33 in No. 2, also see Q. Ahmad, WahabiMovement in India, p. 220-21, 223.

21. *Ibid.*

22. *Ibid.*

23. *Ibid.*

24. For life and activities of Ali Kareem See Q. Ahmad, Proceedings Indian History Records Commission, 1958, Vol.XXXIII, pp.9-15.

25. Tayler, Our Crisis, p. 40-41.

26. For details Charles Ball, II , pp. 100-103; S.N. Sen, Eighteen Fifty Seven, pp. 249-252, Kaye, History of the Sepoy War, Vol. III, pp. 85-86.

27. Letter from Tayler to Lowis, Magistrate of Patna (Death Warrant of Peer Ali Y others), dated 7th July, 1857, Exhibit No. 8, and Letter dated 9th July, 1857, Political Deptt. Central Record Room, Patna Archives.

28. G.W. Forrest, Vol. III, p. 414.

29. S.N. Sen , P. 153.

30. J. W. Kaye, History of the Sepoy War, vol. III, pp. 93-94; also S.N. Sen, Eighteen Fifty Seven, pp. 253-54.

31. W. Tayler, Our Crisis, Chap. III.

32. Parliamentary papers, Vol. 44, Part I of 1857-58, No. 40, NAI.

33. Home Public Consultation, dated 21 August 1857, No. 40, NAI.

34. S.N. Sen, Eighteen Fifty Seven, P. 255.

35. J.J. Halls, Two Months in Arrah in 1857, London, 1860, pp 13-14.

36. *Ibid.*

37. Parliamentary Papers, Vol, 44, part I of 1857-58 No. 263 (C2295), p. 33, Enclosure in No. 3 Narrative of Events, 31 August, 1857.

38. William Tayler, Thirty Eight years in India, 2 Vol., London, 1882, Vol. II, p. 193.

39. S.N. Sen, Eighteen Fifty Seven, p. 255.

40. K.K. Datta, Freedom Movement, I, pp. 26-27.

41. R.C. Majumdar, History of the Freedom Movement in India, p.273.

42. Charles Ball, History of the Indian Mutiny, Vol. II, p.105.

43. Quoted I.G. Sieveking, A Turning Point in the Indian Mutiny, London, 1910, pp.67-68.

44. Ball, Vol, II, p. 108.

45. *Ibid.,* p. 110, Capt. R.P. Harrison of her Majesty';s 37th Regiment to the Adjutant General , dated 31st July, 1857.

46. Samuell to the govt. to Calcutta, dated 25th Sept., 1858. also G.B. Melleson, Recreations of an Indian official, London 1872, pp. 302-329.

47. *Ibid.*

48. K.K. Datta, Freedom Movement in Bihar, p. 30.

49. Major General Lloyd dated 2nd August, 1857, quoted in Ball, Vol, II, p.111.

50. Parliamentary papers, Vol. 44. Part I of 1857-58, No. 26, p. 3, Narrative of Events upto 8th August.

51. Parl. Papers, Vol.44,, pt. I of 1857-58, No. 26, p.3, Narrative of events upto 8 August.

52. G.B. Malleson, Recreations of an Indian official, p. 313

53. Sieveking, A Turning point, p. 106.

54. Military Consultations, No. 408, A. Dated Fort William, 4th Sep. 1857, National Archives of India.

55. Parliamentary Papers, Vol. 44, pt. I of 1857-58, paper No.

c 2294, p. 92 Enclosure No. 76 in No. 2. also K.K. Datta, Biography of Kunwar Singh, pp.116-117.

56. Charles Ball, Vol. II, p. 127.

57. S.N. Sen, p. 261.

58. Major V.Eyre commanding the field force to Asstt. Adjutant General, Danapur Division, Dated 14th Aug. 1857 Military Deptt. Consultation No. 408, dated Fort 'willeaw, 41 caper. 1857, Letter No. 13, NAI.

59. Letter dated 30th August, 1857, from W.C. Costtey, Deputy Magistrate of Sasaram, to the Secretary to the Govt. of Bengal.

60. K.K. Datta, Freedom Movement in Bihar, p.45.

61. Military Consul stations No 367, Aug,. 1857 National Arch.

62. S.N. Sen, p. 261.

63. Sir William Muir, Records of the Intelligence Deptt. of the Govt.

of the North West Provinces, India, Vol. I, pp. 539-540 and Military Consolations, No. 394, 4th Sep. '57.

64. Military Consultations No. 457, 16th Oct. , 1857.

65. Military Consultations No. 511, 6th Nov. 1857.

66. Foreign Secret Consultations, No. 142, 27th Nov., 1857.

67. S.N. Sen, p. 262.

68. William Forbes Mitchell, Reminiscences of the great Mutiny, 1857-59, 1895, pp.138-139 also S.N. Sen, p. 262.

69. Military Consultation, No. 488, 27th Nov., 1857 also statement of Nishan Singh during his Trial vide Datta, Freedom Movement, I, Appendix V, pp. 209-211.

70. From first Brigadier General Macaregor to the Secretary, Govt. of India 10th February 1858, Foreign (Political) Consultations, No. 1386, 30th Dec., 1859. National Archives.

71. Secret Consultations no. 273 of 30th Apr. ' 58.

72. Datta, Biography, p. 144.

73. Secret Consultations, No. 263 , 30th Apr. '58 , National Arch.

74. Charles Ball, History of the Indian Mutiny, Vol. II, pp. 285-287. Also Malleson, History of the Indian Mutiny, Vol. II, pp. 473-474.

75. *Ibid.*

76. Letter dated 22nd Apr. ' 58, No. 4058, from E.A Samuells to the Secretary to the govt. of Bengal, state Central Records office, Patna.

77. For details, Malleson, Vol. II, pp. 473-74.

78. Foreign Secrete Consultations No.503, 28th May, 1858.

79. Foreign Secreta Consultations No.59, 28th May, 1858.

80. Home Public Consultations No. 50, 30th April, 1858.

81. Secret Consultations No. 273, 30th April, 1858: National Archives; also letter dated 15th April, 1858 from the Commissioner of Patna to the Secretary to the Govt. of Bengal, State Central Records office, Patna.

82. Letter from E.A Samuells, Commissioner of Patna, to the Secretary to the govt. of Bengal, dated 22nd Apr. ' 58, No. 4058A State Central Records office, Patna.

83. Foreign Secret consultants, No. 3505/508, dt. 28th May, 1858, National Archives.

84. J.J Hall, Two Months in Arrah, p.58.
85. Home Public Consultations, No. 50, 30th April 1858.
86. Secret Consultations, No. 504 & 521 of 28th May, 1858.
87. Charles Ball, History of the Indian Mutiny, Vol. II, p.287, also Malleson, The Indian Mutiny of 1857, II p.379.
88. S. N. Sen ,p. 263.
89. Secret Consultations, No509,510,523, 28th May, 1858, National Archives.
90. Home Public Consultations, No. 28, 9th July, 1858.
91. K.K.Datta, Biography, p.155.
92. For detail Datta, Biography, Chapter-IX , pp. 96-97.
93. Foreign Secret Consultations, 25th June ', 1858, No. 279,
94. Military Consultations, 28th Sept., 1857, No. 410.
95. Letter dated 5th Sept., 1857 from Commissioner Patna Divn. to the Magistrate Shahabad.
96. Letter dt. 25th Sept., 1858, from the Comm. of Patna to the Secretary to the govt. of Bengal, No. 1515, Patna Commissioner's Records, State Archives.
97. Buckland, p.76.
98. Buckland, p.76.
99. Ibid ,pp. 82-83.
100. For details Datta, Biography, pp.163-171.
101. Foreign Secret Consultations, No. 188, 25th June, 1858 and Nos. 148 to 156, 27th August, 1858.
102. Letter dt. 18th June 1858, from Commissioner of Patna to the Govt. of Bengal.
103. Chattopadhyaya, pp.194 also Buckland, p.85
104. Trial proceedings of Harkishan Singh, from J. Richardson officiating Judge & Special commissioner of shahabad, to E.H. Lushing ton, officiating Secretary to the Govt. of Bengal No. 122, dated 17th Dec., 1859.
105. Letter from the Commissioner of Patna, dated 30th July 1858, to the Secretary to the Govt. of Bengal.
106. Letter dated 8th June, 1858, from A.N. Cole, Dy. Magistrate of Shahabad No. 344, Patna Records,.
107. Sir F.J. Halliday in his minute, Buckland, I, 94.

108. Home Public Cons. No. 35 of 13th Aug.l & No. 28 of 3rd Sept., 58.

109. S.N. Sen, p. 265.

110. Home Public consul., 3rd Dec. 1858, No, 32.

111. Letter, dated 31st oct., 1858 from Brigadier Douglas to the Adjutants General of the Army, Allahabad.

112. S.N.Sen Eighteen Fifty Seven, p.265.

113. Home Public Consul, 26th Jan., 1859, No. 19.

114. Foreign Political Consul. 4th Nov. ,1859, No. 160.

115. Letter from Fergusson, offic. Commr. of Patna to the Secretary to the Govt. of Bengal, 15th Feb., 1860, No. 89, Commr. 's Monthly Bundle, No. 26, State Archives, Patna.

116. R. C. Mazumdar, British Paramountary, Vol. IX, p. 551.

117. *Op.cit.,* and also S.N. Sen, p. 409.

118. S.B. Choudhary, II, 173.

119. Report from E.A.Samuells, commissioner of Patna, to A.R. Young, Secretary to the govt. of Bengal, dt. 25th Sept., '58, No. 1555.

120. Quoted Datta, Biography, p.112.

121. Sir F.J. Halliday in his Minute of 30th Sep. 1858, on the mutinies etc Buckland, I p.88.

122. Datta, Biography, p.155.

123. *Ibid.*

124. Vide R.C. Mazumdar, British Paramountcy, Vol. IX, p,579

125. Vide Datta, Biography, p.176,

126. Ed. K.K. Datta, Unrest Against British Rule in Bihar 1831-1859, State Central Record office, Political Deptt. Bihar, Supt., Secretariat Press, Bihar, Patna, 1957, pp. 43-44.

127. Ibid, pp.26-27 Enclosure 4 in No. 2 Events, 29 Aug. 1859 & part II, Paper No. C. 2316, p. 328, Enclosure 19 in NO. 3.

128. Parliamentary papers vol. 44, part I of 1857-58, paper No. 363 (c. 2295) O, pp. 36-37 Enclosure in No. 3, Narrative of Events, dt. 31 August, 1857.

129. Dr. S.B. Singh, Gaya in 1857, Proceedings of the Indian History Congress, Mysore, 1966.

130. Parliamentary papers Vol, 44 pt. II , paper nos., 5-7 relating to the Muting, pp. 1058.

131. Parliamentary papers, Vol.44, Pt I of 1857-58 paper No. 363 (c2295), p. 61 Encl. I in no. 6. Narrative of events, 12 Sep. 1857.

132. HP Chattopadhyay, the Sepoy Mutiny, 1857, p. 127.

133. Telegraph massage, Gaya Collectorate Records, vol. 10, 1857 Issue side.

134. Halliday's Minute dt. 30Sept. 1858, C.E. Buckland Bengal under Lieutenant-Governor Vol.I, Append., p.75.

135. Parliamentary papers vol. 44, pt. I of 1857-58, paper No. 363 (c2295), p.68, Encl. 2 in No. 6 Narrative of events, dt. 19 Sept. 1857.

136. *Ibid.*, p.76, Encl. No. 7, Narrative of Events, 26th Sept. 1857

137. *Ibid.*

138. Buckland, Bengal under Lieutenant-Governors, Vol. I, p.77.

139. Letter, dated 4th January 1858, from Assistant Magistrate of Bihar to the district Magistrate of Bihar, Gaya Collectorate Records.

140. Buckland, Bengal under lient. Governors Vol. I, p.77.

141. *Ibid.*, p.93.

142. Letter, dated 4th July 1858 from C. Beadon, the Secretary to the Govt. of India to A. R. Young, secretary to the Govt. of Bengal, Gaya Collectorate Records. Also see Biography, p,174.

143. Charles Ball, Hist. of the Indian Mutiny, Vol. I, p.449.

144. Letter dated 20th June, 1857, form A.R. young, Secretary to the Govt. Of Bengal, to all Commissioners, Patna Commissioner's Records.

145. Datta, Freedom Movement in Bihar , Vol. I, p.19.

146. Charles Ball, Vol. I , pp. 449-50.

147. *Ibid.*

148. Home Public Consul., dt. 7th Aug. 1857 No. 11, Foreign Secret consul..,dt. 26th Feb., 1858, Nos. 255-69, National Archives.

149. *Ibid.*

150. Buckland, Bengal Under Lt. Governors Vol-I, p. 72.

151. P.C. Roychouhary, Bihar Dist. Gazetteers, Saran ,p. 61.

152. Buckland, p.74

153. Secret Consul, 30th July, 1858 Uly, 1858, Nos. 195 & 198.

154. P.C. Roychoudhury, Bihar District Gazetteers, Saran, pp. 61-62.

155. Buckland I p. 94.

156. Sir F.J. Halliday's Minute on the Mutinies etc of 30th Sept., 1857, Buckland ,I p.72.

157. Parliamentary papers, Vol. 44. pt. I of 1857-58, paper No. 363 (C2295), p. 21, Enclosure in No. 3, Narrative of events, dated 31st Aug., 1857.

158. Letter, dt. 28th Sept., 1857 from the Magistrate of Muzaffarpur ot the Commr. of Patna.

159. Letter, dated 7th Dec., 1857 from the magistrate of Muzaffarepur to the Commr. of Patna, Patna commr. Records, State Archive, Patna.,

160. Home Public Consul, 20th Aug., 1858, No. 3,

161. Sir F.J. Hallidays' Minute on Mutinies, etc. of 30th Sep., 1858

162. Military (Deptt.) Consul, No. 306 Fort William, 21st Aug., 1857.

163. P.C. Roychoudhary, Bihar Distt. Gaztt. Saran , pp.61-62.

164. F. J. Halliday's Minute on Mutinies etc., also see K.K. Datta, Freedom Movement in Bihar, Vol. I, 69.

165. Buckland, Bengal Under Lt. Governors, Vol.I, p.26 & p.158.

166. K.K. Datta, Freedom Movement Bihar, Vol.I, p. 59.

167. Buckland, Bengal Under Lieutenant-Governores, Vol.I, p98.

168. Home Public consultations, 14th August, 1857, Nos. 22-26, also Military Consultation, No.356, dated Fort William, 4th Sept., 1856, National Archives.

169. Ibid., also Military Consutation, No. 366, 14th Aug.,1857.

170. Lt. J.M.Graham to the Commander-in-chief, Military Consultations, 4th Sept., 1857, Nos. 356-59 also Dalton to the Govt. of Bengal, 5th Aug., 1857 Letters Dispatched to Govt. From Chotanagpur Commissioner's office, Vol.218.

171. Parliamentary papers vol. 44, Part I of 1857-58, Paper No. 363 (C2295), p.28, Enclosure 4 in No. 2, Narrative of Events dated 29th Aug., 1857.

172. Buckland, Vol. pp.99-100.

173. P.Papers, Vol. 44, part I of 1857-58, Paper No. 363 (C2295, p.29.

174. H.P. Chattopathyay, The Sepoy Mutiny, 1857, o.135.

175. *Ibid.*

176. Bishanath Shahi in his Trial under Act XIV of 1857-58, on 16th April, 1857 Vide P.C. Roy Choudhary, 1857, in Revision Branch, Revenue Deptt., Bihar, Patna, 1959, pp.61-62

177. *Ibid.*

178. K.K. Datta, Unrest Against British Rule in Bihar, 1831-1859, State Central Record Office, Political Deptt., Bihar, Patna, 1957, p.65.

179. Military Consultation, 4th Sept., 1857, No. 368.

180. Final Report on the Survey and statement operations in the distt. of Ranchi, 1902-10. J. Reid Govt. Printing, Bihar, Orissa, Patna, 1926, Para 78, also Home Public consutation, 25th Sept., 1857, No.134-135.

181. P.C. Roy Choudhary, 1857 in Bihar, pp. 134-135.

182. F.B. Bradley Birt. Chotanagpur, A little known provinces of the Empire, London, 1910, p.215.

183. Major J.Simpson, Principal Asstt. Commissioner of Hazaribagh, dated 4th October, 1857, camp Kalapahari near Chitra (Chatra) to Capt. E.F. Dalton, Officiating Commissioner, Chotanagpur, Vide P.C. Roy Choudhury, p.60.

184. Telegraph Messages from Sherghati and Chatra Nos. 83-8, 89, 152 to Calcutta by Major English, vide, Ibid, pp. 55-56.

185. Major Simpson to E.P. Dalton, *op.cit.*

186. Buckland, p. 102.

187. P.C. Roy Choudhary, Chotanagpur in 1857 pp. 61-62, 138-39.

188. *Ibid.*

189. Buckland, Vol. ,p. 100.

190. Manbhum Asstt. Commissioner to Chotanagpur Commissioner, 20th Aug., 1857, Manbhum Distt. old Correspondence, 1856-57, vol. XI, State Central Records office, Patna.

191. Military Consultations, 11th Sept., 1857, No. 360, Enclosure, Letter dated 18th Aug. 1857, from the District Magistrate of Midnapur who reports, on the basis of information supplied by the Rani of Raipur (Purlia) to his superiors.

192. E.F. Dalton to Govt. 23rd Sept., 1857, No. 28, Chotanagpur Commissioner's office Letters, Vol, 218.

193. Dalton to Govt... 16th Sept., 1857, *op. cit.*

194. G.R. Cakes to Govt. 12th Sept., 1857, Manbhum Distt. old Correspondence, Vol, XI, Central Records office, Patna.

195. Bengal Distt. Gazzetteers, Manbhum, p. 65.

196. Buckland, Vol.I, P. 104 .

197. Sir F.J. Halliday's Minute on Mutiny vide Buckland, Vol. I, p. 110-11.

198. *Ibid*.

199. Foreign Secret Consultations, dated 26th Feb. , 1858, Nos. 255 - 69.

200. Buckland, Vol. I, p. 112.

201. Ibid, pp. 110-115, also Bengal District Gazetteers, Smbhalpur, pp. 32-33.

202. S.B. Choudhury, Civil Rebellion in the Indian Mutinies, II, 196, Sambhalpur Dist. Gazetteer, pp.26-27.

203. Sir F.J. Halliday in his Minute on the Mutinies, Buckland, I, p.106

204. K.K. Datta, Unrest Against the British Rule, pp. 66-70, also P.C. Roychoudhary, 1857 in Bihar, Chapter III on Singhbhum, & Sir Halliday's Minute on the mutinies, relevant portions.

205. *Ibid.*, p. 68.

206. R.C. Mazumdar, British Paramountcy, I, p. 552.

207. S.B. Choudhary Civil Rebellion in the Indian Mutinies, II, p.193.

208. Dalton to Govt. 10 Oct. 1857, Vol. 8218, op.cit.

209. Officiating Commissioner of Singhbhum & Munbhum to the Sec. to the Govt. of Bengal, Home Public Consultation dated 29th Jan., 1858, No. 38.

210. Buckland, I. p.105.

211. Datta, Unrest Against British Rule, p. 70.

212. Buckland, I, p. 106

213. Military Consultation, Dated 29th January, 1858, No. 890.

214. Sir F.J. Halliday in his Minute on the mutinies, Buckland, I, p.p. 106-107

215. Bengal Judicial (Deptt.) Proceedings, dated 27th October, 1959, No. 167.

216. Ibid also Military Consult, dated 19th July, 1858, No. 617.

217. Buckland, pp. 107-110, Dalton's Report on the Mutiny of chotanagpur, 1918.

218. Datta, Unrest Against British rule , pp. 74-75, also for cleverness and military preparedness at the time of Raja's surrender see Home (Deptt.) Public consultation youn. NO. 13, dated 11th March, 1859 from Dalton to A.R. Young, No. 39, dated the 21st Feb., 1859.

219. Bengal Judicial (Deptt.) Proceedings of August, 1861, No. s 224-30.

220. Bradley Birt. Chotanagpur, p.227.

221. K.K. Datta, Unrest, p.76.

222. K.K. Datta, Unrest Against British Rule , p. 77.

223. Buckland, I p.118.

224. *Ibid.*

225. Report from Captain E.T. Dalton , Cemmissioner of chotanagpur, dated camp chibasa the 21st June, 1858, to A.R. Young, Secretary to the Govt. of Bengal, Fort William, Chotanagpur Commissioner's Records.

226. *Ibid.*

227. Buckland , I, pp. 1180119.

228. Dalton to Govt. 21st June, 1858, *op.cit.*

229. Buckland, *op.cit.*

230. Public Original Consultation, 14 Jan., No. 35/38.

231. Buckland, *op.cit.*

232. Dalton to Govt., 21st June, 1858, *op.cit.*

233. Buckland, I, p. 120.

234. K.K. Datta, Freedom Movement in Bihar, Vol. I, p. 67.

235. Buckland, I, p. 121.

236. Dalton to Govt., 30th Sept., & 8th Dec., 1858, molitary Consultations, dated 29th October, 1858, Nos. 163-64 also Public Original Consultation, 24th Dece. 1858, No. 38-39.

237. L.S.S. O 'Malley, Bengal District Gazetteers, Palamau, Calcutta, 1907, p.40.

238. Dalton to A.R. Young, No. 44, dated 16th August, 1858, Public Original Consultation, 10th Sept., 1858.

239. S.B. Choudhary, II , p. 184.

240. P.C. Roychoudhary, 1857 in Bihar, Chpotanagpur & Santhal Parganas, P. 146.

241. H.P. Chpottopadhyay, The Sepoy Mutiny, p.135.

242. British Paramountcy, I, p.552.

243. Lt. Governor of Bengal in his Minute on the Mutinies, *op. cit.*

244. Foreign Miscellaneous Records No. 383, National Archives, New Delhi.

245. J.C. Jha , Some Light on the Mutiny in Chotanagpur, Proceedings, Indian History Congress, Twenty Eight Session, Mysore 1966; for similar views see Dr. R.C. Mazumdar,British Paramountecy, p.554, P.C. Roychoudhury, 1857 in Bihar,Chotanagpur And Santhal Parganas Chapter-VI.

246. Datta , Freedom Movement , I,p. 61.

247. Sir F.J. Halliday in his Minute on the Mutinies, vide Buckland, I, p. 88.

248. Datta, Freedom movement in Bihar, Vol. I, p. 67.

249. R.C. Mazumdar, British Paramountcy & Indian Renaissance, P a r t — I , p. 644.

250. Disraeli quoted, Charles Ball, History of the Indian Mutiny II, pp. 418-20.

251. K.K. Datta, Freedom Movement,I,p.71

252. Act. XIV, XV, XVII, XXV, XXVIII, etc.

253. Datta, Biography, p. 180.

254. Ibid , pp. 180-81, 184-85.

255. Tayler to the Govt. of Bengal, 25th May, 1859.

256. Charles Ball, History of the Indian Mutiny, Vol. II, pp. 100 103

257. Minute of the Governor-General, 4th March, 1859, for critical examination of Tayler's proceedings, see S.N. Sen, 1857, pp. 249-252.

258. Malleson, Recreations, p.313

259. J.W.Kahye, Vol. II,p.145

260. Charles Ballo, II, p. 127.

261. Datta, Biography, p. 184 & Append. XXI.

262. Buckland, I, p.94

263. Ibid, P. 75

264. Charles Ball, I, 449-50.

265. Buckland, I, p. 107

266. Ibid, p. 113.

267. Ibid, p. 121.

268. K.K. Datta, Freedom, I, p.94

269. Trial proceedings of Harekishan Singh, vide Datta Biography Append, IV, pp. 197-208. Ibid , P. 58.

270. Biography, pp. 184-86, Letter dt. 14th 1859, from A.Money Magistrate of Shahabad.

271. Statement of cases under the provisions of Act. XIV of 1857 vide P.C. Roy Choudhury, pp. 61-63.

272. Letter from Dalton to the Govt. 30th Sep., 1859, No. 224.

273. Bradley Birt, Chotanagpur, p. 227. Raj Arjun Singh died at Banaras in 1890 leaving behind him only son Kumar Nerpat Singh, P.C. Choudhury, 1857 in Bihar, Chotanagpur, p.87.

274. P.C. Choudhury, 1857 in Bihar, Chotanagpur, p. 87.

275. D.G. Manbhum, p. 66.

276. Letter form J. Simpson, Principal Asstt, Commr., Hazaribagh, dated camp, Kala Pahari near Chapra 4th Oct., 1857 to E.J. Dalton, Offg. Commr. Chotanagpur.

277. O 'Malley, D.G. Palamau, p. 40.

278. An extract, dated, Camp Ranchi, Ist Nov. 1857 signed by Major Mac Donnel, Commanding fieldforce of Ranchi, Chotanagpur.

EPILOGUE

Bihar, the land of Imperial Magadhans, the Mauryas, the Guptas, and of holy Buddha and Mahavira occupied a remarkable place in the history of ancient India, and to some extent also in medieval times, particularly during the short reign of Shershah. But it lost it's glory in modern times, more so during the Company Raj.

With the Muslim conquest Bihar lost its old glory, importance, and even independent status. It's fate and fortune hung in the balance, sometimes linked with the Muslim-rulers in Bengal, and at others with that of Delhi, both struggling for the supremacy over the area. Bihar, though always served as the stepping stone to the sovereignty in Bengal, yet in the scheme of government it remained tagged on to Bengal as an inferior partner, receiving step-motherly treatment, not only throughout the middle-ages as Dr. Qanungo had opined, but upto 1912 when Bihar was finally separated from Bengal.

The year 1703 A.D. was a dismal year for Bihar. It was in the beginning of this year that Bihar was united with Bengal, for prince Azim-us-Shan, the favourite grandson of Emperor Aurangzeb was given the Subahadarship of Bihar in addition to Bengal. However, he appointed a separate Naib Nazim and Naib Diwan for the Subah of Bihar. A significant downward change was brought in the political status of the province in 1719, when Murshid Quli Khan, till then the Subehdar of Bengal and Orissa and the 'Diwan' of Bihar, was also made the 'Nazim' of Bihar. Thus, he became the real Subahdar of the three provinces. Bihar was incorporated into Bengal as a junior partner and was to remain so for about two centuries to come.

Since Murshid Quli Khan the provinces, for all practical purposes, began to be ruled as an independent kingdom, owing nominal allegiance to Delhi. The people in Bengal, Bihar and Orissa no longer cared what happened in Delhi. They had fixed their eyes on the 'Mushnad' at Murshidabad. Thus, the centre of interest for this part of the country shifted from Delhi and Patna to Murshidabad, the capital of the ' Nawab-Bahadur', and later on to Calcutta, the capital of'Company Bhadur'. Bihar and its capital Patna lost not only it's independent status, but also political and commercial interest, which it had enjoyed earlier being mid-way important centre between Delhi and Bengal. As Patna lost its political glory and glitter, Calcutta gained in importance. Moreover, with the weakening of the central authority, rebellions and disorders, plots and plunders became the order of day. Heavy exactions of almost all the provincial governors sapped the province of its economic vitality.

With the decline of the mighty Moghuls there had started in India the multifaceted degeneration in society and polity, in culture and moral values. And, at the same time, there emerged new factors and forces on the political scene of India. The clime and the socio-political culture proved to be a fertile land for political adventurism. The consequent emergence of regional powers in place of a strong central authority coincided with the advent, on the political arena, of Europeans in the garb of merchants. It added a new but unfortunate political dimension to the history of India as well as to the history of Bihar and Bengal. The weaknesses of decadent Indian body-politic could not escape the keen obsering eyes of those advanced Europeans who came to India invigorated with new renaissance materialism of modern Europe. They whetted upon their ambition of empire-building in India. It was the misfortune of Bengal and Bihar that when they needed capable and strong rulers like Murshid Quli Khan and Alivardi Khan, who despite continuous Maratha incursions and Afghan insurrections had kept under control those ambitious and designing Europeans, there came in succession rash Siraj-ud-daula, Selfish Mir-Jafar and communal Mir Qasim. The result was obvious. The wild dreams of establishing the Britons as political power began to became a reality well in the time of cunning clive itself.

However, if those princes and debased aristocracy who were selfish to the core, are to be blamed for this Himalayan misfortune, the Marathas, dreaming to be the political successors to the great Moghuls, are no less responsible. Maratha Sardars like Raghuji Bhonsle of Nagpur, with a view to expand their sphere of influence, began to conquer new places and people. But their novel method of conquest and their behaviour were far below their higher ideal of the 17th century, and which alienated the good-will of the people. By their plundering raids on Bihar and Bengal, the Marathas not only shattered the economy of the provinces, but also paved the way for the Company-Raj by accelerating the pace of decay, disintegration and disorder. Aliwardi, though a good ruler and just administrator, and capable of imparting justice and peace, had to spend ten long years, with all his energies and resources, in containing the Maratha-menace, instead of devoting them to the welfare of the people and organisation of the good government. Despite his best efforts the people were ravaged, raped, pillaged and uprooted by the Maratha-raiders. The result was that the people lost faith in the House of Alivardi and reposed them in the English at Calcutta who provided ready shelter and protection. Consequently, deployments, resistance or battles, and duplicities or diplomacy of Siraj-ud-daula, Mir Jafar, Mir Qasim and Shah Alam II proved of no avail. 'Nawab Bahadurs were replaced by 'Company-Bahadur' in Bengal and Bihar. Clive himself established the Company first as the defect-power, and then, after the Buxar and the Grant of Diwani, as the legal sovereign in the three provinces. But he left the actual administration in the hands of the old machinery of Nawabs. Even then the people of Bihar began to distaste and oppose the foreign domination. In fact, the people of the province were not ready to accept the verdict either of Plasy or Buxar. Rebellious activities of Raja Ram Narain, the Deputy in Bihar, and of other Hindu or Muslim Rajas and Zamindars after these battles are indicative of the fact.

Warren Hartings, in 1772, stood forth directly as the Diwan, and for all practical purposes as Nazim also, on behalf of the Company-Bahadur. He began to transform the machinery of merchants into the machinery of Government; and at the same time, tried to consolidate the power of the Company in various parts of Bengal and Bihar. It was then that the real resistance to the English-rule began, and the Imperial Britons had to encounter serious challenges to their infant power in Bengal and Bihar. As a matter of fact, the people of Bihar were never amenable to the alien rule. Their first active opposition came to surface in 1781 during the revolt of Raja Chait Singh of Benaras. J. Reginald Hand, Deputy Collector of Shahabad (1886-90), after examining the records of the period has rightly described this revolt as the political event of consequence in the context of early English administration of Bihar. "The revolt did not remain confine to the citadels of Ramnagar in Benaras. In fact, it proved to be 1857 in miniature which aimed at the 'expiration of the English.' Taking advantage of their late misfortune, powerful rajas and zamindars from Patna, Gaya, Shahabad, Saran, Monghyr and Bhagalpur districts of Bihar 'raised a conflagration from Allahabad to Monghyr'. Even regular 'Daks' were disrupted, and the whole bank of the river (Ganga) were lined with armed men who boarded or fired upon their boats indiscriminately. The situation was so much alarming that Governor-General Warren Hastings repeatedly advised his wife not to stay even at Bhagalpur but to proceed to Murshidabad. Obviously enough, the revolt of Raja Chait Singh had assumed wider dimensions. In fact, it's wide repercussions caused by the large scale participation of the landed aristocracy had a decided influence on the future policy of the English administrators, and in no small measure it was responsible for hastening the Permanent Settlement in the provinces.

The armed resistance to the growing English power was also presented in the form of guerilla war and depredations by the Hill-men and their chiefs like Raja Jagannath Deo and his son Roop Narain of Tappa Chandauri, and Rani Sarbeshwari of Sultanabad (Maheshpur Raj) in the Jungle Terrai from Raj Mahal to Colgong in Bhagalpur. The problem consumed much of the time, resources and even energies of such able English officers as James Burton, Barker, Captain Brooke, Browne and Augustus Cleveland who brought forward a new system of administration to pacify the Hill people. The Hill-system of administration with the Hill Assembly of Sardars and Manjhis and the carving out of the 'Damin-Koh' for the hill people, finally resulting in the creation of a non-regulation district of Santhal Parganas after the Santhal Insurrection, stands testimony to the fact.

Taking lessons and inspirations from the Maratha incursions to harass the ruling power of dislike, the nomadic bodies of Sannyasis and Fakirs (Hindu and Muslim ascetic warriors) also came out to resist the growth of the English-rule in their own way. In the latter part of the 18th century armed Sannyasis and Fakirs raided the travelling English parties, factories, cutchehries and treasuries of the Government and zamindars in many part of Bengal and Bihar. By their plundering raids, they not only threatened the collection of revenue but also the peace of mind of early English administrators, as is obvious from the contemporary records. The Government labelled these Sannyasi and Fakirs as a set of lawless banditi and so have done a host of writers. But if seen in the proper perspective and taking into account the origin, history and martial habits of the armed Sannyasis and Fakirs, their employment generally in the armed services of the Indian rajas and princes hostile to the Company, their bravery and faithfulness as soldiers, timings and targets of their plundering raids, it is hard to dismiss them as a set of lawless banditi. Though, they continued the profession of arms, their plundering raids ceased with the end of the 18th century when they found the Company Raj 'a fait accompli'.

The fierce opposition to the English power was also offered by the tribal people and their semi-tribal chiefs and rajas of South Bihar. The tribal areas of the forest and hilly tracts stretching from Midnapur to Manbhum, Singhbhum, Barabhum, Dhalbhum and Chotanagpur upto Palamau, violently reacted to the sudden imposition of the British-rule. To consolidate their power in all parts of their territorial jurisdiction the new rulers brought new system and new people as their representatives even in secluded and secure areas whose tribal people and their chiefs and Rajas had maintained their freedom, life-style and administrative system throughout the ages. Even the greatest of the Great Mughals could not completely subjugate this region. In the extension of the English power the people of the region saw real danger to their age - long way of life, and as such they offered stiff resistance to the growing control of the English authority. We find a chain of organised resistance and rebellions in the region throughout the Company-rule by the tribal and non- tribal people led by their chiefs, who were dignified among his raiyats with the title of the Raja. Mention may be made in this regard of several Chuar rebellions including the rebellion of 1799-1800, Munda and Uraon rebellions of 1811, 1817, the Hos or Larka-Kol's rebellion of 1821, the great Kol-Insurrection of 1831-32, and the Bhumij-Revolt of 1832-33; and above all the formidable 'Hul' or Insurrection, in 1855-56, of the aboriginal Santhals from the present district of Santhal Parganas, then divided between the old districts of Birbhum, Murshidabad and Bhagalpur. The Sanathal Insurrection, which represents a typical example of the tribal resistance, proceeded from their economic grievances and the inefficiency of the administration. When their grievances were not redressed, their complaints went unheard, the half-savaged exasperated Santhals, under the leadership of four brothers— Sidhu, Kanhu, Chand and Bhairab, came out with their bows and arrows to put an end to the ' Zhulaum' (tyrannies) of Hakims and Amlahs (officers), and deceit of the Mahajans (money-lenders and traders). The Govt. could suppress the revolt only after declaring Martial-Law and a full scale war with the most inhuman barbarities. However, the blood and sacrifices of thousands of tribal people, their chiefs and Rajas, did not go in vain. Recognising the special position of the tribals, the Division of Chotanagpur was created in 1854 and a non-regulation district of Santhal Parganas was carved out for the Santhals in 1856.

The history of modern Bihar is incomplete without a reference to the Wahabi-Movement which brings to the forefront the long sustained Muslim-resistance to the rule of the English infidels. Though, this most remorselessly anti-British movement was all India in character, its progress and sustenance owed substantially to Bihar in general and Patna in particular. The loss of political power by the Muslims which afflicted them in many ways—politically, economically, socially, and religiously, was resented most not only by the Muslim ruling houses and nobility, but also by the Muslim-masses. It was not without battles, rebellions and revolts that the Muslim-rulers gave in. After the failure of their princes and subedars to resist the growing power of the English, the people came forward to shake off the alien-rule. To make this political struggle broad based their leaders prudently thought to unfurl the green banner of 'Jehad'. It is in this background that the Wahabi movement originally started by its founder Sayed Ahmad 'Barelvi' as a socio-religious movement, was transformed into religio-political creed. For freeing the country from the infidels, Syed Ahmad planned to raise a fighting force under the standard of Wahabi-order. And , Patna, with Sadiqpur family of Wilayat Ali, Enayet Ali, Shah Muhammad Hussain, and Farhat Hussain, providing the leadership with devotion as 'Khalifas' or spiritual vice-regents, and sacrificing every thing, hearth, home, property and lives-for the cause, had the rare distinction of being chosen as the first organised centre of the Wahabis. During the subsequent years Patna-Wahabis amply justified the confidence reposed in them by Syed Ahmad. In fact, for about half a century Patna remained the chief Wahabi-centre in India, supplying continuously men and material for the long sustained struggle against the infidels. Patna Wahabis were also instrumental in the Patna conspiracy of 1845-46 in which the conspirators successfully managed to plant mutiny in the Native Infantry Regiment No.1 at Danapur.

The Wahabis as an organised body did not take active part in the great movement of 1857-58 which came as a climax to anti British feelings, fights, rebellions and revolts. However, the Wahabi leaders of Patna were arrested by William Tayler, the redoubtable Commissioner of Patna as a precautionary measure.

Despite all the resistance movements, battles, rebellions, revolts and conspiracies the English rule became a reality which was consolidated through evergrowing and ever tightening administrative control.

The battle of Plassey made the English King-makers in Bengal and Bihar, and that of Buxar the King itself. Mir Jafar and Mir Qasim made them Zamindars of a limited tract of country; and after the battle of Buxar the Moghul Emperor Shah Alam II raised them to the office of the 'Diwan' of the three provinces of Bengal, Bihar and Orissa. Thus the 'Company-Bahadur' received 'Diwani ', the right to collect and reimburse the revenues and to administer the civil-justice of the three provinces, from the Emperor and by arrangements and engagements with successive Nawabs of Bengal, they also got the 'Nizamat', the military control and administration of criminal-justice and police. The merchant-sovereigns, as they now had become, did not realise the 'obvious-moral' of assuming the direct responsibility for the good government of the people of the provinces and left the actual administration in the hands of rutted and rotten machinery of the Nawab, undertaking only the superintendence of the collection and disposal of revenues. This 'dyarchy' established by Clive proved an 'anarchy'. The writer turned administrators of the Company were concerned to 'attain easy fortunes and to leave a land for which they had no affection'. The people of the provinces experienced such skilful, searching and strong tyrannies and oppressions which were unknown and unparalleled in the history of the world. The people were beggared and starved, their suffering being multiplied by the terrible famine and the Company reached on the verge of bankruptcy. Hence, while the Company in 1772 decided to standforth themselves as 'Diwan' and sent Warren Hastings to Bengal as its Governor with specific instruction to anbolish the 'dyarchy' of Clive and to make complete reformation in every branch of Government; the British Parliament in 1773 enacting the Regulating Act and suspending for the time being collection of 'Crime-tax' from the Company, acquiesced in the political role of a private trading company.

Though Warren Hastings as the Governor-General of Bengal gave consuming thought not only to the consolidation of the power of the Company but also to the enormous task of transforming the machinery of merchants into the machinery of government, yet he was bound to fail as this was the first attempt and he had to work under certain limitations. Within the limits provided by the British Parliament (Under the Act of 1773) and instructions of the Directors, and keeping in mind the ancient usages and institutions of this land, Hastings had to erect a government to which the country powers and people could look with respect and awe. Moreover, revenue was the prime concern of the merchant-rulers. Though a good organiser, Hastings, unfortunately was not equally good at the intricate matters of revenue. As a result, his 'strenuous and loyal endeavors' proved a period of experiments and a 'ghastly failure' judging from the happiness of the people. His administration left a trail of misery, famine and insurrections.

The Government established by Cornwallis was essentially

a government based on racial superiority and class exclusiveness. The natives were excluded from all posts of trust and dignity. This resulted not only in the loss of employment opportunities but also led to the debasement of their confidence, character and moral, eating into their intellect and vitality.

The Permanent Settlement in which 'nothing was settled, and little was known except the Government assessment, secured for the Company immense financial gains and powerful zamindars 'into solid supporters to the British interests and power. But this settlement of land revenue with eviction laws and exorbitant rent-rate collected vigorously ruined both zamindars and raiyyats, the latter being the worst sufferers. The raiyyats were left at the mercy of zamindars. Indeed, the raiyyat had 'no rights, and he was left to fight it out with zamindars'. But he was too week against the zamindars, and courts of law were beyond the reach and means of raiyyats. Granting of 'pattas', (declaratory leases) for safeguarding their interests, remained a pious wish, and illegal exactions of zamindars went on uninterrupted. The fact led to the Finance Committee of 1880 to report that the rents of the raiyyats in Bihar had during the last fifty years been illegally and arbitrarily enhanced out of all proportions. The whole condition of the agricultural industry were such as to render it precarious. It only produced beggary, litigation, and corruption.

Ever increasing number of litigations brought forth by the new land settlement and new judicial system which was at the same time defective, costly and corrupt beggared the people of the provinces and extinguished the age-old atmosphere of cordiality and harmony from the society, keeping the zamindars and tenants, rich and poor quite apart. As a matter of fact, the Permanent Settlement destroyed the village-community, changed the structure of society and created new property relations.

The police system of Cornwallis proved to be an extensive failure. It failed to give protection to the person and property. Reports from various districts, e.g. Tirhut, Bhagalpur, indicated that the robberies had increased enormously. Darogas were corrupt and unable to manage the powerful zamindars and extensive territories under them. In 1808, Police Superitendent was appointed but by 1810 he had to supervise the whole of the vast territory of the Presidency of Bengal upto the Division of Patna. Ancient rural police was neglected, yet a civil constabulary was not established till 1865.

The East India Company, trader-sovereign with trade monopoly as they were, administered the territories under them and operated their trade and commerce as they subserved the interests of their mercantile company and nation, but worked to the great detriment, nay to the destruction of the native people, their institutions and economy. It is a known fact of modern Indian History that since the English victories in the battles of Plassey and Buxar, particularly after the grant of Diwani, unbelievably immense wealth of the three provinces of Bengal, Bihar and Orissa made its way to Great Britain. We have the testimony of an English authority, Charles Grant, who said: "In thirty years following the acquisition of Bengal provinces, this nation (Britain) by public and private channels, derived from them alone, exclusive of its other eastern dependencies and of the profits of goods remitted fifty million sterling. "On the one hand, servants of the Company returned home with fabulous fortunes settling there as Indian "Nawabs" and reserving a seat in British parliament, on the other, the whole trade of the Company began to be financed from the surplus of the Indian revenues, particularly the revenues from the three provinces. The mercantile motive of the Company became too apparent after the charter Act of 1833 whence their commerce was altogether terminated and they depended entirely on the revenues from India for the recovery of their assets and dividends. Instead of good government of the provinces and people under their subjection they became concerned more and more with the revenues. Every administrative step was measured on the rod of economy which was practised even at the cost of efficiency in administration and welfare of the people. The fact is quite evident from the administrative history of the period.

Coming of Lord Moira to India as the Governor-General coincided with the passing of the Charter Act of 1813. His appointment and preceding discussions, investigations and reports relating to and passage and provisions of the Act were indicative of an era of utilitarian liberalism and reforms in

England as well as in India. The Act of 1813 diminished the commercial interest of the Company by abolishing its trade monopoly and compelled it to give more attention to the good government of the people under its rule in India. However, till the assumption of office by Lord William Bentinck the attitude of the Indian administration in several respects was more conservative than that of the authorities at home. Moira modified the policy of Cornwallis and began the practice of Indianisation of uncovenanted services. To begin with the natives were appointed as Munsiffs and Sadar Amins in the Judicial Service of the Company. However, they were not empowered to try the cases of Europeans and Americans. The increasing use of native agency in the administration of justice received a setback on assuming the charge of supreme government by John Adams who revived the policy of Europeanisation. But the inadequacy of their number resulted in the pending of civil suits in large number which stood in the district of Purnea at 1,667 and in Tirhut at 3,168. Lord Amherst again augmented the use of native agency with increased powers and emoluments, but there was no corresponding increase in the number of Indian judicial officers. For example, in the district of Saran there were only 8 Munsiffs for 15 Thanas.

Though the Directors had recommended a liberal admixer of native with European authority in the magisterial as in other departments of civil administration, yet their representatives in India were quite reluctant to associate Indians in the administration of criminal justice. As a matter of fact, 'principles of Cornwallis here died hard'; and very limited powers were allowed to the natives in this field.

Earl of Moira, though for different reasons, opposed the extension of stipendiary police beyond the establishment of 'Daroga'. As such civil constabulary was not raised and chaukidari (rural police) system was limited to the head-quarters of Magistrates, that too, only in the division of Patna in Bihar. Again, Moira considered seriously the idea of separating the offices of Judge and Magistrate as early as 1815, yet it was not till 1823 that the two offices were separated in the districts of Jungle Mahals, Ramgarh, Purnea and Tirhut. This separation could not be extended to other districts due to inadequacy of covenanted servants.

Lord William Bentinck, though a true representative of the new spirit of the liberal era in England, had to work under the expediency of economy in the wake of various wars. For bestowing on Indians the best results of the western activities, he introduced in India, the system of English education and initiated a series of social and administrative reforms. Further, he augmented the process of Indianisation of services by appointing the natives to uncovenanted judicial, executive and revenue posts. However, his other measures proved defective and half hearted as he wanted to combine efficiency with economy. For example, Moira had reconstituted the Board of Revenue in the process of decentralisation, yet these Boards with vast territorial jurisdictions failed to secure efficient and effective management of the revenue administration in the absence of personal communication between the Board and the District Collectors. Bentinck found the answer in the institution of the office of Divisional Commissioners of Revenue and Circuit who were to supervise a moderate tract of the country. This also conformed to the Benthamite principle of individual officer against the collective Board. But to unite economy with efficiency, Bentinck annexed to the office of Divisional Commissioners of Revenue also the duties and powers of the Courts of Circuit and that of Superintendent of Police. Moreover, only 20 Divisions were created for the whole of the centrally administered territories of the Company. Out of these 20 Divisions only 3 Divisions, namely, Saran, Patna and Bhagalpur, appertained to Bihar. Later on, when the Division of Chotanagpur was constituted the division of Saran was abolished.

Throughout the whole period of our study the general situation of peace and security continued to be the perennial problem; and even then there was nothing final in the police administration. Not only that the ancient rural police system was neglected, and civil constabulary was not raised, but also the superior office of the Superintendent of police always remained a matter of experiment. The separate post of the Superintendent of Police was revived in 1837 but was abolished in 1854. It was only in 1861 that the tug of war between the Divisional Commissioner of Revenue and the Superintendent of Police for the superior control and supervision of the police came to an end; and the police administration was organised on modern lines.

The alien Britons with a view to perpetuate their colonial rule not only imposed their system of administration but also the system of education put forward by Macauley which with a total emphasis on English language and literature produced white-collar mentality among the natives and neglected altogether the science-technology and agriculture.

Along with common causes as a natural corollary to bondage, artificial union of Bihar with Bengal proved to be the most important political factor for the backwardness of Bihar. It was unfortunate that instead of palliating the evils consequent upon the unnatural union of the three provinces of Bengal, Bihar and Orissa effected during the latter Moghals, and confirmed under the 'Diwani', the Company's Government added a vast territory to the Presidency of Bengal which long (till 1912) remained under-administered as the particular administration of Bengal was tagged with the general administration of the Government of India. Even in 1853, While the three provinces required three separate Governors-in Council, the whole of the lower Provinces of Bengal, as a measure of economy, was provided with a Lt. Governor without a council. If this was the fate of Bengal where the people could shout aloud, what can be said of Bihar, a dumb people, who believed in action, not in shouting? Even at this late stage special position of Bihar as a separate province was not at all taken into consideration, and Bihar appended to Bengal as a junior partner remained altogether neglected for more than half a century. Take the case of the Upper Provinces of Bengal. This North-Western Provinces with comparatively a shorter span of its seperate Lt. Governorship (constituted in 1836), despite famines, witnessed more development of agriculture-irrigation, education and other public works, whereas Bihar's progress in all these fields had been insignificant.

With the transfer of the seat of government of the province of Bihar to Calcutta, and discriminatory policy of the Company, Patna and its neighbourhood which even at the beginning of our present study had been a flourishing international centre of trade and industry, and oriental learning, lost all its former glory and prosperity under the Company-rule. In fact, the condition of peasantry, agriculture, and industry in Bihar as compared to their counterpart in Bengal was, indeed, lamentable.

Racial discrimination in the matters of civil and criminal justice prompted the planters and others of ruling-race to perpetrate their oppressions and crimes on the native peasants which continued unabated. The fact was acknowledged by the European indigo planters themselves before the Police Committee in 1838. Cruelties and oppressions of the indigo planters began to decrease after the 'Nil-Darpan' episode and publication of the Report of the Indigo Commission (1860), followed by appropriate and vigorous measures taken by the Lieutenant-Governor of Bengal. But the case of peasants and raiyyats of Bihar was not considered with such details as that of Bengal. There was none to look into such complaints and no measures to protect the raiyyats from the cruelties of indigo planters in Bihar. The reasons were the distance of the seat of government from Bihar and the resulting stepmotherly treatment of the Government and leaders of Bengal. There were no Dinbandhu Mitra (the author of Nil-Darpan) to dramatise the pitiable plight of the peasants, no Reverend J. Long, the publisher and no Seton-Karr, Secretary to the Govt. of Bengal, in Bihar to create a great sensation through the official publication of the English translation of Nil-Darpan. The peasants of Bihar groaning under the tyrannies of European-Indigo planters had to wait till 1917 for the arrival of Gandhi to alleviate them from their sufferings.

The unnatural union of Bihar with Bengal affected adversely the former even in other ways. Moira and Bentinck tried to mitigate the effects of the policy, initiated by Cornwallis, of the exclusion of Indians from the services, by appointing them to junior revenue, judicial and executive posts. In this field also Bihar remained a loser, for Biharies lagged behind in English education due to their early apathy towards the same. The result was that English educated people from Bengal flooded Bihar. Descendants of those 'prosperous' Bengali officers can still be found in good number in most of the towns and cities of Bihar. It was in the last quarter of the 19th century that the Govt. of

Bengal took some measures to encourage English education in Bihar and to reserve certain jobs in Bihar exclusively for Biharies with a view to check the flow of Bengalis from Bengal to Bihar. However, this issue later on proved to be the main plank for the emergence of the movement for the separation of Bihar from Bengal and 'Bihar for Biharies, leading to the creation of the separate province of Bihar in 1912.

Thus a century of alien English-rule beginning with Plassey and followed by political, administrative, socio-religious and educational changes raised a great and active volcano of discontent and disaffection which growing in volume and intensity year after year erupted fiercely during 1857-58, when the very life, system and honour of the people seemed to be threatened.

India had been ruled by alien conquerors many a time in the past, but there had been a marked difference between the English conquerors and their predecessors. The imperial Britons always remained aliens in the true sense of the terms. With the growth of their territory and power, grew the sense of their racial superiority and arrogance and with that widened the gulf between the ruled and the ruler. We have the testimony of high ranking English officers from Bihar, of those momentous years preceding the great revolt, that they were separated from millions around them and isolated from their hearts by an utter absence of individual feeling or sympathy. Further, the people were in a very restless and disaffected state and they had' generally conceived the idea that there was an intention on the part of the Government to commence and carry through a systematic interference in their religion, caste and their social customs. An anonymous petition supposed to be from the principal inhabitants of the province of Bihar claimed that the grievances of the people would run to a volume and that when their religion were destroyed and they were deprived of the means of earning their bread, (this referred to the preference begin given to the English educated people in services) life would be burden to them. The petitioners further claimed that the Zamindars and Rajas of Muzaffarpur, Arrah, Chuprah, Azimabad, Sahebganj and Bhagalpur and sepoys attached to the jails and collectorates of these districts had formed themselves into a party and had made preparations for battle to defend their religion and honour. Events proved that it was not an empty claim.

Bihar, true to its traditions, played a glorious role, under the leadership of Kunwar Singh and Amar Singh, in the great movement of 1857-58. The motive of Kunwar Singh for joining the rebels might be debatable but once the octogenarian hero 'joined' the movement, he fought to the end of his life even against heavy odds, and sacrificed everything for the cause he was fighting for. Moreover, he opposed the alien-rule in a wider theatre of war, achieving more and brilliant successes than any other leader. And, not the least, Kunwar Singh inspired a band of fighters' against the mighty British empire. As a matter of fact, his name, as the then Lt. Governor of Bengal and Bihar rightly remarked, had "always been a tower of strength to the rebels in this part of the country."

Amar Singh, the younger brother of Kunwar Singh, though reluctant in the beginning to join the movement, proved the foremost leader of the revolt in Bihar. While Kunwar Singh had been out of Bihar to fight at various fronts, Amar Singh took command of the home front providing the most needed and able leadership to the rebels. In fact, it was he who in the absence of Kunwar Singh kept alive, against heavy adds, the flames of the great movement in Bihar. And, it was with the death of Amar Singh that the movement came to an end. Though not a great general like his immortal elder brother yet like his celebrated brother, he fought with grim determination, vigorous efforts, rare tacts of guerilla warfare, exemplary courage and bravery, securing an exalted place amongst the leaders of the great revolt.

Beginning with the mutiny of the 'Sawars' of the 5th Irregular cavalry from an insignificant village at Rohini in Deoghar on the 12th June, 1857, the whole of Bihar, from West to East, from North to South-from Patna to Purnea and from Champaran to Chotanagpur, was soon engulfed in the greatest anti-British upsurge. If Patna in the beginning of July, 1857, had the distinction of having a people's 'revolt', a popular outbreak without a military rising, an event unique in the annals of mutiny'; the movement in Arrah and adjoining districts achieved the honour, even according to the English standards, of assuming the national dimension with "all the dignity of a national revolt."

Gaya (Bihar) with excitement among all sections of the people and anxiety among the officials and other Europeans remained disturbed during the whole period. European bunglows and jails were attacked and prisoners released. Thana in Jehanabad was burnt and the Daroga cut to pieces. The 'insurgent Sawars' at Sugauli murdered their high handed Major Holmes, his wife, their little son and the European Post-Master. The commotion was wedespread in the whole of North Bihar. The districts of Muzaffarpur, Saran, Chapra, Tirhut and Purnea long remained disturbed due to hostile activities of revolutionaries.

South Bihar did not lag behind in fighting the foreigners. The British power was fiercely challenged in Chotanagpur also. Hazaribagh, Ranchi, Sambhalpur, Singhbhum and Palamau and the districts of the Division were ablaze. We have the testimony of the then Lt. Governor that during the whole period of the outbreaks, the Division of Chotanagpur had been a source of anxiety and uneasiness and from time to time of embarrassment and difficulty. In fact, no Division in the whole of Bengal had been subject to such continued disturbances as this province.

If Gaya, Patna and Shahabad produced martyrs like, besides Kunwar Singh and Amar Singh, Jeodhar Singh, Sarnam Singh, Har Kishan Singh and his four brothers Seedha Singh, Needha Singh, Meghur Singh, Debi Ojha and Ibrahim Khan, the Division of Chotanagpur also came forward with a long list of celebrated leaders like Raja Arjun Singh of Porahat and his brother Kunwar Baijnath Singh, Nilmani Deo of Panchet, Thakur Bishwanath Shahi of Barkagarh, Pandey Ganpat Rai, ex-Diwan of the Maharaj of Chotanagpur, Tikait Omrao Singh and Shaikh Bhikhari, Udwant Shahi, Nilambar Shahi and Pitambar Shahi, Jamadar Jai Mangal Pandey, Kurban Ali and Nadir Ali, Chemu, Shiboo and a host of others who met death or suffered otherwise heroically.

With their superior military might, better organisation and plan, skill and strategy, diplomacy and vast resources backed by a powerful nation; and with the active help of friendly Indian princes (including Nepal Darbar) an Zamindars, loyal battalions and regiments (including the Sikh Regiment), the British, with a sense of higher ideal to save their national glory and Empire, could suppress in Bihar, too, the Movement of 1857-58 , which they took as one of the greatest national calamities. As in other theatres of war, so also in Bihar, the suppression of the Great Revolt was marked by terrible ruthlessness and vengeance. Gradually, the whole of province was brought under Martial Law. The Governor-General in Council approbated through para I of the Circular dated 31st July' 57, the zealous exertions of the local civil authorities for the apprehension and condign punishment of the mutineers and deserters to show that the just fate of the Mutineers was death, and that the British Government was powerful enough to inflict the penalty. Several special Acts with harsher provisions for the apprehension, trial and punishment of the different category of rebels were enacted and enforced in 1857-58. Repression and reprisals knew no limits. Blowing through guns or hanging, long term imprisonment, transportation, confiscation of properties of the rebel leaders, burning or destruction of houses or villages of prominent leaders, imposition and forcible realisation of collective fines from villagers who joined the rebel leaders enmasse, and disarming and even flogging of such people, were general features of punishment.

Thus with great violence and vengeance the Great Revolt was suppressed in Bihar. As a result of this movement, the rule of the mercantile sovereign, the 'Company-Bahadur,' came to an end and the power was assumed by the British Crown. However, no change was effected either in the structure of the government or in the plight of the people of the province.

On coming close to the study through preceding chapters two themes, running side by side, are clearly discernible. On the one hand there was gradual growth of English political sway with ever growing and tightening administrative control based on the policy of racial discrimination and mercantile motive of economy and on other, continuous opposition to it. The people of Bihar—whether Hindus or Muslims, tribal or non-tribal, from plains or plateau, Fakirs or farmers, rulers or retainers—came out at one time or the other against the British conquerors. In fact, opposition forms a running theme of the history of the period under review. The people began to distaste alien supremacy just after the battle of Plassey when the impact of the English ascendancy was first felt. The armed resistance, beginning with Buxar and the grant of Diwani, became widespread and stiff from 1772, whence the 'Company' assumed directly the Nizamut along with the Diwani of the three provinces. It ended with the great Revolt of 1857-58, when practically the whole of Bihar rose against the Company-rule, and gave in after the defeat in their last and the biggest bid to overthrow the foreign-rule. Intervallum witnessed a series of risings, raids, rebellions, movements and even conspiracies.

Thus, the people of Bihar though never accepted the rule of the East India Company with alacrity, yet their opposition proved futile, for they were sporadic and disunited. With the exception of the Wahabi-Movement, and the movement of 1857-58, they lacked consistency, unity of purpose, organisation and leadership. In their fight against the English, who were a nation with superior organisagtion and modern knowledge of science-technology and war-machine, the native people were never united with a sense of greater and nobler cause of nationality. Even during the Great Revolt the Wahabis did not support the movement (of 1857-58) as an organised body and many rajas and regiments fought and worked for the alien-rulers. Consequent upon the failure of all the rebellions and movements, the yoke of slavery became still heavier not to be shaken off easily. The fate of Bihar became the fate of all Hindustan.

How a subject people could think of their glory, progress and prosperity, all of which had become the things of remote past ? The multifaceted degeneration which had started with the decline of the mighty Moghuls was complete with a century of the 'Company-Rule'. Evils of bondage with all its natural corollary and the unnatural union of Bihar with Bengal as an inferior partner made the province backward and the people stagnant lagging behind in every field of human activity.

Bibliography

1. PRIMARY SOURCES :

Unpublished Documents

(a) RELEVANT VOLUMES OF :

(i) Patna Commissioner's Records (Bound Volumes, Monthly Bundles, Mutiny Bundles).

(ii) Bhagalpur and Chotanagpur Commissioner's Records

(iii) Records of Chotanagpur Commissioner

(iv) District Records of Bhagalpur, Hazaribagh, Munger, Purnea, Tirhut, Saran, Shahabad.

(v) Singhbhum, Manbhum old correspondence

(vi) Old Zamindari Records

(vii) Political Agent/Governor-General's Agent, South West Frontier agency Despatches and receipts, Miscl. Despatch Book.

(viii) Correspondence of Major Roubhsedge.

(b) RELEVANT VOLUMES OF :

(i) Bengal Public (1763-1823), Secret, (Criminal) Judicial, Revenue (From 1781) Miscellaneous, Revenue (Judicial) (1791-83) Consultations/proceedings.

(ii) Select Committee Proceedings.

(iii) Committee of Circuit Proceedings (1772-1773) (also printed, vols-1-3 in one, Calcutta, 1926-27).

(iv) Board of Revenue Proceedings (170 volms.)

(v) Board of Trade Proceedings.

(vi) Proceedings & Minutes of the Controlling Council of Revenue at Patna (1770-1773), 9 Volumes.

(vii) Proceeding of the Provincial Revenue Council at Patna (1774-1780)—25 volumes.

(viii) Commercial General letters from the Court of Directors: Judicial Letters from the Court of Directors.

(ix) Judicial Letters from the Court of Directors.

(x) Bengal District Records.

(xi) Muzaffarpur Collectorate Records.

(xii) Patna Judge's Court Records.

(c) **RELEVANT VOLUMES OF :**

G.G. Proceedings /Consultations /Records

(i) Home Department- Public , Secret, Separate, Military, Miscellaneous

(ii) Foreign Deptt. - Political, Secret, Miscl.

PRINTED DOCUMENTS

1. Old Fort William in Bengal, ed. C.R. Wilson, Vols. I &II, London, 1906.
2. Early Records of British India, ed. J.T. Wheeler.
3. Calendar of Persian Correspondence in 10 Volumes N.A.I., New Delhi
4. Fort William -India House Correspondence (Relevant Volumes) (Indian Records Series, NAI)
5. Selections, from the Unpublished Records of Government, 1748-1767 (Edited by J.Long); Calcutta, 1869.
6. Selection from the State Papers of the Governor-General of India-Warren Hastings (Edited by G.W. Forest), BH. Balackwell, 1910.
7. Selections from the letters, Despatches and other State Papers preserved in the Foreign Department of the Government of India, 1772-85), Vols. I-II (Edited by G.W. Forest) Calcutta, 1890.
8. Selections from the State Papers of the Governor-General

of India, Lord Cornwallis, 2 Vols. (Edited by Sir G.W. Forrest); Oxford, 1926.

9. Bengal and Madras Papers Vol. II and III, Calcutta, 1922.

10. Correspondence of Charles, First Marquis Cornwallis, 3 Volumes, (edited by Charles Ross), London, 1859.

11. Collections of Treaties, Engagements and Sanads relating to India & Neighbouring Countries, Compiled by C.U. Aitchision, Vol.I, Calcutta, 1909.

12. A Narrative of the Transactions in Bengal, Vol. 1-3 , by Henry Vansittart, London, 1766, 1st Indian Reprint, edited by A.C., Banerjee, Calcutta, 1976.

13. A View of the Rise, Progress and Present State of the English Government in Bengal, by Harry Verelst, London, 1772.

14. The Third Report of the Select Committee of House oF Commons, 1831-32.

15. The Fifth Report from the Select Committees of the House of Commons on the Affairs of the East India Company, Dated 28, July, 1812 , Volume, I, II —Edited by W.K. - Firminger, Calcutta, 1917.

16. The Sixth Report of Select Committee of the House of Commons on Revenue, 1782.

17. Narrative of Events regarding the Mutiny in India of 1857-58, and the restoration of authority, & Further papers on the Mutinies in the East Indies, 1857.

18. Parliamentary Papers, Vol. XLIV, 1859.

19. Selections from Unpublished Correspondence of the Judge-Magistrate and the Judge of Patna, 1790-1857, (Edited by K.K. Datta), Patna, 1954.

20. Selections from the Records of the Bengal Govt. (Edited by H.Rickets) Calcutta, 1855.

21. Selections from the Correspondence of the Revenue Chiefs of Bihar (1781-1786)'; (edited by J.F.W. James), Patna, 1919.

22. Selections from the Unpublished Records of Government 1748-1767 (Edited by J.Long)); Calcutta, 1869.

23. Selections from the Judicial Records of the Bhagalpur District Office, 1792-1805 (Edited by Dr. K.K. Datta). Patna,1968.

24. Gaya Old Records, 1958, Hazaribagh Old Records (1761-1871) (Edited by P.C. Roy Choudhary), Patna, 1957.
25. Land Revenue Policy of the Indian Govt. Govt. Printing, 1902.
26. Regulations of the Fort William, Edited by Richard Clare, J& H. Gox, Lincoln's Inn-Fields, 1854.
27. The Regulations and Laws, Baptist Mission Press, 1827.
28. J.H. Harringon—An Elementary Analysis of the Laws & Regulations enacted by the Governor-General-in-Council at Fort-William, 3 Vols., Calcutta, 1805, 22.
29. Extract from Harrington's Analysis of the Bengal Regulations, Calcutta, 1866.
30. Supplement to the Digest of the Regulations and Laws enacted by the Governor General in Council anterior to the year, 1793 by J.E.Colebrooke, Calcutta, 1807.
31. Bengal MS Records (1782-1807), 4 Vols, Edited by W.W. Hunter, London ,1894.
32. Bengal District Records : Midnapore (1763-1774) 4 Vols, (Edited by W.K. Firminger), Calcutta, 1904-26.
33. West Bengal District Records, New Series, Burdwan, (Edited by A. Mitra and R. Guha), Calcutta, 1956.

REPORTS

1. Report on the Administration of Bengal, 1872-73.
2. Report of the Police Commission, 1860-1961.
3. Report of the Royal Commission upon Decentralization in India, Volume-I, London, 1909.
4. Report on the Administration of Bihar, Patna, 1913.
5. Report of the Indian Police Commission, 1902-1903, Calcutta-1909.
6. Report of the Bihar Police Commission, Patna, 1961.

GAZTTERS

1. Hunter, W.W. - The Imperial Gazetteer of India, & to XXIII, Oxford, 1908 (relevant volumes).

2. O' Malley L.S.S., Bengal District Gazetteers:
   (a) Singhbhum, Sereaikela and Kharsawan, Calcutta, 1910.
   (b) Bengal District Gazetteers, Palamau, Calcutta, (1907)
   (c) Bankura, Calcutta, 1908.
   (d) Midnapore, Calcutta, 1911.
3. Macpherson, T. S., and Hallet, M.G., Bihar and Orissa District Gazetteers, Ranchi, Patna (1917).
4. Lister, E, -Bihar and Orissa District Gazetteers, Hazaribagh, Patna (1917).
5. Coupland, H. Bengal District Gazetteers, Manbhum, (1917).
6. West Bengal District Gazetteers, Govt. of Bengal, New Series, edited by Mitra & Guha.
7. Bihar District Gazetteers, Govt. of Bihar, New Series, edited by P. C. Roychoudhary.

(e) SETTLEMENT REPORTS

1. Final Report on the Survey and Settlement operations in the District of Manbhum, 1918-25, edited by B.K. Gokhale, Patna, 1928.
2. Final Report on the Survey and Settlement operations in the District of Ranchi, 1902,10, edited by J. Ried., Calcutta, 1912.
3. Final Report on the Survey and Settlement of Pargana Dhalbhum in the District of Singhbhum, 1906-11, Calcutta, 1912, edited by J. Ried.
4. Final Report on the operation for the preparation of a Record of Rights in Pargana Porahat, 1905-7, edited by T.S. Macperson, Calcutta, 1908.
5. Settlement Report of the Santhal Pargana by Macpherson.
6. Champaran and Muzaffarpur Survey and Settlement Reports editeds by J. Stevenson Moore.
7. Darbhanga Survey and Settlement Report (1904) edited by J.H. Kerr.

Books

Ahmad, Qeyamuddin - The Wahabi Movement in India, Calcutta 1966.

Ascoli, F.D. - Early Revenue History of Bengal and the Fifth Report, Oxford, 1917.

Aspinal, A. - Cornwallis in Bengal, Manchester, 1931.

Auber, Peter. - Rise and Progress of the British Power in India.

Baden -Powell, B.H. - The Land Systems of British India vol, I, Oxford, 1892, Oriental Publishers, Delhi.

Balfour - Encyclopedia of India, Vol. III.

Ball, Charles - History of the Indian Mutiny, 2 Vols., London, 1858-59.

Ball, V. - (Translated & Edited) Taverneir's Travels in India, London, 1808.

Banerjee, A.C. - Indian Constitutional Documents, Vol. I, Calcutta, 1961.

Banerjee, A.C. & Ghosh - A Comprehensive History of India.

D.K. (Ed.) - Vol, IX (1712-72), Delhi, 1978.

Banerjee, D. W. - Early Administrative system of the East India Company in Bengal, Madras, 1949

" " - Early Land Revenue system in Bengal and Bihar, Vol.I 1765-72. Longmans Green, 1936.

Basu, B.D. - Rise of the Christian -Power in India, Calcutta, 1931.

Bellew, W.H. - A General Report on the Yusufzais, Lahore, 1864.

Beveridge, Henry - A Comprehensive History of India, London, 1867.

Blechynden, Kathleen - Calcutta Past and Present,

London, 1905.

Bolts, W. - Consideration of Indian Affairs, London, 1772.

Bradley, Birt, F.B. - The Story of An Indian Upland, London, 1905

" " - Chotanagpur, A Little known province of the Empire, London, 1903, 1910.

Broome, Arthur - History of the Rise and Progress of the Bengal Army, Calcutta, 1850.

Broughton, Thomas Duer - Letters Written in A Maharatha Camp, London, 1813.

Browne, James - Indian Tracts, Black Friats, 1788.

Buckland, C.E. - Bengal Under Lieutenant Governors in 2 Vols. Vol. I, Calcutta, 1901.

Buchanan, F. - An Account of the Distt. of (I) Purnea (1809-109), Patna, 1918.

" " - (ii) Bhagalpur (1810-11) Patna, 1939.

" " - (iii) Bihar & Patna, 2 Vols. (1811-12)

Burgees, James - The Chronology of Modern India (14-1894) Edinburgh, 1913.

Busteed, H.E. - Echoes from old Calcutta, London, 1908.

Bowrey, Thomas - A Geographical Account of the Countries round the Bay of Bengal (1669-1679) edited by Sir R. E. Temple, Bart,Hakluyt Society, 1903-1905.

Campbell, George - A sketch of the civil Government,

		London, 1852.
Capper, John.	-	The Three Presidencies of India, London, 1853.
Chand, Tara	-	History of the Freedom Movement in India, 4 Volms, Delhi, 1958.
Chatterji, Nandlal,	-	Mir Qasim, Allahabad, 1935.
Chick, N.A.	-	Annals of the Indian Rebellion, 1857- 58, London, 1974.
Chattopadhyaya, H.P.	-	The Sepoy Mutiny, 1857, Calcutta, 1957.
Chaudhary, Shashi	-	Civil Disturbances During the British
Bhushan	-	Rule in India (1765-1857) Calcutta, 1955.
Choudhary, P.C. Roy	-	1857 in Bihar (Chotanagpur & S.P)., Patna, 1959.
Choudhary, P.C. Roy	-	Sarkar Saran (1785-1866)
,, ,,	-	Bihar, Delhi, 1978
Choudhary, R.K.	-	History of Bihar, Delhi, 1958
Curry, J.C.	-	The Indian Police, Faber & Faber, London, 1932
Cotton, S.	-	Nine years in N.W. Frontier of India, London, 1868.
Conell, Herbert	-	History & Constitution of the Courts and Legislative Authority in India, Calcutta, 1872.
Constable, Archibald	-	(Revised & Edited) Francs Bernier's Travels in the Mogul Empire (1656-1668), 1891.
Datta, K.K.	-	Studies in the History of the Bengal Subah, Vol. I, Calcutta, 1936.
Datta, K.K.	-	The Dutch in Bengal & Bihar

(1740-1825) Patna, 1948.

„ „ - The Santhal Insurrection of 1857-58, Calcutta University, 1940.

„ „ - Biography of Kunwar Singh and Amar Singh, Patna, 1957.

„ „ - Alivardi & His Times, Calcutta, 1963.

„ „ - History of the Freedom Movement in Bihar, Vol.I (1857-1928) in 3 Vols., Patna, 1957.

Datta, K.K. - Unrest Against British Rule in Bihar (1831-1859) Patna, 1957.

Datta, K.K. - (Edited) Comprehensive History of Bihar, Vol. III, Patna, 1976.

Dhar, Niranjan - The Administrative System of the East India Company in Bengal (1774-1786).

Diwakar, R.R. - (Edited) Bihar Through the Ages, Calcutta, 1959.

Dodwell, H.H. - (Edited) The Cambridge History of India, Vol. V&VI, Indian Reprint, Delhi-1963-64.

Dutt, Romesh - The Economic History of India Under early British Rule-(1757-1857) London, 6th Ed.,

Edwardes, M. - British India, London, 1967.

Egerton, Hugh, Edward- A short History of the British Colonial Policy, London, 1913.

Elphinstone, M. - The Rise of the British Power in the East, London, 1887.

Field, C.D. - Landholding and the Relation of the Landlords and Tenants in various Countries, Calcutta, 1883.

Forrest, G.W. - A History of the Indian Mutiny, 3

Vols., London, 1904-12.

Forrest, S.G., - The life of Lord Clive, London, 1919.

Foster, Sir .W. - The English Factories in India 1618-1669, 13 Vols. London, Oxford, 1906-1926.

,, ,, - John Company, London, 1926.

Ghosh, Raisahib, - Sannyasi & Fakir Raiders in Bengal, Calcutta, 1930

Ghoshal, H.R. - Economic Transactions in the Bengal Presidency 1793-1833, Patna, 1953.

Gleig, G.R. - Memoirs of the life of the Rt. Hon, Warren Hastings, London, 1841.

Grant-Duff, James, C. - A History of the Maharattas, Cambray Edition.

Hand, J. Regionald - Early English Administration of Bihar (1781-1785) Calcutta-1894.

Hamilton, C.J. - The Trade-relations Between England & India (1600-1896), Calcutta, 1919.

Halls, J.J. - Two Months in Arrah in 1857, London, 1860.

Hastings, G.W. - A Vindication of Warren-Hastings, London, 1909.

Hill, S.C. - Three Frenchmen in Bengal, Longmans, Green & Co. London, 1903.

,, ,, - Bengal in 1756-57, 3 Vols. (Indian Record Series) London, 1905.

Holmes, T.R. - History of the Indian Mutiny, London,

Hunter, Sir, W.W. - The Annals of Rural Bengal,

Indian Reprint, Delhi, 1975.

" " - Rulers of India Series- Earl Canning, Oxford, 1899.

" " - Marquess Dalhousie, Delhi, 1961.

" " - Our Indian Mussalmans, London, 1871.

" " - History of British India,

" " - Rurla life in Bengal, London, MDCCLX Vol-VII- Gaya & Shahabad; Vol. XIII- Tirhut & Champaran; Vol.XIV- Bhagalpur & Santhal Parganas; Vol. XVII-Sighbhum, Manbhum & Tributary Tertiary States of Chotanagpur.

Hunter , Sir W.W - Statistical Accounts of Bengal, London, 1869.

" " - The Indian Empire, 1893.

Hutchins, Frances, G. - The Illusions of Permanence, NewJersey, 1967

Hutton, J.H. - Primitive Tribes in Modern India & the West.

Ives, Edward - Voyage from England to India, London, 1773.

Jha, Jagadish Chandra - The Kol-Insurrection of Chotanagpur , Calcutta, 1964.

" " - The Bhumij Revolt (1832-33) , Delhi, 1967.

Johnston, Sir Harry - Pioneers in India, S. Strand, London.

Jones, Moncton - Warren Hastings in Bengal, Oxford, 1918.

Joshi, P.C. - (ed.) Rebellion, 1857, Delhi 1957.

Kaye, John William - The Administration of the East

India Company, Reprint, Delhi, 1966.

,, ,, - A History of the Sepoy War in India, 3 Vol, London, 1864-78.

Keith, A.B. - A Constitutional History of India, 1600-1935, Mathuen, 1937.

Lyall, Alfred. - The Rise and Expansion of the British Dominion in India, Indian Print, Delhi, 1973.

Majumdar, R.C. - History of the Freedom Movement in India, 3 Vols., Calcutta.

,, ,, - The Sepoy Mutiny and the Revolt of 1857, Calcutta, 1962.

,, ,, - (Edited) British Paramountcy & Indian Renaissance, Bombay, 1970.

,, N. - Justice & Police in Bengal (1705-93),Calcutta, 1960.

Malleson, Col. G.B. - History of the Indian Mutiny, 2 Vols, London, 1878-80.

,, ,, - Decisive Battles of India, 1746-1849, London, 1914.

,, ,, - Recreations of an Indian official, London, 1872.

,, ,, - The Indian Mutiny of 1857-Reprint, Delhi , 1977.

Malcolm, Sir John - The Life of Robert Clive, 3 Vols, London, 1836.

,, ,, - The Political History of India (1784-1823) London, 1826.

,, ,, - (Edited) Sketch of the Political History of India , London, 1811-15.

Marshal , John - John Marshal in India Ed. S.A.

Khan, London, 1927.

Martin, Montogomery - Eastern India, Vol. II.

,, ,, - Wellesley's Dispatches, 4 Vols, London.

Mehr, G.R. - Syed Ahmad Shahid and other Volumes, Vols 4, Lahore, 1953,56.

Milbern, W. - Oriental Commerce—2 Vols, Revised by E. Thornton, 1825.

Mill, James & Wilson, H.H. - The History of British India, 10 Vols. London 1858.

Misra, B.B. - The Central Administration of the East India Company, Oxford University Press, India, 1959.

,, ,, - The Judicial Administration of the East India Company (1773-1833) Manchester, 1959.

,, ,, - Mahatma Gandhi's Movement in Champaran, Govt. of Bihar, 1963.

Mishra, S. G. - History of Bihar (1740-1772), Delhi, 1970.

Moon, Penderal - Warren Hastings and British India, Hodder, Stoughton.

Mundy Peter - Travels of Peter Mundy, Ed. R.C. Temple, London, 1862.

Narain , V.A - Jonathan Duncan at Varansi, Calcutta, 1959.

Nolan , E.H. - Illustrated History of the British Empire in India , London ,1862.

O'Malley, S.S.L. - (Ed.) Primitive Tribes in Modern India & The West, 1941.

,, ,, - History of Bengal, Bihar & Orissa Under British-Rule, Calcutta, 1925.

Orme, Robert, - A History of the Military Transaction of the British Nation in Hindustan .... Vols. I-III, 1778-80, 1803.

Pandey, S.N. - Education & Social Changes in Bihar, Varanasi, 1975.

Phillip, C.H. - The East India Company (1784-1834) Manchester, 1940.

Price, J.C. - Notes on the History of Midanopore etc. V. I, Calcutta, 1876.

Rawlinson, H.C. - Intercourse between India & the Western World, Cambridge University Press, 1926.

Raye, N.N. - The Annals of the English Settlements in Bihar, Kamala Book Depot., Calcutta, 1927

Raynal, Abbe - A Philosophical & Political History of the Settlements & Trade in the East & West India , Vols 6.

Roberts, P.E. - History of the British India, Oxford, 1962

Roy, A.C. - The Career of Mir Jafar 1757-65, Calcutta, 1953.

Sarkar, Sir Jadunath - Fall of the Mughal Empire, Vol.I, M.C. Sarkar & Sons, Calcutta 1932.

,, ,, - (Ed) History of Bengal ,Vol I-II

,, ,, - A Short History of Auranzeb, Calcutta, 1979

Sardesai, Gobind - New History of the Marathas, Vol. II, Sakharam, Bombay, 1948.

Scrafton, Luke - Reflections on the Govt. and Company of Indostan, Edinburg,

1761,

Sen, S.N. - Eighteen Fifty Seven, Delhi, 1957.

Sen, S.P. - The French in India, Calcutta, 1948

Seton-Karr, W.S. - The Marquess Cornwallis (Rulers of India Series)

Sieveking, I.G. - A Turning Point in Indian Mutiny, London, 1910.

Shore, Fredrick, J. - Notes on Indian Affairs, 2 Vols., London, 1837.

Singh C.P. - The Ho-Tribe of Singhbhum, Delhi, 1978.

Singh, S.P. - Regional Administration in Bihar, Calcutta, 1977

Sinha, B. P. - (Ed.) Comprehensive History of Bihar Vol, I, Patna, 1974.

Sinha, J.C. - Economic Annals of Bengal

Singh, S. B. - European Agency Houses In Bengal, Calcutta, 1965.

Starchy, John - India, its, Administration and Progress, London, 1903.

Stewart, C. - History of Bengal, Calcutta, 1918.

Talyler, William - 'Our Crisis', Calcutta, 1918.

" " - Thirty eight years in India, 2 Vols. London, 1882.

Thompson & Garrat - Rise & Fulfillment of British Rule in India, London, 1934, Allahabad, 1958

Thornton, Edward - History of the British Empire in India, Vols., I-VI, W. H. Allen & Co. London, 1841-1845

Trotter, L.J, - History of the British Empire in India, etc.,.. London. 1866.

Wilson, C.R. - The Early Annals of English in

	Bengal, Calcutta, 3 Vols. 1895
Wilson, M.	History of Bihar, 1880.

Proceedings, Periodicals & Journals

1. Proceedings Indian Historical Records Commission,
2. Proceedings, Indian History Congress
3. Calcutta Past and Present
4. Journal of Asiatic Society of Bengal
5. The Calcutta Review
6. Journal of Bihar & Orissa Research Society
7. Journal of Bihar Research Society
8. Journal of Indian History
9. The Quarterly Review of Historical Studies
10. Journal of Historical Research

Index

T

V

W

Z